A NEW JESUS

The life and deeds of the man Jesus triggered off the immense Christian religion nearly two millennia ago, but his most sublime and profound teachings were either largely disregarded or strongly reshaped by the practical needs of the early Christian Church. This old religious package, which still survives today, no longer satisfies the current wave of practicing Christians and others seekers who are searching for clear answers to their pressing spiritual questions: What is the purpose of my life, and of all life? Where did I come from? What will happen to me after I die? Who am I? Why is there such injustice and suffering in the world, and why doesn't "God" do something about it? And so on. Only a small collection of Christian mystics, saints and prophets since Jesus' day have found satisfactory answers to these questions through their individual devotional and intuitive efforts.

It's time now to release these original teachings of Jesus from their doctrinal, legendary and religious package. This book attempts to identify them, set them free from the grasp of tradition and upgrade them to meet the spiritual needs of contemporary seekers. It utilizes for this purpose the powerful and proven method of *intuitive inquiry*. This approach is distinct from rational means for generating knowledge, which are fundamentally inapplicable to a task such as this. We utilize instead the skills of an expert intuitive, *Kevin Ryerson*, whose record for obtaining both lost and entirely new information of many sorts has been truly outstanding. Many of his past contributions have been validated scientifically.

In this first attempt to apply the method of intuitive inquiry to the life and teachings of Jesus you will find perceptive answers to the main questions, including a filling in of several gaps and the resolution of distortions and contradictions in the New Testament Gospels and related Christian writings. It also offers answers to the fundamental questions posed above and shows how to apply these answers to enhance your personal life with rich, new understanding and a fresh and genuine spirituality. The book closes with a modern restatement of the spiritual philosophy Jesus offered to his apostles and later generations—and to you.

OTHER BOOKS BY THE AUTHOR AND CONTRIBUTOR

- Kautz, William H. *Opening the Inner Eye: Experiments on the Practical Application of Intuition in Daily Life and Work* (New York: iUniverse, 2005).
- Kautz, William H., and Melanie Branon, *Channeling: The Intuitive Connection* (Harper and Row, 1987).
- Kautz, William H., & Melanie Branon, *Intuiting the Future* (HarperSanFrancisco, 1989).
- Henry, Ronald & Kevin Ryerson, *The Future Healer: Spirit Communication on Healing* (New York: iUniverse, 2007)
- Ryerson, Kevin & Stephanie Harolde, *Spirit Communication: The Soul's Path* (Bantam Books, 1989).
- Kautz, William H., *The Story of Jesus: An Intuitive Anthology* (New York: Trafford Publishing, forthcoming)

A NEW JESUS

REDISCOVERING HIS DEEPER TEACHINGS
THROUGH INTUITIVE INQUIRY

REVISED EDITION

WILLIAM H. KAUTZ,
Sc.D.

in cooperation with expert intuitive

Kevin Ryerson

iUniverse, Inc.
Bloomington

A NEW JESUS
REDISCOVERING HIS DEEPER TEACHINGS THROUGH INTUITIVE INQUIRY-REVISED EDITION

Cover photo credit: Dreamstime, LLC., Brentwood, TN 37027 www.dreamstime.com.

The author wishes to thank Kevin Ryerson for his willing and very capable contributions to this book; Jack Goldberg for his attentive consultation on Judaism, which contributed to Chapter 2; and Dr. Paul Grof for his constructive comments on the Introduction and Chapter 14.

Figure Credits:
Figure 1: courtesy of Institute of Antiquity and Christianity
Figure 2, courtesy of xxglennxx (in public domain)
Figure 3, courtesy of Geza Vermes, from The Changing Faces of Jesus
Figure 4, courtesy of Starseed International
Figure 5, courtesy of yashanet

iUniverse books may be ordered through booksellers or by contacting:

iUniverse
1663 Liberty Drive
Bloomington, IN 47403
www.iuniverse.com
1-800-Authors (1-800-288-4677)

ISBN: 978-1-4620-3658-5 (sc)
ISBN: 978-1-4620-3659-2 (ebk)

Printed in the United States of America

iUniverse rev. date: 08/02/2011

CONTENTS

INTRODUCTION

"As a human being you have a right to know what you are doing here, trying to live a life. Where did you come from, and where you are going? What is the point of struggling for several decades and then dying? Who are you in the greater scheme of things? Why is there so much suffering in the world and why does evil so often go unpunished? . . . How can you possibly live your life effectively and fully without somehow resolving these issues? . . . Believe me, my friend, the answers you seek are not secret wisdom reserved for a few devout seekers. They are readily accessible to all who desire them and are willing to make room for them in their belief systems."

We have very good reason to believe today that the man Jesus not only understood these deeper matters but taught them to his apostles. The quest to bring to life his deepest teachings still continues after nearly twenty centuries of searching by saints, scholars, mystics, prophets and a contingent of lay seekers committed to answering these questions. Despite occasional individual insights we possess today no broadly accepted body of consensual knowledge about Jesus' deeds and his more profound teachings.

Many Christians today suspect that there must be more to Jesus' teachings than the few moral directives and life principles presented in the Gospels and later historical and Christian doctrinal writings. This lack exists mainly because these documents do not answer the basic spiritual questions just stated, which sit quietly in the back of our minds as "unknowns," sometimes even believed to be "unknowable." A few of the wisdom teachers who have arisen out of devotional Christianity during the past two millennia say they have found answers, and they generally agree on their content and significance, though their explanations are phrased in the language of their times and are typically hard for us to understand today. In any case they often seem abstract, unspecific or incomplete, therefore not directly applicable to ordinary life without extensive interpretation and a select filling-in of the gaps.

We know today that the most profound teachings of the man Jesus were largely obscured during the creation of the Christian church and over the centuries of its development to follow—perhaps for good reason at the time, but obscured nevertheless. Can we not bypass these religious writings and somehow tap Jesus' sublime wisdom more directly, thus enriching and enhancing our lives in the twenty-first century?

Past pursuits to understand Jesus' message from the surviving writings alone will probably never reach closure. This is largely because profound truths cannot always be neatly packaged in the words of human languages unable to hold them well—not to mention the minds of individual seekers not yet ready to receive them. Like learning to walk, speak and relate to other humans, most such truths must be learned anew through direct involvement by each learner. Descriptions and explanations, lectures and books, stories and dramas and lively examples can all help, of course. And like the taste of strawberries, the awe of looking at the heavens and the pleasures of intimate love, *there can be no substitute for the direct personal experience* of discovering Jesus' main teachings for oneself and incorporating them into one's own life. This personal discovery is an inherent part of the process of achieving the kind of deeper understanding we are seeking here.*

Few persons seek out such intimate involvement on their own until they are "ready," until the right moment, which may arise gradually but typically occurs as a singular mind-opening like a revelation or insight accompanying a life crisis. When it occurs it can turn an idle background curiosity into a compelling need to answer the underlying questions. We will soon see that Jesus addressed these issues head on. We can accelerate our own readiness by learning for ourselves what he discovered, with a

---

* Let it be clear that I am using the term *understanding* here (and elsewhere) to designate personal comprehension through *all* of one's faculties, not just the intellect, and the term *information* to include statements about people's intentions, opinions and feelings as well as "hard" factual information of an objective nature. *Knowledge* refers to broad understanding so well integrated with prior knowledge that it may serve as a basis for decision and action.

little attention in the right direction and using an appropriate means of inquiry.

Herein lies the purpose of this book: to aid the personal and very human search for these almost ineffable answers. We provide this aid to you not so much through facts and arguments as by inducing key insights into your contemplations. We will do so by employing a unique orchestration of stories, descriptions and explanations about Jesus' life and teachings, this time with a little help from our intuitive friends. Carefully conducted intuitive inquiry is our method of choice.

· · · · ·

This book is targeted at those who are approaching the "right moment" and are therefore motivated to explore these basic questions for themselves. All who have come this far are eligible. We do not assume an academic, religious or non-religious background or any particular set of beliefs or non-beliefs about Jesus.

Our presentation brings together two endeavours not usually enjoined. The first is the age-old exploration of Jesus' deeper teachings, as just mentioned, and especially those hinted at but still not clear in the original historical documents and later Christian writings. The second is the application of "another way of knowing" besides the critical, academic and intellectual method normally employed in the Western world for historical analysis and acquiring new knowledge generally.

A main hope for this unusual marriage is that the second endeavour will aid the first. That is, by applying "direct knowing" methods such as intuitive inquiry to the still unknown portions of Jesus' life and teachings, we may come to understand more clearly what he was trying to communicate to his apostles, followers and later generations. As in any good marriage, though, we expect a profitable interaction: the message will impact in turn upon the means. A successful demonstration of the power of intuitive inquiry, especially in an area such as this one, at the edge of what is practically knowable, will testify to its usefulness on similar topics in other fields.

The choice of Jesus' teachings as an application area for intuitive inquiry is a fitting and natural one because our knowledge of these teachings is at present *information limited*. That is, we are held back in the understanding we seek not so much by natural barriers, institutional pressure, clouded thinking or insufficient motivation—as is the case in so many human undertakings—but more by *a lack of specific information* about what Jesus said, intended and did. Intuitive inquiry is a powerful means for providing such missing information, even if it was never written down or otherwise preserved for later generations. *Prior studies have shown that missing information is readily accessible to carefully conducted intuitive inquiry.* Evidence for this strong claim will be given in Chapter 2.

· · · · ·

The only "original" historical sources about Jesus himself and his teachings consist of the four Gospels of the Christian Bible's New Testament, plus about thirty surviving and questionable fragments of other ancient writings. Sadly, all these sources are sorely lacking in useful content because they are biased, omit essential details, do not agree well with one another and/or were modified by editors long after they were written. As a result they are incomplete and contradictory and often misleading. They cannot be trusted for accuracy, reliability and completeness.

These shortcomings exist in spite of the powerful role Christianity has played in the evolution of Western society over two millennia. The Christian religion and its enduring legend were certainly triggered off by the man Jesus, but (as we shall soon see) almost all subsequent writings about him are a reflection of other societal forces and activities and do not reflect at all well what he was trying to teach and demonstrate in his life.

Our purpose in presenting this material is not to provide factual, authoritative and "proven" alternative information, such as scientists or scholars might do, but rather to offer credible options which you may use to resolve for yourself the major uncertainties, omissions and contradictions in the Jesus story. You are encouraged to utilize this new information to add fresh perspective and depth to your understanding of Jesus' message, and a strong inspiration for your personal and contemplative inner search. Only through this kind of inner process can you arrive at a deeper personal understanding of the truths contained in Jesus' unusually powerful teachings.

To be specific, you are invited to regard the intuitive descriptions to follow as possible alternatives to whatever beliefs you originally bring to the table. *They are not commandments, nor are they appeals that you accept them as facts from an external source that seems to be authoritative.* Rather, use them as a platform and starting point for your own inner search, so you may uncover your personal truth through them.

We will be restating this important point several times as reminders before this book closes.

· · · · ·

The modern scientific age in which we live today has impressed upon all of us an underlying belief that the truth of any matter is to be found through critical analysis and rational proof. It is easy to forget that our forefathers had no such expectation. Science's contributions to common knowledge and our present way of life (beginning in the seventeenth century) are impressive indeed, but they pertain almost entirely to the *material* world. For non-material matters scientific knowledge is weak indeed and must rightly be supplemented with intuitive, mystical and contemplative approaches for gaining new knowledge. It is these latter faculties which our predecessors relied upon as their prime means for understanding and even for survival. In the Western world the inner mode of knowing has by now been almost totally eclipsed by the rise of science.

Our society has sunk into an excessive dependence upon science's paradigm, or way of thinking, along with its limited model of reality and the associated loss of important human values. We will do well to re-explore the intuitive and mystical alternative for what it can do for us here. If human history is any indication at all, it is telling us that, in our continuing search to learn the meaning of human life—to find answers to the fundamental questions stated above—we cannot continue to neglect this less visible and therefore less recognized realm of our existence. This is the realm lying behind and beyond our sensual and rational faculties and materialistic values. We must turn *inward* for the answers we seek.

· · · · ·

We offer *intuition* as the most effective and accessible means for reaching these deeper and wiser parts of ourselves, for learning how they work and for incorporating into our lives the missing knowledge they can bring to us. We will seek the help of individuals who have chosen to develop their natural and inherent intuitive faculty into a strong, workable skill. Called here *expert intuitives,* they have demonstrated over the past fifty years (and even before) their ability to access many kinds of both new and lost information, well beyond what the intellectual mind can generate. This information is vast. It appears to include everything potentially knowable, even that not yet known by anyone alive but verifiable later by familiar means.

Intuition is the mental process employed by the greatest mystics and sages of all ages and all cultures in the world to obtain deep understandings about themselves and life itself. Mysticism and sometimes even intuition have a mixed reputation because so many ungrounded individuals are classified as mystics or psychics, but that does not change the fact that some of them saw very deeply and clearly and have greatly aided the development of human civilization. We can be grateful to them for tapping directly into the inner human resource—whatever it is—from which all knowledge comes, and for acquiring deep wisdom there, reporting back to their societies and eventually aiding us today.

We know now that it is not necessary to struggle so hard and suffer such anguish as did these explorers in their day. Intuitive inquiry, which is essentially a kind of formalized mysticism, is a universal gift. *Everyone* has the ability to develop and use it for his own and others' benefit. Moreover, it is not all that difficult to do so.

It makes only good sense, then, to apply this powerful means of knowledge generation to the problems of our times—individual, familial and societal—that require new information, knowledge and understanding for their solutions. Where better to begin than to try to understand the malaise of meaninglessness and lack of values that affects so many persons in our modern Western world? Jesus had much to say about this problem. Let us access this knowledge ourselves by digging intuitively into his teachings. We may probe even more deeply than the historians, theologians and mystics of the past were able to do.

· · · · ·

What you will read in this book is an example of modern intuitive inquiry at work. The main text consists of an annotated and organized transcript of four long interviews with renowned expert intuitive *Kevin*

Ryerson° on the life and teachings of Jesus. It presents Ryerson's responses to about one hundred questions on the most ambiguous and controversial topics in the Biblical record of Jesus' biographical life and especially his central teachings. His responses go well beyond what is preserved in the Gospels and other ancient documents and what evolved later out of Christian activity.

Ryerson is an expert intuitive with a long and successful track record. Over the past few decades he has provided accurate and relevant information on a broad range of subjects, ranging from specialized scientific, philosophical, spiritual and historic matters to intimate counsel on the personal lives of hundreds of individual clients.[1] We have in Ryerson's many accomplishments good reason for paying close heed to whatever he has to tell us about Jesus.

This study is actually a byproduct of a much larger project for gathering intuitively derived information on Jesus' life and teachings from a variety of sources. It was a natural outgrowth of the work of the *Center for Applied Intuition*, the institution which developed the method of intuitive inquiry used here and with which Ryerson and other expert intuitives were allied for a decade. This extensive collection of intuitive data on Jesus is being integrated into a credible and meaningful report so as to inform and inspire a broad class of seekers.

The new material from Ryerson is part of this collection. It was not originally intended to be offered separately but only to fill in gaps and resolve some questionable issues within the larger body of data. It turned out, however, to have a reasonably coherent and independent value of its own, especially on the most uncertain aspects of Jesus' education, his preparation for his early ministry, his intentions and his message. We therefore chose to publish it separately, ahead of the main report.[2]

My own (WHK) role in this project has been as interviewer, editor, administrator and author of this Introduction, Chapters 1 and 2, the final integration (Chapter 14) and the commentaries within chapters. I am solely responsible for these four non-intuitive tasks.

Ryerson's words were recorded, transcribed, edited and arranged into chapters, following roughly the narrative sequence in the Gospels (mainly Matthew's). In the text to follow questionable, unknown and filled-in words

---

° These one- to two-hour sessions were conducted with Ryerson on 5 January, 25 June and 20 August 2004 and 7 January 2007.

and interpolated references are inserted in brackets [. . .]. Paragraph and long-sentence breaks have been inserted and punctuation added as must be done for any transcription of recorded speech. Footnotes have been included for cross-referencing and to explain possibly unfamiliar concepts and terminology. References to Biblical, historical and other supportive sources are cited in the Endnotes, Bibliography and Recommended Reading sections. A few descriptions and several citations to Ryerson's earlier book *Spirit Communication*[3] have been included when relevant.

• • • • •

We are assuming for this book that our reader is generally familiar with the Jesus story as presented in the Gospels, though not necessarily to the extent of a religious scholar, minister or theologian, for example.

We use the term "Jesus" in these pages rather than the common designation "Jesus Christ" as a reminder of his humanity over his much argued divinity as a god walking on earth, and to distinguish his personal name *Jesus* or *Jeshua* from his assigned title, "the Christ." (Many Christians do not know that the term "Christ" is simply the Greek word for "Messiah.") The name "Jesus the Christ" might be better, though this designation carries an unfortunate apocalyptic connotation. And Christ is certainly not Jesus' family surname, as some seem to use it.

The term "God" is employed broadly here to designate an omniscient, ubiquitous, and all-compassionate presence and an omnipotent creative force, without any particular religious or secular definition. Each reader is therefore free to retain his personal concept of God, even if it is a definition he chooses to reject until he is ready to enlarge it as his understanding grows. Sometimes we defer to the frequent and fairly neutral expression the *Deity* or the *Divine* to signify this presence.

Finally, the pronouns *he, him* and *his*, as well as *man* and *one*, are intended to include both male and female genders except where particular males are indicated. God is assumed to be genderless but is called "He" by convention.

CHAPTER 1

THE HISTORICAL JESUS

"The advent of historical reason meant distinguishing the factual from the fictional in accounts of the past. . . . To know the truth about Jesus, the real Jesus, one had to find the Jesus of history. . . . Biblical scholars rose to the challenge and launched a tumultuous search for the Jesus behind the Christian façade of the Christ." [Robert Funk, Founder of *The Jesus Seminar*[4]]

It is clear now, after centuries of historical, archeological, theological and even psychological scholarship that we will never come to know the true Jesus—even the Jesus of history—at least not from these disciplines. If we are to understand what Jesus actually did and said we are going to have to rely upon another source of information, "another way of knowing," that has the capacity to dig more deeply into the realm of knowledge than either scholarly research or theological faith is able to do.

Before launching into such a novel and non-traditional inquiry, however, we need to first learn what is deficient in the available writings and traditions about Jesus and how these deficiencies came about. Then we can appreciate the various historical, religious and spiritual issues involved and can ask the right questions of alternative sources of information. Only in this way can we learn what we do not yet know, and would like to know.

William H. Kautz, Sc.D.

Jesus in History

It's not that these historians and other scholars haven't seriously tried to discover the truth about what Jesus was like and what he did and said. The effort has been extensive indeed. The difficulty was rather that they were forced to rely upon only a thin skein of facts in the few surviving historical documents. These comprise primarily the four Gospels of the New Testament and secondarily around thirty so-called *apocryphal* texts.

The search for the historical Jesus began about two hundred years ago in Germany when a few dedicated and courageous theologians sought to distinguish the *historical* Jesus from the theological and faith-based Jesus of traditional Christianity. It was pure heresy at the time![5] Other efforts outside of Germany followed. One was a personal, revised version of the Gospels by American Thomas Jefferson (published only late in his politicical career).[6] Albert Schweitzer, in his now famous treatise, *The Quest of the Historical Jesus*, reviewed the body of scholarly work up to 1900 and refined it in his own escatological way.[7] Parallel studies by secular historians and Judaic scholars examined the Palestinian world in which Jesus grew up and carried out his ministry.[8]

The pursuit then moved from the churches to the universities and from Europe to the United States. Religious scholars poured over these ancient documents, searching for hidden meanings and analyzing words, phrasings and cross-relationships. They diligently sought the truth of what must have "really" occurred in Jesus' life and the messages he actually preached, trying to cut through what was recorded. There were always issues of accuracy, authenticity, authorship and dating of the ancient writings, and controversy naturally ensued. Also problematic were the highly varied interpretations introduced into the writings from each age and culture. In retrospect, it is doubtful now whether such meticulous analysis and dissection is justified, in view of the informal and sloppy way in which the Gospels appear to have been written in the first place and later edited. To be sure, the best analysis cannot make up for a severe lack of reliable data.

Figure 1. The Nag Hammadi Codices

Almost all of the surviving Christian apocrypha exist today only as fragments rejected from the Church's canonization of the Christian Bible in 325 CE.[9] Some were lost until rediscovered in the twentieth century. The large *Nag Hammadi Library*,[10] for instance, includes a few old Gospels atributed to Peter, Thomas and Mary Magdalen,* along with subsidiary material. Other fragments and a recent *Gospel of Judas*[11] turned up elsewhere.† The *Dead Sea Scrolls*—which predate Jesus and are not Christian apocrypha—describe the Jewish sect of Essenes, which may have

---

* The *Nag Hammadi Library* is a collection of fifty-two Coptic texts discovered in Egypt in 1945 and dated to 350-400 CE. They include several apocrypha, some of which are translations or copies of older post-Jesus Gnostic documents for which the originals are lost. (See Meyer 2007 and a later section of Chapter 3.)

† The *Gospel of Judas*, just recently rediscovered, translated and made public, portrays Judas as following Jesus' instructions in offering him up to the Sanhedrin. It also suggests that the teachings in this Gospel were given specially to Judas and not to the other apostles. Its unidentified author may be Judas himself or someone else. See also the references to Judas at the beginning of Chapter 12.

influenced him.'[12] Some apocrypha emerged from early Gnostic sects.[†] The books of the New Testament apart from the four gospels describe the early Christian evangelic movement fairly well but say little about Jesus himself. The secular historical documents mentioned above barely mention Jesus.[‡]

This long pursuit for the historical Jesus culminated recently in the *Jesus Seminar*—a gathering of about one hundred religious scholars, who retranslated and carefully screened for historical credibility the 1500+ sayings and nearly 400 events (acts) in the Gospels and closely related documents.[§13] Their fifteen-year effort found that 82% of the sayings and 84% of the events had to be rejected—not as necessarily *wrong,* or with the claim that they did *not* occur, but simply not supported by the available historical data. This exclusion includes the most salient and popular aspects of the Jesus story: the virgin conception, the popular birth and infancy narratives, most of his miracles, his resurrection and later appearances and more. While the parables and his moral teachings remain, much of Jesus spiritual message, such as that presented in this book, has been left out. It

---

[*] The *Dead Sea Scrolls* consist of a collection of about 900 ancient documents, dated from 150 BCE to 70 CE,) discovered in 1947 in a cave near Qumran in the Israeli West Bank of the Dead Sea, near where an Essene community is believed to have existed. Most are copies of ancient Hebrew Biblical, apocryphal and sectarian documents, but others consist of new material describing the beliefs and practices of the Essene community. They have contributed much new historical understanding of early Judaism. [Vermes 1987, Wise 1996]

[†] The *Gnostics* were a varied collection of sects in the Middle East in the centuries just preceding and following Jesus. They practiced a set of beliefs generally more mystical and advanced than those prevalent at the time. Some adopted portions of Jesus' teachings not already picked up by the emerging evangelistic movement and even considered themselves to be Jesus' followers. They are credited with creating, or at least preserving, a number of the apocryphal Gospels. [Pagels 1979, Borg 1996]

[‡] Secular histories of the Middle East by historians such as Flavius Josephus, Philo of Alexandria and Pliny the Elder describe life in first-century Palestine and some historical events. They mention Jesus' brother James and John the Baptist, and confirm some Biblical portions of Jewish history, but they say nothing significant about Jesus himself or what he said and did. A passage on Jesus in Josephus' detailed *Antiquities of the Jews* has been recognized as a forgery since the 17th century. [Josephus 1987, Williamson 1981, Bostock 1855]

[§] The Jesus Seminar project was conducted as a public and accountable forum for debate and evaluation of conflicting insights and interpretations on Jesus' words and deeds. Its conclusions were reached by a four-level voting process among the scholars. Rather few of the votes were fully consensual.

is very likely that several of the excluded events are actually true, and you will find some in this present story.

All in all, reliable information about the man Jesus and his early teachings is very, very sparse. If this 80%+ of excluded events and sayings are indicative of the true state of affairs, or even partially so, then totally new information, apart from the historical record, must be brought to bear before we can speak with confidence about who Jesus was and what he taught. New archeological discoveries are always possible, of course, but they are unlikely to occur, invariably raise yet more unanswerable questions and offer little hope for present purposes.

Almost every serious treatment of Jesus' biographic life begins with an apology of this sort for the paucity and unreliability of available historical information about him.[ix] We are forced to qualify our own inquiry similarly. This limitation must be made clear at the outset, if for no other reason than to help counteract the widespread but mistaken belief, which almost all of us hold to some extent, that the stories about Jesus which have come down to us today are factually and historically valid. They are nothing of the kind.[*]

The Interminable Gap

The collection of available historical records of Jesus' life do not begin to satisfy modern standards for biographies and histories. The most important biographical issues about Jesus' early years (before age 30), his family life, colleagues, education, work, personality, religious life, community relationships and his physical manner and appearance are all unknown. They remain the subject of speculative art, biography and historical fiction, which are all very well but a far cry from what we would like and may claim to be the truth.

While some of the events and sayings reported in the Gospels may be factually true, in spite of the lack of historical evidence, we have no acceptable way of knowing which ones. Even apart from his early years we possess no credible consensus on who Jesus really was as a person and what he actually did and said during his so-called ministry. We are certain only that he was an itinerant preacher in first-century Galilee who taught

---

[*] Searching for the historical Buddha is even greater a waste of time because credible documents about his life are even more lacking than for Jesus. Fortunately, and in contrast, writings on his teachings appear to have survived in better shape.

through parables and aphorisms with a message of love, peace and good will. He said that everyone should love God and his neighbor. He "cured" a few people of their illnesses. It is fairly sure that he had connections with the man called John the Baptist and with several disciples who carried on his work after his death. He went to Jerusalem at one point where he generated controversy, displeased the authorities and was killed under judgment by the Roman Prefecture Pontius Pilate. This much we can say we know for sure.

Almost all of the remaining Gospel accounts about Jesus, including much of his preaching, have to be regarded as unknown and for the most part a *legend*—imaginative, metaphoric and typically human, but a legend nevertheless. These elements arose variously from Judaic and Greek traditions, the Gospel writers themselves, other followers and the fathers of the early Christian Church—but not from Jesus. This fact is now widely accepted by scholars, and no convincing evidence exists to indicate otherwise. Therefore we are not entitled to quote most of the Gospels nor the subsequent Christian literature as authoritative sources about Jesus' life. We can only speculate, guess, interpret and "believe," which is what saints, clerics, historians and laymen have done for nearly two millennia. The wide differences among their writings testify clearly to this fundamental ignorance.

To fill out the story you might fall back upon the faith of Christians over the intervening centuries—or your own faith—as an alternative source of "information." Some ancient Christians were undoubtedly very discerning and were able to bring forth from their devotions elements of truth about Jesus and his teachings. Unfortunately, we have no credible basis on which to distinguish their valid discoveries from mere personal impressions and projections based upon what such followers wished to be true. While their insights may have been inspiring and meaningful to them personally, as do many mystical experiences, they are of little use as contributions to collective, consensual knowledge about the man Jesus, which is what we would most like to have.

The Gospels describe fairly well the first stage of evolution of the institution of Christianity. We may be cautiously grateful for this grand contribution, which has served so many people and is still strong in the world today despite its obvious limitations. We shall soon see, however—if it is not already apparent—that Christianity has only a limited relationship to Jesus' main teachings, which are our primary concern here.

How Did This Divergence Come About?

The numerous distortions in the Gospels and related documents arose from several factors. It will be helpful in our interpretations to understand this unfortunate evolution.

For one, the Gospels were written two and three generations after Jesus' death by men who never knew him. They "would not have recognized him if they met him on the street."[14] They were not objective historians or responsible on-the-spot reporters but empassioned evangelists. They were committed to converting others, setting up enclaves of followers and putting in place a new set of beliefs that would appeal to their congregations and survive the political and religious pressures of the day. Their first few written records were little more than personal notes, recollections from memory and hearsay preserved through the oral tradition. They were heavily biased by the worldview, common beliefs and cultural norms prevailing at the time. This factor alone accounts for most of inconsistencies and distortions among the Gospels.*

As these notes were copied and passed around the early Christian enclaves they were freely modified, and perhaps translated from Aramaic to Greek, to fit local audiences and needs. The standards of the time allowed one writer to speak for another and revise his writings without permission or acknowledgement, and even without identifying himself. As a result many changes were made and the true authors of most of the Gospels and apocrypha are not known today with any certainty. The originals are no longer available, and the order of the copies (which came first) is also in doubt.

This same practice was followed later by Church officials, who made their own selections and carried out their own editing, further changing Jesus' words and the reported events at will to suit their political purposes.†
We know now that over the first two centuries after Jesus' death the Church fathers screened and modified all four Gospels, ostensibly to help unify

---

* The four Gospel accounts overlap, to be sure, but multiplicity does add to their credibility. The many copied statements reveal that each author except Mark had access to major portions of the prior Gospels and chose to select from them while adding his own corrections and contributions.

† It is almost certain that a few of early Church fathers understood Jesus' teachings very well but were in the minority among those who were shaping policies of the new church.

the fragmented early Church under a single authority. This led in the fourth century to the canonization of the four Gospels into the Christian New Testament, essentially the version we know today. At this point the Gospels became Church documents in support of doctrinal solidarity rather than historical and biographical accounts. The residual apocrypha were declared heretical and illegal, and most were destroyed.

A Seriously Misleading Heritage

It is mainly these gaps and distortions that have contributed to today's lack of an informed and trustworthy consensus on other than the barest events of Jesus' life—what "really happened." We especially do not know with any certainty what we should believe about the legend we have inherited today. It would probably not matter much except for one inescapable fact: *the erroneous belief in the alleged authority of the Gospels and Christian legend is distorting the central messages of Jesus' teachings.*

For example, serious errors have resulted from the common belief in the *literal* veracity of the Gospel story. It was often claimed to be "divinely inspired," and by implication to be unquestionably and literally correct. Metaphoric statements were taken literally without question. This mistaken belief persisted over the centuries and is still common in several sects today.

Despite the widespread and powerful impact of the Gospels on Western civilization and beyond over the last two thousand years, much of Jesus' essential wisdom is missing. It is largely hidden by the distorted legend and its associated doctrinal material. While the central spiritual wisdom (to be expounded in later chapters) is elegant and simple, it is obscured and not now readily accessible except for Jesus' moral teachings, and must be diligently sought after rather than simply read in a book or listened to in a sermon. We see that the present legend is not so much the true story of Jesus' life and teachings but more a testimony to mankind's on-going need for guidance, inspiration and leadership. The legendary alternative still has value, of course, though it's not what we're looking for.

Over the course of this and the several following chapters (3 to 13) we will be explaining and substantiating these claims with numerous examples, and will be searching out and clarifying Jesus' central, original and most strongly spiritual teachings—especially the powerful message he offered to his followers and the world.

16

Sorting Out the Gospels

The Gospels are best seen as a collection of inspired and valuable gems mixed in with faulty, questionable material. Let's try first to identify as best as we can the valid portions of the Gospels from those which have been added or modified. To enable this discrimination we shall apply to this mixture a strategy and a criterion.

Our *strategy* will be to identify first those portions and statements that we can firmly assert are true and valid, mainly on broad, human grounds, and then use these valid portions to reject others that contradict them.

We are dealing here with both the episodes, acts and *events* in Jesus' life and with what we may call his *teachings*, for lack of a better term. Loosely connected events may be independently valid or not, but teachings must hang together and form a consistent "system of thought," we might call it, if they to be meaningful. The events (Jesus' deeds) are useful as examples in support of the teachings and to help resolve ambiguities in them. The teachings provide a better opportunity for distinguishing the credible portions from the incredible.

The *criterion* comprises three elements: first, we may use the overlapping body of human knowledge preserved within the cores of the world's major religions as the highest truths mankind has been able to come up with; second, we have the earliest and most doctrine-free portions of the Gospels, which are therefore the most credible of Jesus' recorded sayings; and third, there are a few consistent, positive themes running through all the Gospels with which no one can reasonably argue.

Two Realms of Being

> "The most important subject that can be addressed is the relation of the human being with the Divine, with truth itself." [Kabir Helminsky[15]]

Jesus' central teachings consist mainly of a collection of *moral principles* and *spiritual concepts*, along with explanations and examples to show how these fit together into a coherent thought system that can be followed and practically lived. The most fundamental of these principles and concepts are not unique to Jesus but are shared among the major religions and philosophic systems of the world. They have been worked out and preserved since antiquity in the esoteric branches of these religions. These branches may be respected because they have been concerned with central ideas and themes rather than doctrines and belief systems. The key overlapping portions among them have been singled out into what is now called the *Perennial Philosophy*,[16] a term coined by Leibnitz and popularized by Aldous Huxley. It is the common denominator or core which underlies and is inherent in all of the world's major religious and spiritual teachings.[17] It may be summarized like this:

- *Primordial reality: there are two realms of reality*: the familiar everyday realm of physical objects and living creatures (the first realm), and a more subtle and profound realm of consciousness, mind and spirit (the second realm). The second is not a polarized opposite of the first but rather a source that embraces and includes the first. It is timeless, spaceless and not directly perceivable by the senses or by instruments.
- *Participation: human beings partake of both realms.* We are not only physical beings but also spiritual beings, intimately linked to the second realm. Each of us has, at the center of his being and in the depth of his mind, a center of transcendent awareness, a personal *essence* which is his link to the greater Reality to which he belongs.
- *Accessibility: every human has the inherent capacity to recognize this sacred ground of being, this second realm.* Each one of us can test the validity of his inner connection by experiencing it directly when his mind is still, open and uncluttered with thoughts. Such an inner pursuit is the purpose of all spiritual practice.
- *Priority: the recognition of one's inner spiritual nature is the highest goal and greatest good of human existence.* To realize this goal is to discover one's true Self and one's true relationship with the greater Reality to which he belongs.

The main ideas in this Philosophy are not typical religious beliefs but *principles* supported by centuries of validation through human revelation, reflection, experience and application. They have been well tested and gradually refined by mankind's greatest wisdom teachers, religious and otherwise, of our planet's major cultures. For these reasons alone we have to take them seriously. We can safely accept them to be as basic and sound to man's understanding of the nature of his existence as anything that humanity has devised.

We may recognize these four principles in the early history of Christianity, especially in the offshoot called *Gnosticism*. To the present point, they may be found in Jesus' sayings in the Gospels, though he stated them in terms more understandable to his contemporaries than if he were speaking directly to us today. He spoke of the *kingdom of heaven*, which obviously refers not to a physical location or a political or geographic territory but to a *state of consciousness*—precisely the second realm of human existence. He spoke of this kingdom as man's origin and destiny, the greater Reality of which he is a part and an on-going source of spiritual nourishment. He also made it clear that through this kingdom each human is intimately connected to all other humans, who share the same inner source he called his *Father God*. He contrasted it with the material, ego-driven, daily world (first realm) which is a particularized projection downward from the second realm and is the place of man's daily life, trials and tribulations.*

The point of connection between the two realms, which Jesus clearly recognized, is often called one's Higher Self, *essence* or *soul*. He declared that the kingdom, or second realm, is accessible to everyone and should be a top priority, the most important task he may undertake in his entire life: "But seek ye first his kingdom . . . ," and "Thou shalt love the Lord thy God with all thy heart, ..."[†18]. He also affirmed that this attainment of the second realm is not a fortuitous event caused by external factors but is a self-determined and transformative awakening, chosen by the

---

* This two-realm model is a simplification of Wilber's "Great Nest of Being" [Wilber 1998], which recognizes several levels of existence from Elemental Matter to Soul and Spirit. It is itself a step down from Hindu and other systems which have up to twelve levels. The two realms in the Perennial Philosophy simplify further by combining all levels into just two, those below and those above the boundary of emerging awareness.

† I am using traditional Christian terminology and concepts rather freely for lack of anything better. It needs to be kept in mind, however, that to discern proper meanings for some of these ambiguous terms often requires going beyond religious tradition and what most of us have been taught in our younger years. Some of these terms (faith, sin, salvation, etc.) are discussed in Chapter 10 and recapitulated in Chapter 14. The loaded religious meanings of terms such as *soul* and *redemption* do not fit well the definitions used in this book. For others, such as *atonement and grace,* barely mentioned here, you are on your own to define them for yourself as they arise.

individual himself. This is the essential step of his spiritual growth and the recognition of his true identity and eventual fulfillment.

In the central portion of Jesus' teachings we find a direct expression of the Perennial Philosophy.

The Sayings Gospel Q

The "Sayings Gospel" Q is not a separate document but an extraction of about eighty sayings of Jesus that occur in Matthew and Luke—but *not* in Mark.[19] It is reasoned that Matthew and Luke, who had access to Mark's earlier Gospel when they wrote, must have derived these eighty sayings from a separate source, termed "Q" (for German *Quelle*, or *source*), which paralleled Mark's Gospel but was distinct from it and probably written earlier. Most Biblical scholars now agree with this reasoning and conclude that these pre-Christian sayings in the Q Gospel are much closer to Jesus' original teachings than those reported in the balance of the four Gospels. We may therefore turn to this Sayings Gospel for utterances much more likely to have come directly from Jesus himself.

The Gospel Q contains no narrative, no accounting of Jesus' birth or death, no Christ or Messiah, and no information about second comings, salvation or Jesus' divinity. The apostles are barely mentioned. It includes the familiar Sermon on the Mount ("blessed are the . . ."), which is a set of positive values and moral instructions on how one may live a worthy and blessed life; which personal qualities one should strive for and which avoided; and what constitutes personal fulfillment.[20] While these acclaimed statements by Jesus are not contained in the Perennial Philosophy, they are completely consistent with it. They provide down-to-earth guidelines on *how* to manifest this Philosophy in one's personal life.

Most of the sayings in Q are homey teachings that could have been addressed to rural peasants in Galilee. They are typical of how Jesus must have begun his ministry, before he had to deal with urban audiences and the Judean priesthood. They are illustrated with practical examples from daily life (plowshares, mustard seeds, bride-maidens and falling seeds, for example), and they appear in the allegories and parables which run throughout the Gospels. As one modern scholar puts it, "Jesus, in the Gospel Q, is neither Christ nor the Messiah, but rather part of the long line of Jewish prophets. He is a charismatic teacher, a healer, a simple man filled with the spirit of God."[21]

Many of these sayings in Q are not unique to Jesus but appear in other world religions as well, just like the Perennial Philosophy presented above.[22] Some (such as forgiveness and brotherly love) were part of his Jewish legacy but were neither emphasized nor widely practiced in Judaism at the time.[23] A few have found their way into Western law and offer a practical counterpart to the spiritually inclined Perennial Philosophy. Almost all can be immediately accepted as sayings coming from Jesus.

The Gospel of Thomas is also a sayings Gospel, an independent production obviously not derived from Q.[24] One third of its sayings overlap with Q. Others, apparently Jesus' advanced teachings given only to his apostles, are highly symbolic and in some cases obscure.[25] It is difficult to know whether these arose from Jesus or were borrowed from other sources or were just poorly recorded. Only a portion of its unique sayings can be accepted at this point as Jesus' sayings.

A Message of Love

In both the Gospel Q and the other Gospels Jesus repeatedly and strongly stressed to his audiences an overriding message of *love* as a key thread running through all of his teachings. He explained in detail how one should live so as to manifest the universal love of God; to love all other persons, even one's enemies; and to practice love's various derivatives such as kindness, mercy, humility, forgiveness, honesty, non-violence, non-judgment, generosity, patience, generosity, care and trust. He warned against human behaviors that avoid or block love's natural expression: revenge, blaming, condemning, hating, harming, judging, envy, anger, intolerance, impatience, greed and so on. He offered aphorisms for detecting these absences of love within oneself: the blind cannot lead the blind, he said; pay attention first to what is most important; when the eye is clear then the whole being is light; and so on.

This broad message of love and its active expression are instantiated and supported by Jesus' chosen way of life, by most of the Sayings Gospel Q and in his parables, which can be easily understood by almost anyone. We may therefore safely include Jesus' words about *love* and its derivatives as a part of the Gospel record that may be credited to him.

These three portions of the Gospels, and a few lesser ones to be encountered later on, may be accepted as genuine and originating from Jesus himself, without further biographical or theological argument.

Exclusions

In contrast, many other of Jesus' alleged sayings, explanations and utterances in the Gospels may be rejected as *not* coming from him because they contradict these valid portions.*

To begin, we may reject immediately Jesus' alleged proclamations of God's dire punishments for those who do not toe the mark, simply because such punishment would never be imposed by the loving Deity he espoused. The Jews of his day envisioned an apocalyptic day of judgment when all souls would be judged and rewards and punishment handed out. We know now that, however God might be defined as representing the second and higher realms of existence, He does not function this way. The whole notion of rewards and punishments is *man's* doing, not God's. There is no overseeing, capricious and sometimes angry God who doles out pleasures and suffering in response to man's behavior, once He has created a *Natural Law*† of automatic consequences of actions in the first place. Such old ideas (common in many old religions) arose mainly from over-personalizations of God according to man's limited imagination at the time, and especially his insistence on punishment as necessary for his "sins" whenever he believes he has committed them.

In addition, for Jesus to induce in his listeners a *fear* of such punishment is not consistent with his compassionate nature. He sought to *dispel* men's fears, not create them. His alleged threats must be rejected as not coming from him.

Blaspheming the Holy Spirit cannot be an unforgivable sin,[26] as Jesus is supposed to have said, if we accept that God and all life are inherently and unconditionally forgiving, a point made repeatedly.[27] This statement could not have been his own, though it could be reworded to make a valid point: rejection of the Holy Spirit has serious personal aftereffects.

Jesus' reference to his priestly opponents as "a brood of vipers" and "fathers of the devil"[28] must be similarly denied. He certainly opposed

---

* Again, see the reports of the Jesus Seminar for a comprehensive discussion of these contradictions [Funk 1993, Funk 1997].

† I use the term *law* here with some misgiving. Since the legal laws we are accustomed to and live under are social, they incorporate many approximations in the interests of simplicity and enforceability and they call for punishment when broken (if you are caught). In contrast, what we are calling *Natural Law* here is closer to the laws of physics, for example. It is precise, universal, firm, inviolate, automatically enforced and does not include punishment.

their heartless behavior and rightly declared them to be hypocrites,[29] but he could not himself have uttered these heavy condemnations against their persons. He taught non-judgment and condemned no one. His accusation of Judas as a devil surely came from the Gospel writers and the Church, both of whom were looking for someone to blame for Jesus' death. Other accounts suggest that Jesus greatly loved Judas.

Jesus' quoted statements about himself as King, Lord and one uniquely chosen by God to be the personal savior of mankind disagree strongly with his validated teachings. He may have earned such titles in the eyes of others but he could not have claimed them for himself. He acknowledged his close relationship with his "Father" and his awareness of several universal qualities, but he taught that all men, including himself, are equal before their Creator. His positive teachings override Gospel statements about his personal claims to superiority.

For Jesus to affirm that God was his "Father"—a notion taken over from Judaism—was a powerful teaching metaphor for his Jewish audiences but it was certainly not meant to be taken in literal or familial terms. He realized through his own awakening that God exists within himself, just as it does for all men. To say that he "was God" would be an easy misinterpretation for those who wished to deify him. He probably claimed he was a "*Son of God*" but this term was already in use at that time to refer to all Jews. He sometimes called himself the *Son of Man*, perhaps a kind of representative of mankind to God, though this title is used imprecisely in both the Gospels and ancient Jewish literature and has to be interpreted selectively.

Jesus' alleged claim to be the Messiah (Christ) is also ambiguous. He certainly saw himself, at some point in his life, as a fulfillment of Old Testament prophecy in an enlightened sense, but the Jews used this term with a different meaning. They were expecting a God-sent deliverer from their miseries, and most specifically their Roman rulers. After all, whether you meet someone else's expectations is up to them, not you. Thus, some of Jesus' self-references as Messiah are valid and some are not.

Jesus claimed mainly to be a message bearer and emissary—a voice of God, if you will—just as other avatars in world history have done. He said he was an aspect or manifestation of God, as are all humans. He was quite aware of his built-in link with a higher reality, with his God. He recognized that most humans are not so aware, but they could be.

There are also several obvious factual contradictions among the four Gospels. For example, John and the synoptic authors differ on the length of Jesus' ministry: from one to three years.* There are also widely different interpretations of Jesus sayings. We know that the assumption that the Gospels are independent biographies is not correct, because each author except Mark relied on the previous ones and apparently sought to add what he felt was left out. There is much textual overlap, however, many events being duplicated but significant events *not* repeated, that we have to regard most of the latter as disagreements: the event was not repeated because the second author did not believe it occurred (such as Jesus walking on water and quelling a storm).

In addition to the above contradictions some of the Gospels' descriptions of Jesus' and others' intentions cannot be believed as stated because there is no credible way in which the writers could have learned about them. For example, Jesus' so-called "temptations" during his lone post-baptismal retreat on the mountain were certainly not the sort of intimate experiences he would have bragged about to anyone.[30] The words of his Gethsemane prayer, as fitting as it is, was said to be spoken in isolation, with no one close enough to hear him. And how could Luke, who never knew Jesus and was not around during his birth and youth, have known what Mary "pondered in her heart"?†[31] These and other similar claims could only have been manufactured.

These several contradictory Gospel statements, and a few more to be identified in later chapters, may therefore be rejected as inaccurate, misleading or downright wrong.

Between these contrasting examples of validity and invalidity there still lies a large body of Gospel text for which we cannot easily discriminate what is valid and what is not. We must rely upon another basis for filling in the remaining gaps in the story, resolving the ambiguities and identifying the inconsistencies. We will find this basis not in documents, scholarship and theology but through an entirely different way of gaining knowledge.

---

* John has Jesus attending three Passovers while the Synoptics account for only one.

† Unless he obtained this information intuitively, of course, but there is no other indication that he was functioning this way.

Christianity and the Gospels

What has been the role of the Christian religion in the Biblical account of Jesus? While this book is about Jesus, not Christianity, we still need to be aware of the difference between the two if we are going to unravel the truth about Jesus himself. This is largely because, as already noted, the records are highly weighted toward doctrinal Christianity, with the result that they are erroneously overvalued today as reliable sources about Jesus himself.

The majority of the distortions in the Gospels arose directly out of particular needs of the early Christian Church, mainly in the interests of unification and dissuading followers from prior existing allegiances. Others arose inconspicuously and indirectly because the writers were influenced by their culture and by the new Church as it evolved, even though this influence did not always show up explicitly in their writings. We can imagine well enough in retrospect how these distortions came into the minds of the Gospel writers and later editors as they sought to create a new Church.

The Gospels survived, but with a large Christian overlay. They have great value but do not do proper justice to Jesus' teachings.

Christianity in History

Let it not be misunderstood: the Christian religion which emerged from the early Church has been a unique and unquestionably powerful, effective and worthy social factor in Western man's evolutionary development over the last two thousand years. Just like other major world religions it has spawned valuable scholarship, unified social values and laws and generated a huge legacy of architecture, literature, music and art. It drew people together into cooperative and collective enterprises more than had ever occurred before in human history. While its political policies varied from benevolence to treachery, it insisted that every human, even a heavy sinner, is worthy and loved. It provided hope in the form of an idyllic heaven, immortality and forgiveness for sins. It gave Western man a set of positive metaphors and other symbols to sustain him through his miseries, even though they were embodied in a questionable legend. But this is what legends are for: to hold symbolically in the form of *beliefs* whatever of value cannot be maintained over time in the form of factual history and sets of principles.

Despite its shortcomings and terrible misuses the Christian religion has driven and nourished the spiritual lives of hundreds of millions of people. It has inspired the thought and work of countless contributors to society in many lands and callings. Highly successful in overall human terms, it is today the most salient religious influence in the lives of more than a billion people, and a strong underlying force in Western secular society and even throughout the planet.

Our position here is not to tear down Christianity but rather to encourage its enhancement and enrichment through a better understanding of what Jesus was actually teaching. In this way its adherents can choose to apply this deeper understanding in their individual lives, group endeavors and large-scale societal activities.

This is not unlike the process we follow when we raise a child. We do not continually criticize and judge it for being immature, or discard it for its frequent learning mistakes. Rather, we value, nurture and support it as it matures. We take pleasure in participating in its creative growth so it may someday become responsible, self-fulfilled and a positive force in the world.

This is the same charge before each one of us as he tries to work out his personal relationship with the behemoth of Christianity, and to find his peace with it whether he be Christian or not. It's only fundamental error today is its incompleteness, or immaturity.

Many saints, prophets and devoted practitioners over the ages have experienced the Christian life very deeply. Their contemplative devotions generated insightful interpretations, novel insights and the resolution of some of the shortcomings in the Biblical account of Jesus. A few of these practitioners found "hidden" truths within the Gospels and were able to write about them for later generations. The Christian contribution to the Perennial Philosophy arose in just this way. Also (barely) preserved by their efforts are the principles of soul growth, reincarnation and karma (to be explored in later chapters), which Jesus almost certainly espoused but are only hinted at in the Gospels. Thanks in large part to this minority of Christian explorers we are better enabled today to experience for ourselves Jesus' finer teachings and his grander vision. They have given us a head start, so to speak. We may dig even more deeply on our own now by building upon this background for ourselves.

Perhaps most important, we may come to accept Jesus' master claim that God is not to be found *external* to man—as has been tacitly assumed by most Christians for a hundred generations—but lies rather *within* each one of us. While he said this very clearly, this central message has been largely neglected, obscured or disregarded in Christianity. To reclaim it one need only acknowledge this grand presence within himself, which is not so hard to do, then relate to it intimately and draw understanding from it. Could there be a simpler path to higher wisdom, greater compassion and a new awakening?

Implications

Was Jesus aware of the organizational and theological controversies which would ensue after his death? Did he foresee the distorted form his vision would take and the drastic, inhumane methods that would be employed to propagate the Christian legend in his name? Did he realize that so many of his guiding principles would be all but lost as Christianity carried into the world its own version of his vision and message?

He certainly had the capacity for great foresight, so we can easily believe he was generally aware of this dynamic but limited future. He even "prophesized" portions of the most terrible consequences. He may well have seen it as the only possible alternative if man were ever to grow out of his primitive, warlike state into a higher nature in which he could accept his own in-built Godliness and live harmoniously with his fellow humans.

Jesus may have not only realized these social changes but deliberately *created* the complex legend about his life, as a survivable vehicle capable of holding a portion of his message over time.

If we accept this perspective we may suppose that the terrible catastrophes (wars, crusades, inquisitions, genocides, etc) *were on course to happen anyway,* and could have been much worse without Jesus' injection of the principles, values and vision he was able to contribute. It appears that man can enlarge himself only in his own reckless way, even though he is being constantly reminded of his better nature, including the help Jesus offered, and that he is always free to respond more positively if he so chooses.

What is hardest to understand is why so little has been done in the long evolution of Christianity to correct the large divergence between the religion and the central principles Jesus taught. Apparently the same human needs have persisted for a symbolic, dogmatized and ritualized religious institution, a personified God-man as figurehead, a personalized savior from sin and a lingering hope for salvation in an indefinite future. Indeed, these needs are built into the Christian creed and are still widespread in the Christian world today.

Individuals who no longer find this Church offering personally supportive tend to step out of Christianity and seek their own way in another religion, or as agnostics or atheists entirely outside of the domain of organized religion. Many have followed a solitary spiritual path and discovered all by themselves their inner God-nature and all it has to reveal to them. But the option to find it within Christianity as it stands is still open, and still possible.

Conclusion

We may conclude that Christianity has only partially followed the track Jesus originally offered. Its base of knowledge and practice is only weakly related to Jesus' teachings. As an organized religious institution it is rooted instead on manufactured doctrines and persuasive *legend*—not even on the more reliable historic facts and certainly not on the central teachings of the man for whom it is named. Even though the Jesus movement grew obliquely out of his exemplary life and sayings twenty centuries ago, Christianity is not the only and not necessarily the easiest and most direct gateway to a deeper understanding of the deeper message he taught.

It is this deeper understanding that we seek in this book. To find it we will explore in the next chapter an alternative path for learning about Jesus' life and teachings.

Review

History

The historical data on Jesus are far too sparse to constitute a reasonable biography of him.

The available Gospel record contains many distortions induced by their writers and the early Church and never corrected later. With the help of the world's spiritual literature, the earliest Gospel records (Q) and Jesus' specific teachings about love and its derivatives, we may identify and discard the worst of these distorted passages.

The true events in Jesus' life and the message he was teaching have been greatly weakened and are all but lost in the Christian legend, yet they were enough to trigger the Christian religion and nourish it globally for nearly two millennia.

Despite its great accomplishments (and terrible misuses), the institution of Christianity has rather little to do with Jesus the man and his main messages. We need a fresh source of information if we are to learn about Jesus' life and teachings. We must find another way of knowing.

CHAPTER 2

Another Way of Knowing

"Of all the hard facts of science, I know of none more solid and fundamental than the fact that if you inhibit thought, and persevere, you come at length to a region of consciousness below or behind thought . . . and a realization of an altogether vaster self than that to which we are accustomed. . . So great, so splendid is this experience that it may be said that all minor questions and doubts fall away in face of it." [Edward Carpenter]

Yes, there is indeed another source for learning about what Jesus was doing and teaching.

We spoke earlier about the Christian saints, prophets, sages and mystics who sought and found deep revelational knowledge within their devotional practices. These singular individuals were able to achieve an unusually deep understanding on the origin, purpose and meaning of human life, and some of them say they won a measure of personal transcendence as well. The accounts of their amazing discoveries contain valuable insights about Jesus' teachings, well beyond the Christian religious tradition.

To be sure, their experiences were often mystical and highly personal. Their explanations bordered on the ineffable as they tried to express, in words not able to hold them, what they found through the more deeper realms of their own consciousness. They often spoke wisely of the source of human suffering, the nature of Godly presence in man's life, and what it means to be in attunement with God through prayer or by some other means. Their insights offer valuable testimony to the spiritual wisdom that lies at the core of the cumbersome religious package through which they were forced to seek their understanding.

A similar story is repeated in other religions and cultures of the world about their own avatars. Their best writings parallel the Christian experience and compare well with it. This body of illuminating literature is still accessible today through books and on the Internet. Anyone may study and learn from it.[32]

The Nature of Intuition

How did these prophets and others achieve this high state of consciousness and such an exceptional mode of inner inquiry? Their approaches varied but we now know that they were early examples of an innate and universal human mental capacity for obtaining "hidden" knowledge and understanding.

We also understand better nowadays how one may attain this inner state of awareness and receptivity. One need not join a religious order, adopt quaint beliefs, retreat to a cave in the mountains or undergo decades of monastic discipline. Some opening and cleansing of the mind are normally necessary but the heart of the effort lies in an age-old mind process for gaining knowledge and insight *directly,* bypassing ordinary thought, intellectual reasoning, doctrinal study, ritual prayer, physical hardship, personal sacrifice and similar traditional hurdles.

This human ability to acquire knowledge apart from reasoning, sensing and remembering is called *intuition.*

Intuition over the Ages

Intuition is an ancient human capacity, known even in Grecian times when it was called *nous* (later *gnosis*), a term which referred to innate or direct knowing as distinguished from knowledge acquired through the senses or thinking. Intuition has been prevalent and practiced throughout the world and through most of history as the accepted "way to know things." With the rise of intellectual thinking in the 17th century, however, it fell into near obscurity in the civilized world. Science took over as a very practical alternative for generating knowledge, at least about material matters. The deliberate practice of intuition is still in active use today as a natural and accepted ability within small cultures that escaped modern

Western civilization, and among a few Western individuals who have chosen to recover this lost skill.

While intuition is not manifested much today we all still practice it, inadvertently, weakly and unconsciously, as part of what we consider to be ordinary thought.[33] It is an invisible partner to intellectual activity and a significant factor in the small and large decisions we make as we live our daily lives and experience and interpret the consequences of these decisions. Intuition is also the mental faculty responsible for occasional insights into our deeper nature and the greater order of things. This includes our personal knowledge about how the human body, mind and heart function; our closest relationships; the complex tribulations of our societies; and the particular concept of God one fashions for himself to accept or reject.

In short, each person's intuition is *his personal communication link with the second realm* described by the Perennial Philosophy. The second realm was known to the world's wisest teachers throughout human history as man's spiritual center, where he recognizes (normally sporadically) his origin, discovers his true identity and experiences his unity with the greater Reality of which he is a part. It is his main contact with this spiritual center, thus touching into both his personal truth and profound world truths.

Allowing Intuition to Work

While everyone possesses this intuitive capacity as a given ability, only a few choose to develop it into a workable skill and deliberately apply it to assist themselves and others. Their collective experience demonstrates that they are able to provide totally new knowledge on almost any topic, and to a depth that appears to be limited only by the inquirer himself. These few individuals, called here *expert intuitives,* will be our means of choice for obtaining the additional information we seek about Jesus and his teachings, and especially that which is not accessible by conventional means.

Intuitive knowledge transcends the limitations of ordinary language and thought. We cannot always justify intuitive information with reasons and arguments, nor do we need to as individuals; we just *know* it, as we know that dogs exist, our children love us and the sun rises in the east. The most profound inner experiences and insights by the world's inspired seekers can be credited to this "opening of the intuitive gate" so that deeper knowledge could be reached. It was not "proven" to them; they just *knew* they had reached it.

When intuitive information is received by expert intuitives it comes mainly through their *feelings*—though most feelings are not intuitive at all. The practice of intuition may be recognized in the non-rational processes of meditation, solitary prayer, inner attunement, our best dreams, some psychic experiences and the serendipitous insights that sometimes accompany both crisis and ecstasy. Besides the prophets and mystics, many renowned artists, philosophers, businessmen and scientists acknowledge intuition for their best discoveries and ideas. In these cases the insights typically burst suddenly into consciousness without rational thought, sensual input or memory.

Intuitive insights need not occur only spontaneously, however; they may arise deliberately by establishing a receptive state of mind and asking the right questions. Intuitive skill is readily learnable by anyone who has a serious intention to do so. A small amount of training and usually some emotional clearing are all that are required to awaken intuition, enhance it, bring it under conscious control and then focus it with intention on whatever you wish to know. This is what *expert intuitives* have learned to do.

These strong claims on the power of intuitive inquiry for acquiring new knowledge have been demonstrated many times over for a wide variety of topics, inquirers and conditions of inquiry.[34] The specific information that expert intuitives have brought forth has been used constructively for their own purposes, to assist other persons, in support of group projects and for the greater human welfare. Much of this intuitively derived information has been independently verified to be accurate and responsive to the questions asked, when scientific or other accepted means of validation were at hand and the information was sufficiently specific to be tested.

Intuition and Belief

Before you can totally and internally accept any new information, intuitive or another, you must integrate it into your personal base of pre-existing knowledge and life experience. Your mind is able to do this very well, for it is continually comparing new fragments of information and experience against everything you already know, checking for consistency.

While this integration process is largely unconscious, your conscious mind plays a role because it must give "permission" for corrections to be made whenever contradictions are encountered. When it is unwilling or unable to reconcile the new with the old, intellectual and/or emotional conflict result and show up as a challenge to existing *beliefs*. A common consequence of receiving new information—and especially intuitive information—is therefore to force the recipient to *examine his beliefs* consciously and select what is valid and acceptable to him and what should be rejected.

Unfortunately, the majority of the core beliefs people carry with them are acquired early in life and typically reside outside of ordinary awareness. They are regarded as a "fixed" part of the personality, if they are regarded at all, and appear to be essential for personal well being and security. They reside in the subconscious mind, where they tend to solidify and become difficult to change. Because they differ from genuine, accurate knowledge about the real world, they are responsible for much human misery as contradictions arise and as one attempts to defend them. In society they can lead to terrible discord and controversy, as is quite obvious from the long history of human conflicts which arose directly out of incongruous and very unreal beliefs.

It is certainly better to have *some* beliefs rather than none, of course. You are probably not aware of some of your old, incorrect beliefs because they remain unchallenged until a sufficient contradiction occurs with the real world. For example, people survive for decades with the belief that their death is the end of their existence, or that they are entirely the product of their parents' genes, or that Jews cannot be trusted, or (at the extreme) that they are justified in killing others who do not honor their God, even if they themselves are killed in the process. Such beliefs can produce great suffering before they are changed.

Beliefs can be upgraded to fit the world into which one has matured by first *recognizing* them—bringing them into awareness. Religious beliefs are usually the hardest to detect in oneself because they were adopted so easily and without question at a young age from parents, teachers and one's culture. They lie quietly and unchallenged within the subconscious mind, often for decades or one's entire life. They are often assumed to be not beliefs but incontrovertible fact. Once identified and confronted, however, religious beliefs can be easier to upgrade than others because the contradictions with reality are so blatant. The holder is then strongly compelled to change them—sometimes very suddenly.

Beliefs and Knowledge

It is important here to distinguish between beliefs and genuine knowledge. We do not "believe in" trees or electricity or the love from our parents—we *know* these things exist and they are real to us—but we might believe in UFOs, the gold standard, the virgin birth, that the number thirteen is unlucky or that Muslims are evil. Beliefs play an important role in the mind as *tentative, temporary and candidate knowledge*, and we very much need them in the course of our lives. They are held conditionally and under consideration for acceptance as true, but are still doubted and uncertain. They await deeper insight, testing or refinement from further experience before we are willing to correct and integrate them into a personal knowledge base. Your beliefs can *lead* to knowledge, at which point they are no longer tentative and do not need to be tested, defended, explained or argued for. The term *belief* is then no longer appropriate. You simply *know*.

When the eminent psychologist Carl Gustav Jung was asked if he believed in God, he replied, "I don't need to. I *know* God."* His answer says it well and reminds us that it is important to identify our beliefs and upgrade them into knowledge—to *know* God for ourselves, for example.

Genuine knowledge is inherently valid, permanent, supportive and never a true danger. It may be said to be as close to *truth* as is humanly possible at any point in your growth. Like beliefs, you may be unaware of much of your knowledge because it is so close to home, and so familiar that you are not inclined to question or examine it. Beliefs, on the other hand, while also familiar, are always a bit of a threat. They are subject to change and a compromise with the truth. They entail a fear that you will be misled by them. Indeed, a good test for a belief is whether you feel inclined to defend it if challenged.

Beliefs are powerful shapers of behavior but fall under your conscious control as soon as you become aware of them. After all, they are not imposed upon you; you created them in the first place and you can change them as soon as you choose to do so. As your beliefs grow into knowledge your attitudes and behavior cannot help but change for the better because they reflect the real world rather than the random workings of your mind.

---

* This quote is from an old interview with Jung. In a later interview Jung says, "I will never say that I *believe* God exists." See for example:
http://wiki.answers.com/Did_Jung_believe_in_a_God.

Beliefs affect clear intuitive reception too, because they can easily disagree with newly received intuitive information by modifying or blocking it. To be a competent intuitive you must first convert potentially interfering beliefs into knowledge—or at least reduce them to an acknowledged and innocent ignorance. It is this cleared state of mind that characterizes expertness.

Accessing Intuitive Information

As mentioned in the Introduction we will be utilizing in this book the abilities of expert intuitive *Kevin Ryerson*[*] for our inquiry into Jesus' life and teachings.

Like all expert intuitives Ryerson does not "possess" the information he provides, like an encyclopaedia or a scholar who has accumulated a life-full of it. Rather, he is a vehicle or channel who *transmits* the new information from a higher source of knowledge outside of his personal memory and his acquired experience.

What is this mysterious reservoir of knowledge? Every major religion and philosophic system has a name for it: *God's Book of Remembrance, the Akashic Records, the Book of Life*, the *superconscious mind*, the *collective unconscious* and others. It is not known exactly what this huge knowledge base is or exactly how it works, at least in familiar or scientific terms. There is no doubt that it exists and can be accessed, however, for centuries of intuitive experience testify to it. This includes an untold number of modern intuitives who have shown their ability to tap it for rich information. The information they obtain can be very broad in extent, cover many fields, and be given to great depths and in great detail. It extends into the remote past and the far future (to the extent that the future is predictable at all). It is typically unknown beforehand to the expert intuitive, and sometimes not known by any living person. These present-day expert intuitives have shown conclusively that the information they obtain is consonant with the highest human values and concerns. It has turned out to be generally accurate whenever it was verifiable and was actually tested.

Ryerson accesses this huge reservoir of knowledge by setting aside his thinking mind and entering a sleep-like trance state. (Trance is not

---

[*] For more detailed information about Kevin Ryerson and his work see the biographical summary at the end of this book.

inherent to intuitive reception, for some expert intuitives remain fully conscious.) In this state he accepts questions posited to him and speaks the answers. On awakening from this level of consciousness he has little or no conscious memory of what transpired while he was not present. When in trance he may use terminology and concepts for which he has no conscious knowledge. In general the information he relates is typically well beyond what he consciously knows and his past experience. There is no doubt that at least most of it originates outside of his personal memory. He deserves credit for the role he is playing in transmitting the information, but is not responsible for the information itself.

Ryerson is as generally familiar with Jesus and Christianity as are most of us, and he has a well developed general spiritual understanding from his decades of work as a counsellor, lecturer and teacher on metaphysical matters. He has not been formally educated in these areas, however, and is in no sense a Biblical scholar, historian or religious specialist. His mental skills, language and subconscious memory continue to function in trance. They enable him to relay to the *superconscious* mind the questions posed to him, and to convey the information he receives from it to a listener in clear English. His conscious mind is largely bypassed.

Corroboration and Mode

While intuitive information may be accurate at its superconscious source, by the time it passes through the intuitive's subconscious and is expressed in words it may contain errors. Years of experience with intuitives has shown that when working with *expert* intuitives the distortions are very few. Still, so long as errors can occur at all, *new intuitive information should always be verified or corroborated from other sources* before it is relied upon for decisions and critical actions.

There are several ways to do this, depending upon the kind of information sought. For some types scientific or similar formal means of testing may be applied. For other types one may compare it with information stored in libraries or accessible on the internet. For still others it may be cross-checked with other expert intuitives for the purpose of creating an "intuitive consensus." For predictions and certain innovative ideas it may be possible to just hold the intuitive information and see if it checks out.

For personal, historical and inspirational information, such as that developed in this book, these means of corroboration are not usually possible. Some degree of verification can sometimes be done by the user himself, perhaps through his own intuition—it has to "feel right"—but often we can only experiment personally with it and gradually come to know its validity. This is the same process we normally employ for most of the news we receive from other persons or through the media, for example.

The Center for Applied Intuition (CAI), which developed the intuitive inquiry method used here, applied it to several problem areas during the 1980s. Ryerson collaborated as one of CAI's several staff intuitives on both scientifically and socially oriented research projects, and also provided personal counseling to hundreds of clients (and hundreds more in his private practice). He performed in this manner for researchers, public audiences and individual inquirers for most of his adult life. Significant portions of the information he provided were verified independently as opportunities arose to do so. These validated portions were not casual claims that could have been made by any knowledgeable person, nor were they lucky guesses out of several failed attempts. They were singular, definitive and testable assertions, often with much complexity and depth.

The quality of information provided by an expert intuitive such as Ryerson is quite different from that given by your neighborhood psychic, astrologer or card reader. Such amateurs may utilize their intuition to some extent but only rarely do they offer the integrity, reliability, accuracy and responsibility possessed by a truly expert intuitive. Ryerson's "channeling," as it is sometimes called, has passed very well these various tests on answers to the questions asked of him.

We therefore have in Ryerson good reason to pay attention to whatever he tells about Jesus and his teachings.

Just as with various other expert intuitives who work in a trance state, the information Ryerson provides is spoken by an intermediate consciousness which calls itself "John" and claims to be John the son of Zebedee, youngest of Jesus' apostles and the author of the Gospel which bears the name "John." I naturally have questions about this particular identification, but accept it at face value until it should prove itself wrong—which it has not yet done. I encourage you to do the same.

John has a personality and speaking style distinct from Ryerson's.[*] His language is a bit archaic though readily understandable. As Ryerson says, "John's manner of expression is what we would think of as 'biblical,' both in his language (*ye* and *thee*), and in his many references from that time period."[†35]

For ease of reading I have edited out John's frequent phrases "as though," "such as" and "so-called" when they do not contribute to understanding. Otherwise my editing has been superficial and minimal.

Variations and Purpose

Ryerson is not the only expert intuitive who has provided detailed factual information about Jesus. At least ten credible accounts, and a dozen more which are somewhat less credible, have been published within the last fifty years. Taken together they constitute a rich data base of potentially useful information about Jesus' life, deeds and sayings. These data are currently being integrated and evaluated in a comprehensive report.[36]

Do these multiple intuitive accounts agree with one another? For Jesus' *teachings*, yes, the corroboration among them is very good and they support one another well. The few deviations appear to arise from poor questioning or from differences in terminology and concepts which were imprecise from the start. For the *narrative* events in Jesus' life, however, there are substantial differences among them. This is to be expected from the nature of intuitive inquiry and in view of the purpose for which the information was sought. It works like this.

The value, mode of expression and even the content of new intuitive information is always related to the intended *purpose* for which it is being sought. This appears to be a unique feature of intuitive inquiry when compared with other means of knowledge acquisition such as journalistic interviews, empirical experimentation and science generally, all of which rest on an assumed premise of objectivity: the inquirer is assumed to be separate from the topic of inquiry and is just observing or listening. Intuitive inquiry, on the other hand, is inherently subjective and participative. It is not a unilateral process in which information flows just one way. Its primary purpose is to serve the needs of the inquirer

---

[*]   See Chapter 7 for a clarification of this identity.

[†]   John often brings in parallel teachings from Buddhism, Vedanta and Taoism.

and lead him *to inquire within himself* for the information he is seeking. Yes, relevant information is provided, but its content always pertains first to his present state of mind and well-being, and only secondarily to the specific information he thinks he wants. In other words, the goal of intuitive inquiry is more to *inspire* and *encourage* the recipient than to *inform* him as in a lecture by a scholar, a book by a specialist or a television documentary.

Intuitive inquiry therefore strongly reflects the state of mind of the inquirer and seeks to induce understanding in a personal and sometimes indirect way. The inquirer's understanding may be *triggered* by an intuitive insight, just as it is by a casual remark, a phrase in a book or an image in a dream. Its significance does not lie in the triggering signal itself but rather in his recognition of its deeper implications and his willingness to accept, assimilate and integrate these implications into his existing base of knowledge. This is the main role of intuitive information in general, regardless of the specific information conveyed and the particular means of delivering it.

When factual information can aid an individual's understanding, and he is able to absorb it and utilize it, it is provided. In personal inquiries this is not usually the case, for the inquirer's resistance in the form of preconceived beliefs and personal desires too often prevent him from hearing and applying the information he could benefit from. Thus, the information given to him is shaped more by what he can absorb and use than by the specific facts he desires. This was evidenced repeatedly in hundreds of personal intuitive sessions arranged by CAI and performed by Ryerson and other expert intuitives.

This inquiry process can be compared with a compassionate parent's responses to the curiosity of a five-year old child, or how a wise guru deals with a naïve chela: answers are given in proportion to the recipient's existing stage of understanding and in a form that induces the inquirer to probe deeper within himself. Again, factual content is secondary in importance and may even be held back when it conflicts with a greater benefit.

When asking about Jesus' life, therefore, the intuitive answers which are given are more likely to reflect the inquirer's particular beliefs and personal needs than the subject matter itself. These beliefs and needs can vary greatly from one person to another so we should not expect literal consistency among the responses at all times and to all inquirers. This is so whether they rely upon their own intuition or that of expert intuitives. Inquirers not so burdened with these obstacles can expect clearer answers to their questions. The questions asked of Ryerson in this book were the result of considerable preparation and clearing but they represent this author's version of the cultural need for understanding, and cannot be said to be perfect. How you interpret and accept the answers won't be perfect either.

For factual information on scientific and historical matters this personal biasing and resistance are not so likely to be a problem because the issues at hand are less likely to involve the inquirer himself; hence the remarkable success of such explorations. Most of Jesus' *basic teachings* are also in this category, as noted above, for they consist largely of fundamental principles and their associated concepts, which belong to everyone. The information given follows a common theme, with closely similar declarations and explanations for almost all inquirers.

Subjective Reception

Obviously, one should never accept blindly *any* new information—intuitive or other—but he should first try to compare it with what he already comprehends. The new information may turn out to be absolutely correct, the "gospel truth," or it may seem irrelevant, distorted or entirely wrong. Most often, its accuracy and relevance are uncertain or unknown, and it can only be held in abeyance, perhaps as a belief, awaiting further clarification. While much of this contemplative, evaluative phase of assimilation is unconscious, as explained earlier, it still has a conscious component which is an essential part of knowledge expansion. That is, the new information has to "feel right" or "make sense" before it can be integrated.

For this step of checking and integration, intuitive information works just as do myths, legends and lyrical songs. Their value lies not so much in their literal, factual content but more in the underlying, richer and often nonverbal messages they carry—just like a song of love, a poem, an adventure story, a tale of dragons, or the tale of Jesus' birth in a cave with farm animals. They may be fairly compared with historical fiction (even though it is neither history nor fiction), for there is no expectation of factual validity and the historical facts, the character descriptions and the complex interactions and underlying themes in the story are blurred and not clearly right or wrong. The mixture works, however, to open a reader's mind to new ideas, possibilities and understanding of human nature and perhaps himself. As one intuitive puts it, "Myths and symbols are often closer to reality than what are called hard facts, since so-called hard facts are often distortions of the outer senses."[37]

The Christian Bible itself may be read in this same way, and many persons do so.

This observation suggests that when you read Ryerson's intuitive information you should discern for yourself its accuracy and meaning *for you*. Let this be your preferred method for learning what "really happened" in Jesus' life. It will reveal what the various events signify for yourself, even if only symbolically, and therefore which of Jesus' various teachings are the most relevant contributions to your present state of understanding. This subjective mode of working with intuitive information is the *only valid way* in which to understand and incorporate it into your personal life. Literal analysis and criticism will benefit you very little.

Once again, you are invited to regard the intuitive descriptions as possible alternatives to whatever beliefs you originally bring to the table. They are not factual statements, commandments or appeals that you accept them as such. Like the historical novel, you are to use them as a starting point for your own inner search so you may uncover a piece of your personal truth.

Who This Book is For

This book is directed, therefore, to those who are willing and able to receive new information in this receptive, subjective way.

You do not need to become an expert intuitive yourself to allow this mode of subjective learning to work in your behalf. It is enough that you remain *open* to the new information and willing to hold it *in abeyance*, without judging it to be right or wrong and without trying to fit it into an established belief structure—at least until a later moment of personal reflection when your inner knowing process will be more active and thus safer from intellectual and emotional interference.

In contrast, the reader who expects literal explanations and external, authoritative answers to his questions about Jesus will be dissatisfied by the information offered in this book—and indeed, with intuitively derived information on any topic and from any intuitive source. We can only remind him that the most important knowledge he already possesses and trusts in his life was obtained not solely through his logical mind, senses and external sources, but rather through *his own intuition* operating in the invisible background. This is actually how the human mind functions: it uses both its intellectual and intuitive faculties together. Awareness of the latter is typically weak, especially in this day and age. Practice in working with high-quality intuitive sources can help you remedy this unfortunate weakness.

The appropriate measure of value for all knowledge you obtain intuitively—by yourself or through an expert intuitive—is not how well it ranks against a scale of scholarship or conforms to your existing beliefs, but rather how subjectively and practically relevant it may be to your on-going life. In other words, its mark of quality is not how smart it makes you but how it inspires you toward deeper understanding. On this scale intuitive information has the potential to score much higher than information provided from your relatively laborious, over-thinking mind.

Restatement of Purpose

To summarize, our purpose here is *not* to sell you on any particular set of new beliefs about Jesus, nor is it to tear down as erroneous those beliefs you presently hold, whatever they might be, and leave you stranded. Rather, its main purpose is to *inspire* you with new information and ideas; to *support* your motivation to review your present beliefs (especially your beliefs about Jesus); and to enable you to *upgrade* these beliefs in whatever way you choose.

You may read this book out of curiosity, for entertainment, for potentially useful information or even as a skeptic searching for points on which to disagree and attack. The only requirements for comprehending these new ideas (new to you, that is) is your willingness to hold new ideas in abeyance, without judgment, until they can be assessed later and used to upgrade your existing beliefs.

These two practices—suspension of judgment and upgrading of beliefs—involve both your intellect and your intuition. The latter may be your better ally. Most of us in the modern world are so intellectually inclined that we try to juggle facts and "figure things out" before we attune inwardly to what is really going on.

Relax, therefore, and listen inwardly! You may safely assume that your inner senses know much better than your brain what is true and what is not. Try to accept this assumption. Experiment with its implications. You will not be disappointed!

Review

History

Intuition is the innate and universal human faculty for acquiring knowledge directly, without use of the rational mind, senses or memory.

Intuition has enabled generations of saints, prophets and mystics from all the world's cultures to probe into their own minds for deep knowledge not readily accessible to ordinary thought and experience.

Each individual's intuition is his personal communication link with the "second realm" of existence described by the Perennial Philosophy.

Intuitive skill may be learned by virtually anyone wishing to develop it. Expert intuitives have trained themselves to access the collective unconscious for almost any information or knowledge asked of them.

Beliefs are preliminary ideas awaiting change or verification before they can be upgraded into certain knowledge. They always compromise truth and invite testing and refinement. They can distort or block the acquisition, acceptance and integration of intuition.

Intuitive information, like all new information, should be independently verified in some way before being used as a basis for decisions and actions.

The purpose of intuitively received information is primarily to inspire and induce belief changes, as may be necessary for enlarging one's understanding. To do so may take precedence over factual information.

> "The value of any book isn't in the tangible object itself, but in *the ability of those organized words to inspire thought.* This then becomes the activator of human experience. Therefore, in making these materials available, my primary intention is to inspire thought. Like any other book, [it] will be of value only to the degree that it stimulates an active thinking process within the reader." [Kevin Ryerson[38]]

INTERLUDE

Let us begin this intuitive inquiry by asking Ryerson/John a fundamental question about the long-range implications of this new story of Jesus for the broad class of the world's Christians, including those not likely to read this book.

WHK: (Hundreds of millions of people on this planet are leaning upon the Jesus legend for their spiritual nourishment. In presenting this deeper story of Jesus and the Christ, how should we give due respect to those who are devoted so heavily to the Christian legend, even though it is ambiguous, confusing, historically incorrect and often misleading?)

Ryerson/John: There is much to debate on the dynamics of the legend, even within its two-thousand year history. There's been not so much a *fragmentation* of the legend as *diversity* of the components of the legend. Remember, a legend always contains an element of truth and is based on fact.

Seek, then, to *revitalize* their vision, so that they may reinvent and/or rediscover the elements of the legend that are to serve them more. Consider thyself not to approach this as *deconstructing* what has been given, but [rather] revitalizing the diverse parts of the body of Christ—namely, the very language of the so-called legend. . . .

So this is the recalling: to bring together all the memories, all the diverse elements of the so-called legend, and to breath new life and new vitality into them; to bring together all the parts of the body, the whole, so that these people may be once again *moved* by the spirit and be revitalized by it.

For it is part and parcel to not only their characters but their souls.

In other words, it is not necessary or desirable to destroy or even diminish the Christian legend as it exists, but only to enlarge, unify and revitalize it. This will be our stance in the chapters to follow.

CHAPTER 3

THE WRITTEN RECORD

Because the historical source material on Jesus is so incomplete, biased and distorted as biography, as explained at length above, it cannot be relied upon for historical accuracy, reliability and veracity. Let us begin our inquiry by asking briefly about a few of the historical records about Jesus to see what may be newly learned about them.

Written and Oral Records

As far as anyone knows Jesus never prepared an autobiography or any other writings. He may not even have been literate.*

(**WHK**: Is it true that Jesus never wrote anything down?)

Ryerson/John: Jesus was literate. He often exchanged letters. There survive letters that he had written to the so-called king of Edessa, so there was correspondence.†

---

* Jews are claimed to have learned to read and write in their local synagogue, but the view of scholars is that less than 5% of Galilean Jews were literate. There is no clear statement that Jesus was literate, though it seems likely he was, based upon of a number of circumstantial statements in the Gospels—for example, writing in the sand before the woman caught in adultery.

† Christian history has it that King Abgar V of Edessa in India wrote Jesus, imploring his healing help, and that Jesus replied with a letter, offering to send a disciple after his death. Even if true this does not prove that Jesus wrote the letter himself, of course. A portrait of Jesus is also mentioned. Texts allegedly by Jesus survive but scholars regard them as spurious.

(Why did he not prepare written records of what he did and taught?)

Jesus, like many Essenes, knew the teachings of the Torah, where virtually every word was based upon the Pentateuch, or the Tetragrammiton. It can be found that the Mishna,* the so-called original oral traditions, were still an open and known dialog among the Jewish and Hebrew people and [among] the Essenes.† Although a literate people, particularly from the days of Abraham, and having originated from the cities of the plains and from Egypt, [they] had written languages. The sacred qualities of the Hebrew language emerged so as to conserve the mysteries of the Torah.

Knowing them by rote or by memory, and there being a common denominator, Jesus perceived the passing-on of the *words*. He knew that there would eventually be those who would seek to conserve the words, as this was their natural penchant.

The Essenes were authors of many scrolls but considered that a superior form of teaching was to work directly from the heart, in the oral tradition. Thus, while Jesus did not forbid the writing of the Gospels, he did give instruction, saying, "Behold, ponder not what ye shall say in those days, for it shall be I who speaks through thee."[39]‡

---

* The *mishna* is the early collection of Jewish tradition and law, the basis of the Talmud and originally oral, as noted above. It is regarded as the most significant collection of the Jewish tradition for interpreting the Torah . . . The *Pentateuch* comprises the five books of the Hebrew Torah, which is essentially the same as the first five books of the Christian Old Testament . . . The *Tetragrammiton* is the four-letter designation, usually written YHWH, intended to represent the unpronounceable name of God.

† The *Essenes* were an ascetic and messianic Jewish sect, complementary to the Pharisees and Sadducees. It flourished in the Middle East, at least in Palestine and Egypt, from the second century BCE to the first century CE. Some Essenes lived in religious communities, one of which is now known to have been at Qumran on the Dead Sea near where the Dead Sea Scrolls were discovered. (See more on Essenes in Chapter 5 below.)

‡ Both intuitive and Gospel sources require personal validation by their readers, of course. Neither should be taken as inherently correct or authoritative over the other.

Many amongst the Jewish people, as amongst many people of oral traditions, had highly qualified mnemonics [memories]. For instance, if you were to measure the alpha and beta [brain-wave] activities in those of oral traditions rather than written traditions, you would find the mnemonic centers [memory] of the brain architecture would be highly stimulated—in other words, superior memory.

Jesus, by adhering to the oral tradition, knew that this would force individuals who wished to know him to come into his presence. It was his desire for people to be brought into companionship, thereby creating kindred spirits through direct experience of each other rather than through the written word, which would have tendencies to compartmentalize and isolate society and create administrative forms rather than the true condition of the family.

(Are there more written records from the apostles than those we have available to us today?)

Correct. There are various Gospels that are considered apocryphal but are indeed authentic.

The Gospel of Mark

As one proceeds from the Gospel of Mark, the earliest, to John, the latest, the sequence shows a progression from biographical to devotional, objective to subjective and secular to doctrinal in their persuasion. John's Gospel so disagrees with the three synoptic Gospels that they cannot both be right.

Mark's Gospel, the shortest (16 chapters) and most biographically substantial of the four, emphasizes Jesus' deeds over his teachings and presents a more human than a divine Jesus. Like the other three its authorship is in doubt: who is this Mark? Church authorities assigned it to the evangelist Mark in later years, though this was probably done to add credence to it by attributing it to an associate of Jesus.

(Was the author of the Gospel of Mark indeed a boy who was around Jesus during his ministry, as some claim?)

> He was a young disciple, a youth, correct. The channel speaking [John] was considered the youngest of the disciples—not by many years, however.

(Is this Mark the same as the John Mark mentioned in the Book of Acts[40], a companion to Paul and Barnabas?)

> This would be correct.

(The last ten verses at the end of Mark's Gospel seem to be quite different than the rest. Did Mark actually write these or were they inserted by someone else?)

> Regarding some of the shifts in the Gospels, remember that some things were written from an historic perspective and others in ecstatic states.

The Gospel of Thomas

The apocryphal Gospel of Thomas, part of the Nag Hammadi collection of documents mentioned earlier,[41*] claims to have arisen out of Jesus' private teachings to Didymus Judas Thomas (not the apostle Judas but perhaps the apostle Thomas, a twin, who may also be the author of other apocryphal "Thomas" Gospels[†]). This Gospel contains no narrative, as do the four main Gospels, and there is no mention of Christ, Lord, sin, a second coming or the resurrection. It consists only of 114 *sayings* attributed to Jesus, some of which duplicate those in the four main Gospels. Many of these sayings seem highly symbolic and are difficult to reconcile with either the other Gospels or early Christian doctrine and beliefs.

---

[*] See footnotes about the Nag Hammadi Library and Dead Sea Scrolls early in Chapter 1.

[†] These are *Thomas' Infancy Gospel*, the *Book of Thomas the Contender* and the *Acts of Thomas* [ECW].

(The Gospel of Thomas, a collection of sayings attributed to Jesus, seems terribly ambiguous and even contradictory to Jesus' other teachings. How accurate and important is this Gospel, and how are we to interpret it?)

> Jesus' parables [*sic*] and sayings in the Book of Thomas were considered so powerful that they were isolated from the context of the teachings. This was often the way the man Jesus spoke when he would speak privately to the disciples.*
> At times it was these types of teachings that the disciples yearned for. These were comparable to the Zen ko-an.†
>
> When the man Socrates wished to cause great puzzlement he would often present an individual with an answer without a question, and this would cause great confusion; in other words, it lacked context. When he wished to enlighten an individual he would ask them a question and guide them through the question until it reached its natural clarity or greater wisdom.

(For example, Thomas quotes Jesus as saying, "Every female who makes herself male will enter the kingdom of heaven." What in the world did he mean by this?)[42]

> This [expression] speaks to the so-called kingdom [of heaven]. Jesus knew that people saw the kingdom in various ways, which is why the Gospels give various descriptions of what the kingdom is like. This was an acknowledgment of the various stages of psychic growth of the soul and of the individual.

---

* We should not be surprised that some of Jesus' teachings were not intended for a mass audience but would be given only to those appropriately prepared, including some of his apostles. He is quoted as saying this himself. [Matt 13:13, Mark 4:11-12, 33-34, Luke 8:10] In ancient times there was an on-going commerce in secrets, especially in Jesus' Palestine. Such practices seem undemocratic in this day and age, for we tend to believe that virtually all information should be free and available, as in libraries and on the Internet, but this was not at all the case until recently.

† A *ko-an* is a Zen teaching question, the response to which is intended to be inaccessible to rational understanding, thus forcing the student to rely on his intuitive capacities.

Within the context of the human soul, in contemporary psychology, for instance, it is now known that it [the psyche or soul] contains both male and female, both upon the physiological level and upon the psychological level˙. The concept of a *kingdom* is an archaic word meaning "order of things," likening it to the so-called creation, meaning the natural order or the Eden-like state of things; the ability to see the divine throughout the whole. One can see in this the *ley lines* of the earth connecting all living beings.† Others could see the angels coming and going. And there would be the various levels of al experiences.

But here was a true key. He also says in the Gospel of Thomas, "Those who make the two one shall not perish, or shall not die, but shall have everlasting life."⁴³ What this speaks to is simple: it constitutes the unification of the male and the female of the self—that is, the union of the soul—between what is considered to be both the rational and the non-rational, the analytical and even the intuitive, what is referred to in the Eastern philosophies as the Yin and the Yang, and in this case the male and the female within the self. In Tantra and Yoga‡ it is referred to as the unification of the base chakras and higher chakras.§ This [union] then

---

˙ John is apparently referring to the identification of *animus* and *anima* archtypes within the human psyche, a discovery usually credited to psychologist Carl Jung.

† *Ley lines* are linear geographical alignments of certain ancient buildings, monuments and megaliths. Their origin and significance are unknown and widely disputed. It is not difficult to find lines that pass through three or more of a random collection of points.

‡ *Tantra* is a loosely defined esoteric tradition, an accumulation of mystical ideas and practices which are widespread in the Far East, especially Tibet, and which claim to bring the cosmic power of the universe down into an individual's physical life, including the physical body. Various yogic practices are employed, one of which diverts sexual energy toward this spiritual opening, and this is the aspect for which Tantra is best known in the West . . . *Yoga* is an ancient school of Hindu philosophy that offers a path and a means of spiritual perfection. Its various branches include the "four yogas"—the paths of action, devotion, knowledge and karma—along with the physical body postures of *hatha* yoga, now the most familiar form of yoga in the Western world.

§ According to Eastern philosophy the *chakras* are seven foci of subtle energy in the human body. They lie along the spinal cord and are believed to represent the points where spiritual forces are translated into a material form which the body can utilize.

opens the so-called kundalini,* which opens one to the higher psychic states and allows one to then enter the kingdom, the natural or spiritual order of things.

Fig. 2. Diagram of the Chakras in the human body

(Would it be equally accurate, then, to say that one who is male and "makes himself female" in this sense would enter the kingdom of heaven?)

Right. In other words, if an individual thinks of himself only in terms of gender-based identity he has not yet entered

---

Some modern interpreters associate them with seven of the endocrine glands. See further discussion in a later chapter.

* *Kundalini* is a yogic term referring to a powerful energy, pent up at the base of the spine, which may be released under certain non-ordinary and heightened states of consciousness. It then rises up within the body along the line of the chakras. It is symbolized in Hindu tradition as a snake uncurling upwards. Unfamiliar and often misunderstood in the West, a *kundalini awakening* is usually spontaneous and deeply experiential and often personally transformative. Certain sustained yoga practices are said to be able to arouse the kundalini, with the warning that it should never be forced but allowed to awaken by itself.

the kingdom. For he is then acting out the nature of the soul through the singularity of gender. When he realizes that he is both male and female he enters into a deeper understanding of the nature of the soul rather than merely a material identity.

(So what does this passage from the Gospel of Thomas have for us today?)

If it is looked upon as a book of ko-ans, as in the mystery of the Book of Revelations, it may be said to be the following.

One, it truly embraces many of the mystical teachings which Jesus had taken the disciples aside to speak to them about—the mysteries of the kingdom, the mysteries of heaven that many of them yearned for. For remember, Jesus took them through the journey gently.

When he received his own enlightenment at the baptism by John [the Baptist], and when first approached as he was asked to perform miracles or give a sign, he said, "First come to know me in my own household. Take a meal with me and know first my humanity." So he gently encouraged these individuals to grow according to the degree that their own faith, or belief, might sustain them.

This constitutes [indicates?], then, that many of the teachings of Jesus were very powerful. They were poetry to unify the mind, the body and the spirit. He wished enlightenment [for them] but also to spare them the consequences, [so] that the enlightenment not take them so far out of the world but more so that they could be *in* the world, but not *of* it.

Indeed, Jesus needed his apostles to spread his teachings after his death, not to become mystics or recluses.

The Gospel Q

The Gospel Q, introduced in Chapter 1, has never been found, nor are there any historical references to it as such. There is therefore controversy today over whether such a document ever existed.[44]

(Did an original Gospel Q really exist?)

The Gospel Q exists, and the channel speaking was the keeper of the four sets of manuscripts that were Q. One source for Q was the Gospel of Thomas—the teachings, the *sayings*, of Jesus—but notice there is little historical narration in them—not the flow and the continuity of the life of the man Jesus.

Each Gospel has been known for a particular quality. Some list the events of the [life] of Jesus, others list the miracles of Jesus, others list the *sayings* of Jesus, and others emphasize the overall quality of the life of Jesus. This was because, in order to protect the truth and to validate the testimony, there were four *sources* to be worked with, so that if one was lost, the others could be reclaimed.

These four sources of Q are still contained in the Island of Patmos, in as yet undocumented scrolls in the monastery that holds them there.* There are also sources of Q that are yet to be found [identified?] amidst the so-called Dead Sea Scroll library, for the Essenes began [later] to write down the life of Jesus.† They greatly valued these sacred books. They still exist and remain yet to be discovered.

Jesus [also] had records kept by those who journaled, such as the channel speaking. Otherwise they were [transmitted] through the oral tradition.

---

* *Patmos* is a Greek island not far off the coast of Turkey. It is cited in the Bible's Book of Revelation [Rev. 1:9] by its author "John", who says he wrote this book there. The writing is believed to have originated in a cave on the side of the island's mountain, now a revered UNESCO site. The island contains several monasteries dedicated to St. John, the largest of which contains a large library.

† Most Essene documents predate Jesus' life but a few were written after his death.

(Are these records in Patmos to be found in the basement of the main monastery there, the monastery of Saint John, or where else?)

> There are several copies of same. Some are contained amongst the scrolls and have been misfiled; they are not looked to because they were considered to be merely copies of other Gospels.
>
> The original document is actually secured in the cave that was considered a shelter. It was placed in jars, not unlike Qumran. Perhaps the so-called ground penetrating radar could reveal various cavities within that structure. The cave is historically considered the place of the Revelation.

Review

History

Jesus was literate but preferred to convey his teachings through the oral tradition so that his followers could experience him directly rather than through the written word.

The evangelist John Mark did indeed write the Gospel attributed to him, including the dubious ten verses at the end.

The sayings in the Gospel of Thomas are part of Jesus' advanced mystical teachings to his apostles and require judicious interpretation.

The missing Gospel Q exists as four manuscripts, copies of which still exist on the Greek island of Patmos and could be recovered.

CHAPTER 4

JESUS' BIRTH AND INFANCY

According to the Gospels Jesus' birth was announced in advance to his mother Mary through an angel, and the conception took place through the Holy Spirit. It is alleged that the birth took place in a stable in Bethlehem, with attendance by shepherds and three "wise men" from the East who were drawn there by a special star and some last-minute help from King Herod. After Jesus' birth the family left for a few years' residence in Egypt to escape Herod's murderous inclinations.

On the face of it there is little supportive evidence for us to believe this Gospel story of Jesus' conception and birth. Many scholars reject it entirely as a creation by the early Church, assembled from so-called prophecies in the Old Testament and from Middle Eastern traditions for the birth of any holy person—all adapted in Jesus' case to raise his status as the Church's key idol. On the other hand, the story may be mostly true despite the absence of good historical data. The evidence is indeed scanty, but poor evidence does not mean the story is false, of course.

If the Gospels' birth story is mostly valid then the main questions about Jesus' first few years center around how he was conceived, how wise men were guided by stars to his birth and how he and his parents lived in Egypt (if they went there at all—Luke has them returning immediately to Nazareth.). There is also a secondary question of what is meant by the alleged and apparently conflicting genealogies of Jesus in Matthew and Luke, and by his "belonging to the House of David."

We begin the examination of Jesus' life with these four issues.

Conception

The first question is whether Jesus was conceived normally through a man, presumably Joseph, or "immaculately" by the Holy Spirit or another unusual means.* The debate has been going on for centuries. There are persuasive but unconvincing arguments on both sides but without resolution. Present-day science finds no credible precedent or basis for a spontaneous conception, but this in itself does not rule it out since scientific knowledge is incomplete in this area.

The issue is also circularly entangled with Jesus' presumed divinity. That is, if he were divine from the start then one might say that almost anything could have happened, including an immaculate conception. Or, if he were somehow conceived in such a special manner then he would surely have to be divine. Strange logic!

Jesus is never quoted as speaking about his own conception or birth, and the Gospel accounts themselves are neither detailed nor factually convincing on the matter. Indeed, the entire story is strongly suspicious of early Church manipulation. The conception may have been normal and the Gospels are simply wrong.

We may also quarrel with the wording. Isaiah's prophecy[45] and Luke's statement[46] refer only to a *maiden* conceiving, not necessarily a virgin, though in Jewish society in those days the two states were almost the same. Similarly, the Gospels' alleged visitation of the angel Gabriel to Mary could be interpreted to signify only a special blessing, not necessarily a full-blown conception.[47]

Perhaps it doesn't really matter. However, the different versions have different implications for how one fills out Jesus' unknown childhood and some of the later portions of his life. Did he grow up yearning for a true father? Did the conservative Nazareth community regard him as a bastard and his mother as adulterous? (Bastards and adulterous women were social outcasts at that time.) Did Jesus' birth status affect whether he would consider marriage? How did Mary view her own conception?

(In what sense, if any, was Jesus really immaculately conceived?)

---

* The technical term for this process is *parthenogenesis*. See note below on *hermaphrodites*.

We find that Jesus was born of both a young woman and a virgin. These facts alone would have fulfilled the prophesies and the dynamics of the [Old Testament] scripture, even though he had been conceived of a man and a woman. Jesus' mother was born under the *sign* of Virgo, thus she was truly a Virgo, or virgin. Such was the historical case. The sign of Virgo was historically known in those days. Truly, the original word says there shall be a child born unto a young woman, and his name shall be Immanuel, meaning "Blessed of God.""[48] So here we find no controversy to the context of what has been referred to as the so-called virgin birth.

But we may seek to resolve the mystery even further. Indeed, it is known that there is the phenomenon of the so-called hermaphrodite, a being that contains both male and female, now known to science to be not sterile but that can be self-conceived. Furthermore, thy own scientists have advanced the concept of cloning, where there need be only one principal parent. Even [beyond] cloning they now know that there is the capacity for cell structure to generate a switching of gender, even among mammalian higher life forms.[†]

[It] used to be such [that] the concept of virgin birth, or immaculate conception, was challenged as scientifically unsound. Perhaps now, because it is often said to be a mystery by so-called spiritual sources, science must reassess itself and say that immaculate conception has occurred.

Physiological effects on the body physical are only beginning to be mapped by contemporary science. Yet there is evidence of esoteric physiology in science's more recent

---

[*]   . . .or "God with us."

[†]   A *hermaphrodite* is an organism possessing both male and female sex organs, though the term is also used to designate unisexual reproduction. It occurs in many plants and invertebrates and some fish, sometimes through self-impregnation. Some bisexual animals can specificate as male or female rather quickly as the need arises. It is known but uncommon among larger animals and humans . . . *Transsexuals* are individuals who feel compelled to change their biological sex, a physical change feasible in recent years through hormonal injections and/or surgery. It often leads to serious psychological problems (which may have existed before the conversion, of course). Not surprisingly, there are many controversial aspects of sex modification.

discoveries. For instance, when there is the stimulation of the meridian points there are flows of so-called endorphins,˙ thus the ability to manipulate the physiology for self-conception.

It is better to conceive of this as a *divine* conception, for when the kundalini† energy opens to a higher state in the female anatomy, there is then a capacity for conception that could be monitored [realized?] through the phenomena known as cloning.

The Essenes, on the level of some of the Pythagorean scientists and upon the mysteries of how advanced were the alchemical scientists of Egypt, certainly had the capacity of ritual bathings, prayer and meditation. So self-induced or *spontaneous* conception was conceivable within the potential of human physiology or extraordinary human anatomy.

So the channel speaking would support the concept of the divine birth.

(You have mentioned four possibilities for the so-called virgin birth, or immaculate conception. Which of these actually occurred with Mary?)

These [four possibilities] are metaphorical potentials for the virgin birth. As for that which occurred, it may be so-called energetic conception—in other words, when one literally [makes] oneself male or female as a stated goal.

He [Jesus] was conceived in a manner of his more hermaphrodite-like identity, or what science now refers to as cloning.‡ These can come about on the part of the *soul*, and could be considered a form of psychic engineering, using the psychokinetic forces. There is a measure of this in

---

˙ According to Traditional Chinese Medicine, the *meridians* are a network of channels that extend throughout the human body as a sensitive communication system, similar to neural network but distinct from it. Appropriate stimulation of the meridians through acupuncture is known to relieve pain. Some Western health practitioners postulate that such stimulation releases into the blood stream certain *endorphins*—morphine-like hormones—which can induce pleasure or sedate one against pain.

† See footnote on *kundalini* in Chapter 3.

‡ The apocryphal Gospel of James also states that Mary was conceived immaculately.

contemporary individuals such as Olga Worhall˙ and others, who have been measured in their capacity to use healing energy to manipulate cell structure. So indeed can the soul.

But there is also the capacity that *another* soul may create the vehicle or entrance into the world, with free will and permission, to the point where conception occurs within the so-called virgin womb, as of the individual Mary.†

So John is telling us that we should not be surprised by the story of the immaculate conception of Jesus because it is consistent with scientific possibilities known today and is therefore credible. It could even have been induced by a third party.

The Wise Men and their Star

Wise men or Magi were said to have attended Jesus' birth, guided there by a star or "the stars." Matthew's brief report says, "the star, which they saw in the east, went before them, till it came and stood over where the young child was."[49] While this statement cannot be literally and astronomically correct (stars don't move, though planets move slowly), it seems rather to refer to an astrological forecast that might have brought the Magi as far as Palestine, where the Gospels say Herod provided them with local directions to Bethlehem.[50]

There was indeed a major and unusual conjunction of the planets Jupiter, Saturn and Mars around 7 BCE, about when Jesus is believed (from historical data) to have been born. Could this be what was guiding them? For thousands of years, and in various cultures throughout the world, astrology has been practiced as a planet-based thought system for mapping human character and for prophecy. Astrologers do not agree even today whether the information they provide is represented by the physical locations of the heavenly bodies at the time of one's birth as displayed in the birth chart (or another event), or if it arises from the astrologer's intuitive perception, activated through study of the symbolism of the planets and their movements. Perhaps it is some of each. Superstition and

---

˙ Olga and Ambrose Worrall were famous twentieth-century American healers.

† This last statement suggests that Jesus may have aided his own conception from a non-physical state.

fraudulence naturally abound in such a nebulous field, but this does not mean it is total nonsense.

What we know today is that many skilled astrologers have provided highly detailed and accurate personal information to their clients, well beyond what a psychologist could discern, and have made some phenomenal predictions of natural events well beyond what could be reasonably expected. They say they rely only upon the client's birth chart—which has occasionally been greatly in error! It does appear that an unacknowledged intuitive process is at work. At the same time dozens of carefully conducted statistical studies have failed to find any clear correlation between planetary positions and human personality characteristics.[*51] The mystery of astrology persists.

So there is a serious question whether Matthew's and Luke's birth scenarios ever took place at all. They are delightful stories and still appeal today with Christmas and all that, but are too much a replay of old mid-Eastern legends and Hebrew expectations to be very credible as an original event. Mark and John do not even mention Jesus' birth. Several modern-day intuitives, including Edgar Cayce the "sleeping prophet," support the Gospel's birth story.[52] What does John say?

(Regarding Jesus' birth, we read Luke's [actually Matthew's[†]] charming story about a star appearing in the sky which guided wise men from the East.[53] What did he really mean? Were they tracking the stars as they traveled, or was this simply a metaphor for an intuitive astrological prediction made by these wise men?)

No, it was a traceable conjunction of planets.

(So were they following the conjunction of the planets, or were they following an intuitive prediction?)

---

[*] Actually there is one outstanding exception. The work of Michael Gauquelin has demonstrated definitively that professional achievers (sports champions, actors, generals, etc.) are more likely to have certain planets (Venus, Mars, Jupiter) near the horizon or near the midheaven at the hour of their birth. This finding is based on tens of thousands of births which he has accumulated and analyzed. Most of his work has survived rigorous testing by both supporters and skeptics. Gauquelin has published seven books on his rationale, methods and findings, and 23 meticulously documented volumes of birth data [Gauquelin 1991].

[†] This is my error; this astronomical event is reported in Matthew, not Luke.

Both. The Essenes were masters of astrology. For instance, the Temple Scroll* talks about the twelve gates of the new temple. This speaks of the twelve so-called karma points critical to astrology. The wise men of the East were the Magi, astrologers, and they knew how to calculate a planetary influence. Ye call this astrocartography.[54] There are ways to calculate where that star, or rather the conjunction of planets, would lead them.

(So one can say, then, that this working out was an intuitive prediction?)

Yes, by having a focus. In thy own experience of remote viewing, for instance, having only numerical coordinates, it allows a specific point for viewing the objects contained [located] therein.[55] In astrology, by the predictable nature of the transitions of the planets in their natural orbits, this gives the intuitive capacity, or rather the psychic capacity, to view [in] time and space and specific locations the events before they transpire. Thus the prophecy.

Jesus' Infancy in Egypt

Luke's Gospel has Mary, Joseph and Jesus returning to Nazareth immediately after the birth and purification in the Temple.[56] In contrast, Matthew describes an escape to Egypt but is vague about the time of departure and says nothing about what happened after they arrived there.[57]

(Jesus' parents apparently escaped to Egypt after his birth in Bethlehem. How long was the period of waiting before they left for Egypt?)

They left for Egypt immediately because of the slaughter of the innocents.[58] They dwelled in Egypt for a period of some four to six years, waiting out the death of Herod. This correlates with what is known historically about the passing

---

* The Temple Scroll is one of Dead Sea Scrolls. [Vermes 1987, p. 190ff.]

of Herod,[*] from the time of the formation [conjunction] of the star, the coming forth of Jesus and the approaching of the Aquarian Age.

Jesus' infancy and formative years were spent in Egypt, in particular in the community of Cairo and the community of Nag Hammadan, where there were communities of Hellenistic Jews and Essenes.[†] He received in those seven years many levels of initiation that were unique to the Essenes of Egypt, who later became the so-called Gnostics of Nag Hammadan.[‡]

In Egypt [are] places where the holy family took refuge, within the confines of the city now known as Cairo, and [also] in an ancient synagogue associated with a place tended to by Moses. In that synagogue one of the more ancient copies of writings was found and is still preserved. It is known as an ancient holy site dating back prior to the time of Jesus, to the days of Moses. There is a cave in which the holy family lived and underwent initiation. It is believed to be the site where Moses dwelled in the so-called land of Goshen—in other words, the mouth of the [Egyptian] delta.

Jesus and the holy family also spent time at the site now known as Nag Hammadan, famous for its Gnostic library. Jesus studied there. Even in his adult years before his ministry he gave revelations which eventually became the foundations of the Gnostic and Egyptian influences.

This last remark apparently refers to Jesus' return to the site at a later time in his life.

After Herod's death the family could return to their homeland and begin his instruction in his native Nazareth. So at the age of seven, the leaving of Egypt.

---

[*] It is well established that Herod died in 4 BCE.

[†] See the section on the Essenes in Chapter 5.

[‡] See footnotes in Chapter 1 on Nag Hammadi and the Gnostics.

(The Aquarian Gospel[59] includes several chapters describing the training Mary and Elizabeth allegedly underwent while Jesus was an infant in Egypt. Do you find any validity in this account?)

> We find value. If one is to examine the behavior of ritual schools in Egypt, long buried by the sands and certainly not [accessible], there are certain details that reveal what are only now emerging concerning the mystery practices of Egypt. They remarkably parallel the mysteries described in this inspired work, the Aquarian Gospel.

Ancestry

Jewish tradition placed special emphasis on their expected Messiah coming from the "House of David."[60] Jesus was certainly not the Messiah as the Jews saw it, for he did *not* fulfill the widespread expectation of one who would drive out the Roman overlords, establish a Jewish kingdom on earth and display the usual leadership characteristics of a king. Still, we are left with the question of how much of this Messiah's God-given qualities would in some sense be *inherited* instead of developed naturally or divinely imposed. Did these qualities belong to Jesus through his birth, or were they to evolve during his growing years by his living an especially devout and committed human life?

Let's deal first with the genealogical question.

(The Gospels claim that Jesus was of the House of David. If that's so, how are we to understand the genealogies of Matthew and Luke?)[61]

> They said he would be born of the House of David. In the Hebrew tradition, lineage was passed through the female, thus the lineages of the House of David [apply to] Mary.* However, Jesus' brothers, such as his [step-]brother James, were also of the House of David. These prophets were considered equal candidates to become rulers in the [land]

---

* Matthew and Luke provide different genealogies, one for Joseph and one for Mary. They allow for the possibility that Jesus' mother Mary was also of the House of David.

by their acts of prophecy—though not by an anointment as an administrative king.

Families often traced lineages to see natural talents and abilities passed on to same. The importance of the lineages of Joseph was that James and even the Magdalen were of the lineage of the House of David. When one of the brothers of Jesus, by Joseph, married, this was the natural track of the survival of the House of David.*

Mary [also] gave birth through relationship with Joseph.

(From a modern perspective it's hard to respect the notion of inheritance—to believe that Jesus' genetic inheritance was such a significant factor in the exceptional kind of person he became. Isn't this so?)

It is known that certain characteristics may be passed on even through simple methods of so-called breeding. For example, there are certain desirable physical traits that humanity associates with beauty, and these are passed on in certain forms of domestic lineages. Even certain animals have been developed for personality temperaments. Therefore, it might be said that certain temperaments of consciousness could be passed on through lineages. Those lineages, what actually influence the genes, are the energy, the concentration, the meditation or the meditative lineage, the contemplative lineage.

Ultimately, it is still upon the level of the energy of the soul that the precise temperament [lies]. A person may be gifted with a particular lineage because the energy may still resonate within the genes. If they also receive inheriting factors from another parent, then they diminish or delay the development of those particular gifts that still reside generationally.[†]

---

* John explains (in Chapter 9) that one of Jesus' brothers eventually married Mary Magdalen and they moved to France and continued the blood line.

† John may be alluding here to explanations he has given in other discourses to the effect that an individual's genes are not inherently fixed but can change during the course of his life, depending on how that life is lived. This idea contradicts the traditional

Remember it says, "Sin is passed onto the seventh generation."[62] It may be equally said that blessings are passed onto the seventh generation. Perhaps that is why children born in certain conditions of the seventh generation are considered prophets. This can indeed be cumulative. But it's what the person *does* with the gifts that then become their own final contribution to humanity.

(To clarify, are you saying that some of these subtle consciousness qualities, which distinguish an evolved soul such as Jesus from one that is not so evolved, are actually passed down genetically?)

Cumulatively. For instance, if a person has labored it is spoken that God will bless the future generations. Jesus spoke to this when he said, "Behold, the kingdom of things"—or the order of things—"is not unlike a field." The field may be inherited and a previous generation may have stored a treasure there, but if ye do not go into and work the field, ye will not only not feed thyself of a natural heritage, you will also not discover the treasure that is added unto thee by the previous generations.[63]

What he spoke of is that it is a reasonable expectation that as ye practice a measure of health, through yoga, meditation, prayer, acupuncture or energy systems, then vitality is restored. Indeed, there can be a removing of age from a metabolism, within physiologically measurable results. How much more so, then, when the chakras˙ open, and then the so-called sephiratic† energies—which are the other psychic centers in the body—and the kundalini‡ is opened. It is only natural then that this may influence the

---

theory of genetics, which is already known to be incomplete and is being challenged these days. [Murakami 2006, 2006a] John also explains that an incarnating essence or soul "chooses" its preferred genetic pattern before birth in order to fit its particular needs for growth in the coming life.

˙ See further discussion on chakras in Chapter 13.

† See the discussion in Chapter 13 on the *sephirot* or *sephiroth*, the ten attributes of God as viewed in the *Tree of Life*, and part of the mystical Jewish *Kabbalah*.

‡ See the discussion of the *kundalini* in Chapter 3 and later.

genetic substance of the individual, and that something of his heritage may be passed on.

This is when he spoke of the field, and there being a gift or treasure within the field. But if the next generation does not exercise the conscious properties, these will recede and not be passed on.

Review

History

Mary was able to raise her consciousness to the point that self-conception occurred, so Jesus could be conceived without a male father but through a self-cloning, hermaphroditic process, familiar to the Essenes and known today to occur in certain animals.

The "wise men" from the East who attended Jesus' birth were guided by an intuitive astrological prediction based upon an unusual planetary conjunction around the time of Jesus' birth.

Jesus' family left for Egypt immediately after his birth. For six years he grew and was educated in Essene communities near Cairo and Nag Hammadi.

The Gospels' lineages of Jesus are correct. Some of his qualities can be attributed to genetic inheritance through the House of David on Mary's side. His siblings and Mary Magdalen continued the blood line on Joseph's side.

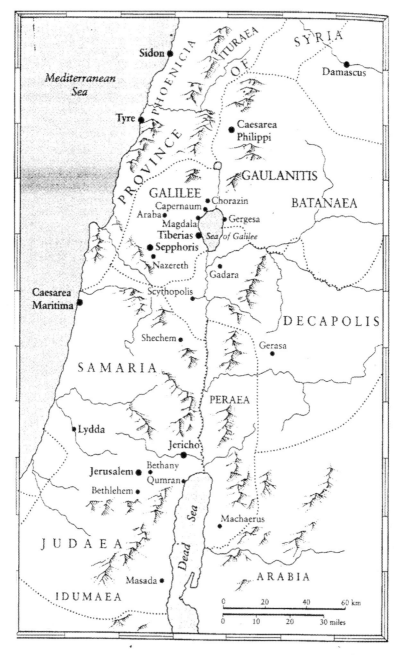

Palestine in the age of Jesus

Figure 3. Map of Ancient Palestine

CHAPTER 5

FAMILY AND CHILDHOOD

The Gospels provide no information at all about Jesus' life during his youth and formative years up to about age thirty, except for a brief visit to Jerusalem with his family at age twelve. It is traditionally assumed that he grew up in Nazareth with his family. The Gospel of Mark says (just once, and vaguely) that he apprenticed to his father as a carpenter.[64] It is difficult to believe, though, that he acquired his exceptional healing qualities, psychic skills and spiritual wisdom from his family, neighbors and the carpenter shop.

There is also the question of how normal he was during his childhood and early adult years. On this matter the Gospels are also silent.* Christian tradition presumes he was a perfect child and could do no wrong, consistent with his traditional position as being an aspect or Son of God. Again, this presumption has no textual basis and is anyway doubtful. We have no good reason to believe he was other than a normal Jewish boy.

Before delving into this period of Jesus' life, though, let us become better acquainted with the community in which he grew up and with his parents.

---

* The apocryphal *Infancy Gospel of Thomas* describes several miracles Jesus performed as a young child, such as animating clay objects and reviving a dead companion, both mentioned in Chapter 5. The *Infancy Gospel of James* describes the conception and birth of Mary by her mother Anne, also claimed to be an immaculate occurrence.

William H. Kautz, Sc.D.

The Essenes

The separatist and redemptive Jewish sect called the *Essenes* thrived in the Middle East even before Jesus' time. The Essenes are mentioned later on by Pliny, Philo and Josephus,[65] all first-century historians, who said they numbered "in the thousands" all over Judea and had their main community just inland of the West bank of the Dead Sea near the village of Qumran. They emerged recently from near obscurity with the discovery of the *Dead Sea Scrolls* in nearby caves.[66]

The Essenes were aesthetic and strict in their practices, eschewing sacrifice, money, commerce and slaves. They interpreted scripture uniquely and devoted themselves to discipline, purity, philanthropy and non-violence. Like other Jews they were expecting a Messiah and they devoted themselves wholeheartedly to the preparation for his coming. They are not mentioned in the Gospels at all, and their relation to Jesus has remained historically obscure, even after the discovery of the Scrolls. Before the Scrolls' discovery expert intuitive Edgar Cayce cited the Essenes as playing an important role in Jesus' education.[67] The first- and second-century Gnostics mixed some of both the Essenes' principles and Jesus' teachings into their own doctrines.[68]

(What role did the Essenes play in Jesus life?)

> Jesus, Joseph and Mary were Essenes, and indeed, Jesus was raised and his earliest trainings were with the Essenes, a fact which can be found in the ancient synagogue at Carmel.˙ Therefore we find that he was intimately linked to the Essenes, and was even said to be of their path. He lived with the Essenes for a time and practiced their extraordinary aesthetic practices.
>
> The Essenes completely set aside all indulgences, not unlike Siddharta [the Buddha], who knew both kings and the practice of aesthetics and tried to develop a Middle Way. Jesus' relation with the Essenes was similar as he became more and more the Messiah. He knew their aesthetic practices

---

˙ "According to Epiphanius [*Panarion*], and Josephus [*The Jewish War*], Mount Carmel had been the stronghold of the Essenes that came from . . . Nazareth." [http://en.wikipedia.org/wiki/Carmel]

for achieving knowledge of angelic states, [which] were not unlike the practices of Enon [?]. But his practices were an intention to bring elegance and refinement so they could become universal and reach out even unto the Gentiles—or, as he considered them, the *righteous* Gentiles [with] whom he had lived and dwelt amongst and whom many of the Essenes had never known.

Jesus spoke continually with the poor; indeed, the Essenes were known almost synonymously with the nickname "the poor." This is why he would say, "Blessed are the poor in spirit," for indeed, they would eventually inherit the kingdom of God.[69] He spoke to this because he had great confidence in the Essenes. He hoped that, when there would be the time of the diaspora, the scattering or the shattering of the Jewish culture unto the nations, that they [the Essenes] could become divine in their own time through the great revelations he had worked. For at the turning of every age, [just as] ye now have upon thee the so-called age of Aquarius, ye know that there is great hope for the transformation of the *whole* of society. [He had] great hope that the Essenes could be that vehicle.

If you study the sacred scriptures of the Essenes [you will see that] not only did they study the Torah but they studied other books attributed to Moses. Study the ancient ciphers [texts] of the Dead Sea Scrolls and here you will see continuous references to the Essenes, [who] perceived themselves as being the Sons of God.

Eventually they became more the conservers of knowledge. Many of the great Kaballah* and mystic teachers of Judaism could trace their roots back to the Essenes. Even among those Jewish persons who were forgiven by the Roman state and were allowed to remain and live in

---

*   The *Kabbalah* (*Qabbalah*) is a secret mystical Hebrew philosophic system, a "path to knowledge," believed to be passed down from Moses and incorporated into Hassidic teaching in the 18th century. Secretly guarded for most of its history, it describes the ten *Sephiroth*, or attributes of God, whose interrelations are depicted in the *Tree of Life*. The main set of commentaries on the Kabbalah is the *Zohar*. See illustration and further discussion in Cjhapter 13.

their historic land [after the diaspora], many of them were Essenes.

This particular endeavor, then, finds historical replication [validation] at the site of Qumran. So if one [studies] the authorship [writings] of the Essenes one finds various manuals; in particular the so-called Manuals of Discipline and others, about the manner in which the Essene was taught from *birth* to discern the nature of angels, taught from *birth* to discern the names of God, taught from *birth to* discern the phenomenon which ye know as the contemporary Kabbalah.*

(Was being an Essene like being a member of a church? Did it involve ritual or preparation?)

To be an Essene [was] more accurately to be amongst a community. The Essenes themselves, although disciplined in their ascetics, did not expect everyone to practice them. Any stranger could visit and petition to learn, and eventually graduate into the inner circle.

Also, it is known that the Essenes kept many astrological calendars. For instance, they often arranged ceremonial weddings among persons according to astrology, unique to the Hebrew calendar but having its parallels in what was known as Greek astrology.† One has to go no further than the so-called temple of Dendera in Egypt to look upon similar calendars which Jesus, the man who became the Messiah, had looked upon himself.‡

There were resuscitation and resurrection rituals often practiced among the Essenes. This is why they would often live to great longevity, like Moses, some to 120 years, sometimes further. This should not be such a great marvel, in that some of your most long-lived individuals, which

---

* For a fuller description of the Kaballah see Chapter 13.
† See the comments and footnote on astrology in Chapter 4.
‡ Dendera is an ancient town on the bank of the Nile in Egypt, and the site of one of the largest and best preserved temples in all Egypt. Parts of it date back to 2500 BCE. It once included a famous zodiac, now in the Louvre, Paris.

ye give unto the phenomenon of genetics, even to this day live well past the century mark. The Essenes accomplished these things consciously, and—this is said somewhat humorously—most of these couples to this day live long periods without the sexual act between them, even though it is permitted by marriage.

Mary, the Mother of Jesus

Mary has been sainted, worshipped, iconosized and otherwise honored in Christianity though we know very little about her historically. The child she bore and raised was indeed exceptional, but what does this tell us about *her*? Subtract the Christian legend about her and we are left with almost nothing.

We may fairly assume that Mary was a good mother, given her special calling, and that she suffered at least as much as do all mothers who have exceptional children in a largely uncivilized setting—and especially when their children are later killed. On one hand she might have been so unaware of what she was dealing with in this unusual son that she was repeatedly surprised, shocked and frustrated. On the other hand, perhaps she knew all along the destiny of the son she had given birth to, and fully expected the unusual consequences that followed.

(The stories I read about Mary differ greatly in how much she understood about Jesus' mission and the way he was carrying it out, including his death. . . . Can you straighten us out on this, John?)

Here we find a real mystery. Even Jesus himself had confusion at times as to his ministries.

Remember that Mary was one among many young Essene women who had received blessed birth. The mother of John the Baptist had also received similar visitations. So, as one amongst many, such birth, such high expectations amongst the Essenes, was considered a certain norm. For the Essenes considered themselves to be the chosen amongst the chosen, and still their number was not lacking.

The miraculous, the energy, the kundalini,* was known and a well established principle amongst the Essenes. This must be taken in the context of growth and evolution. It must also be understood that they knew the perilous nature of the political journey as well as the spiritual journey. So his mother Mary grew even as he did in various psychic states. These are more so described as periods of normalcy. . . .

To place this somewhat humorously, and perhaps even in more proper context, what mother does not believe that their child is always the most special, and at times dotes over them, but at [other] times doubts this when they display childish behavior?

The anchoring of the soul in everyday affairs was sometimes considered the greater psychic achievement than the performance of miracles. So it was in these moments, in states of grace, in everyday familial activities and celebrations. Sometimes when the energetic states, the divine states or the kundalini states, might almost erupt into these scenes, it gave the appearance that somehow the nature of the growth, or the journey, may have been forgotten or set aside.

(For example, when Jesus left the carpenter shop, visisted John and was baptized, was this a great shock to Mary, or did she kind of expect it?)

Such baptisms were common. The idea, however, of having the kundalini open and the Ruach ha-Qadesh† causing a visitation—notice immediately Jesus' first response. After having previous experiences of these disruptive forces, and the over-heightened expectations in a highly politically charged environment, Jesus immediately integrated such an episode by bringing them [the persons] to visit his family and restore balance in the order of things. From her [Mary's] previous experience with startling episodes with this unique being, she appreciated his strategy of bringing his guests

---

* See the description of *kundalini* in a footnote early in Chapter 3.
† Ruach ha-Qadesh is a Hebrew term referring to the spirit or soul in man. In Christianity it is usually refers to either the heart level of love or the Holy Spirit. The latter appears to be the sense in which John is using the term.

to the home, where she entertained them and became knowledgeable of what he was doing.

(And Jesus' death—did Mary expect this to happen?)

> When there was the perishment on the cross, all of them would have a shock of sensibility [as would] any mortal. What startled them all was the capacity of *resurrection*, for they were beginning to wonder what were the *limits* of this extraordinary being.
>
> There was great confusion as to what constituted resurrection. Many scriptures talked about the Messiah being lifted up by angels, which indeed had occurred. But remember, these were tests, or acts of faith.
>
> One final note on Mary. Remember, the man Jesus said upon the cross unto the channel speaking [John Zebedee], "Behold, mother, thy son. Behold son, thy mother."[70] In other words, Jesus, even in this moment of the testing of his faith, wished to see to the continuity of life of his mother, thus turning over the charge of her unto the channel speaking. Even in that moment he wished to make certain that human need was met, by the natural order.
>
> For he knew that even in the resurrection, he must eventually pass from this realm, so the Great Comforter [Holy Spirit], the more universal nature of humanity, [could come]. They should not focus upon *him* as a divine being and an exclusive source of the miraculous. Even *he* knew that his mother would not [then] have the immediate comfort of her living son.

Joseph

Joseph also receives short shrift in the Gospels. He is almost a nobody, for we know even less about him than Mary. We are not told about his difficulties from having such a young wife, raising an exceptional child of destiny and living among provincial neighbors who may have seen him as a cuckold. We'd like to believe he was a good husband and father but we don't even know that. The Christian Church sainted Joseph and created a lively legend and an art around him, but these embellishments too have no basis in recorded historical fact.

(Who was Joseph, and what was his part in Jesus' birth?)

Joseph was the adopted father. He was an extremely unusual man for his day to have such a young wife. Mary was at the age of sixteen, considered the age of consent for marriage. Joseph, as a man of thirty, was considered to be an older man in those days. When he found out about her conception he felt perhaps that she had known another man. But as her swearing that such was not the case, and his profound belief in the potentials of such affairs as being divine, he did not set her aside. He became the adopter and very much the earthly father in the raising of the infant child and the man Jesus.

Mary and Joseph lived together as man and wife. She remained a virgin. This did not mean that she did not conceive and love as man and wife with children, and give birth to children. It meant that in having chosen Joseph as her lover, they became *one flesh*. This is what is meant by the word *virgin*: one who chooses their own lover. This was highly unusual among women in those days, for most marriages were arranged. Even then, the concept of her being virgin did not mean that she did not give birth to Jesus' historical brothers and sisters. This deepened her humanity, as she then lived fully the life of wife, mother and lover, one that fulfills and brings grace to womanhood, thence unto Jesus.

When Joseph eventually passed from natural causes, within the life span of the man Jesus, Jesus wept for him as if he was his own father, the father of his flesh, even though he was conceived of the spirit.

(Was Joseph previously married before his marriage to Mary?)

Indeed, he had been married before. Like many, particularly of the Essenes, he had been betrothed and had lost his first wife.

(Did he have children from this earlier union?)

Correct. We find that they were highly active in the family affairs. Some of them helped him [Jesus] as older siblings and helped him grow in his identity. They were resident at Qumran and at Nazareth. Some lived within Jerusalem, some in Nag Hammadan in Egypt.

Remember, this was when enterprises were carried out by families. Various members would be proficient in various skills. As a carpenter, for instance, it was not unusual for Joseph to have dealings in many substances, which gave family members various skills, not only in carpentry but in trade dealings: oils, woods and other endeavors. Joseph was not only a carpenter. He was an artisan with the capacity and vision to design art pieces of great complexity. Study the artifacts of the households of the day, the complex wood carvings and their symbols. This would give thee a more true or clearer idea of the skills of the man Joseph in those days.

(When in Jesus' life did Joseph die?)

Joseph lived into the early days of the ministry, perishing before the time at the cross. When Jesus said unto the disciple speaking, "Son, behold thy Mother," and he spoke to Mary, his own Mother, this was an acknowledgement that Joseph had passed.

It was in the attendance of his father's funerary rituals that Jesus increased his ambitions to heal death, out of the mourning of the loss of his adopted parent.

Jesus' Early Childhood

(As a consequence of the virgin birth, Jesus was technically a bastard and Mary would be presumed to be an adulteress. How did Joseph and Mary—and Jesus, for that matter—cope with this stigma and the prejudice against them from their neighbors in Nazareth?)

> First, ye must understand that those of soul association for the segment of society that they traveled with, and the whole of Nazareth, was of the Essene order.* [This is] much as ye have regions in thy own country, where if you travel north to south or east to west, there are regional prejudices by which a person of different culture would suffer by their neighbors for their beliefs. They may differ from their neighbors. Some turned throughout the whole of Judea. There were various Jewish sects.†
>
> The Essenes were considered Masters of the mystical laws. Indeed, Joseph and Mary, as has been revealed through other prophets and through historical validation, were members of the Essene community. Therefore, Mary was looked upon within the Essene community as a prophetess, as one who sought to engage in being a vehicle for the Christ. Also, by their very exposure to Greek and Egyptian mythology, for instance, [this] would not be considered a phenomenon beyond their capacity, if it was God's will to be born as such, even amongst the Hellenistic Jews.
>
> Within the historical dynamics of the period, Joseph and Mary's company, the neighbors, would have been Essenes or those inspired by the Essenes, and the Hellenistic Jews or those who were likened to Jews because they lived as Jews—[even] Gentiles who studied with the Essenes. This

---

*   Josephus claimed that a stronghold of the Nazareth Essenes lay at Mt. Carmel, not far from Jesus' home, and some apocryphal stories of Jesus say that he studied there.

†   History records show that the area of Galilee where Nazareth is located was much different from Judea in the south: more agricultural, a less educated populace, a greater Greek presence, less under the influence of the priesthood and relatively free of the strict observances of traditional Jewish law. The Galileans were considered provincial and backward by their Judean counterparts.

would create a broad social infrastructure, keeping right fellowship [for] sheltering the couple from the more harsh judgments that could have been called into account by the Torah. So Mary and Joseph lived under the *protection* of the Essenes.

(That much is clear, but surely there were people in Nazareth who were not part of the Essene community and had no great respect for it. Is that not so? How did they feel about it all?)

Study the Gospels of the Infancy.[71] Many of those individuals—some, at least—respected Jesus as a prophet because he was able to perform prophetic deeds even in infancy and childhood. It isn't as though the couple, having fled to Egypt, necessarily made constant pronouncements of the nature of the birth. They had [been absent in] their early years when they had fled to Egypt. The nature of the birth was unknown except for those who were Essenes.

Therefore, they were accepted as a somewhat unusual couple, Joseph being of a previous marriage, having children and of more advanced years than Mary. All this was not unusual, for often a man would take his brother's wife if the brother had perished. Given the constructs of the marriage rituals and familial conventions, the concepts were not completely unknown. In the infrastructure of the society they could indeed be a family, even an honored family.

But then the synagogues, as the law was practiced in those days, and the communities that were based upon the Torah [were quite different].

(So Joseph and Mary, while they were living in Nazareth, kept the immaculate conception secret from the general population there. Is that indeed correct?)

Not so much as a secret, more so as a mystery. Many families, for instance, would tell of an angel before the birth of a child. Each person had a guiding angel, and they would speak of the angel before the birth. So believed the Essenes. This would not be so unusual. It is merely that they would withhold the announcement of when Mary was with child, and the circumstances.

Ponder thy own society. How often do many people know of the actual circumstances of birth? Often birth is not spoken of. There may be rituals, christenings and other endeavors, but the actual circumstance of birth, and the privacy of the phenomena of conception, are not asked after.

Jesus in Jerusalem

The Gospels say that Jesus visited the Jerusalem Temple with his family at age twelve. Christian art shows him lecturing the Temple priests from a high pedestal.[72] It is easier to believe that he was only asking questions of some lesser staff who would condescend to speak with a country lad of twelve from Galilee. Is the truth somewhere in between?

Even as it is said scripturally, he was . . . debating [with] the various members in the Temple himself, showing that he had grown great in wisdom. He also was there to *learn* through the process of debate, in the form of questions. So the Jesus you know is conserved both in the so-called legend—I would call it autobiographical—in that he went there to learn, and also to be reinvigorated, to be inspired.

The elders, of course, knew about the transmigration of souls and many of their past lives, but they marveled at the things that Jesus knew. He knew these things in his earliest and most lucid moments, almost from infancy.

We read that Jesus also became separated from his parents on this trip.[73]

When Jesus caused concern to both of his parents, as they articulated, he turned to them and said, "Where else would you find me to express myself but in my father's house?" There was as much amusement on his part on these issues of their agitation, as children often delight in their ability to torment, tweak, or "play at" these affairs. So these elements of childhood, as are known in days of innocence, are not only a romantic notion. Indeed, they are a perceivable and natural notion.

Was Jesus a "Normal" Child?

(Unlike many Christians, I prefer to assume that Jesus was not humanly perfect in his childhood and early years, when he was learning how to become a human adult, but was actually quite normal. Wasn't he a boy who made mistakes, played pranks, told little lies and fell in love with young girls?)

Such indeed was the case. The so-called Gospels of the Infancy[74] portray exactly such a figure. The young Jesus carried out the normal activities of a child and yet had heightened abilities, extraordinary abilities. In other words, he was gifted in energy states. He would [often] cause consternation among those observing, not unlike any child particularly gifted or given intellectual or various physical powers.

At times, for instance, he caused fear among his playmates by having the ability to control the fall of energies. One child, for instance, once struck him and would make fun of him. Like a child not fully in the throws of the discipline of emerging adulthood, he struck the playmate dead. But then, knowing *remorse,* raised him up again. Thus indeed was the nature of the infancy that he had [while] still having the abilities of the Divine.[75]

For instance, Jesus would often delight others in his ability to make simple clay figures, and then, not unlike the mind process of so-called psychokinetics, bring mild forms of animation to them for amusement. Also his ability to bring healing to playmates. Remember, other Essene children had similar abilities, not to such a degree as Jesus possessed but they too played with these so-called powers and abilities, sometimes to the discernment [concern?] or agitation of adults.[76]

This is not unlike the temptation that children undergo, for instance, to sour the milk in which bread is being made in order to see the expression it brings to the faces of adults or children who consume it. Pranks like these are normal to *any* childhood, and found no difference amongst that of Jesus.

(Even as an adult he must have put his foot in his mouth from time to time, like telling questionable jokes and making errors in judgment. Just how normal was the adult Jesus?)

Take for example the story of Jesus and the Gentile woman, where he stated that he marveled at her ability to learn. This was where he said, "The food of the children is not for the dogs."[77] This would have been a moment you quaintly referred to as "foot in mouth"; in other words, an embarrassment that he did not [yet] know that his divine mission extended to all peoples.

Also, when a woman was brought to him and said to be caught in adultery he began to reveal some of the [accusers'] innermost secrets, to their discomfort, and to the amusement of those about them who knew of the accusers' behaviors.[78]

In his teachings he often used both humor, and, as reflected even in the known Gospels, laughter in the partaking of wine with meals, for instance. Also, the fact that he taught in gardens shows that he partook of certain pleasures in the aromas of the gardens. The fact that he kept the company of women meant that he appreciated the beauty of women.* All these things are natural to humanity, natural to a youth, his growing into manhood and growing in his humanity. They were all natural to him.

Most extraordinary was his capacity to love those about him.

---

* For Jesus' experience with young women see also Chapter 9.

Review

History

The Essenes were masters of the mystical laws. They engaged in ascetic practices, psychic states, kundalini, healing without herbs and bodily regeneration. Jesus received part of his education from them and had a great hope for their part in a future world. They later influenced the Gnostics and Jewish mystical thought.

Joseph and Mary lived as man and wife and as Essenes in the protection of the Nazareth community. The family included children from Joseph's prior marriage as well as their own. Joseph was an accomplished artisan and an unusual man for his day. Jesus adored his adopted father, who died during his ministry.

Mary was a prophetess in her own right and very aware of Jesus' mission. While she vacillated in her expectations regarding him she was genuinely shocked at his death and startled by his resurrection.

Jesus grew into adolescence as a normal child, including pranks and other childish behavior when he was young. Like some of his Essene playmates he possessed unusual psychic abilities which he sometimes used playfully.

Jesus visited Jerusalem at age 12 for learning and inspiration through questioning and debate. He teased his parents when they lost him and then found him in the Temple.

CHAPTER 6

THE LOST YEARS

We are also completely in the dark about Jesus during his so-called "lost years" from age twelve until he is baptized by John the Baptist at about age thirty, when he is said to have begun his so-called ministry. What might he have been doing during these nearly two decades?

Novels and stories, a few of them generated intuitively, have filled in Jesus' adolescence and twenties in various ways. Some have him working in the carpenter shop with his father, quietly waiting "until my time has come." Others describe much hardship and testing in preparation for his later role, including educational travels to the Far East, wanderings in the desert and initiatory training in Egyptian temples. One says he spent part of this period traveling around the Mediterranean, interacting with a large variety of people as a kind of apprenticeship for his later work."[79] There are many speculations to choose from, and combinations of them are not ruled out, but unfortunately there are no factual data at all to fall back on.

The principal unanswered question for these lost years is how he acquired his esoteric wisdom and healing skills. Did he receive them from the Essenes or the wisdom teachers of his day in Palestine or elsewhere? If so, which ones, where were they and from which traditions did they come? Or did he already somehow possess his knowledge from the start, perhaps as a special gift or because of his allegedly divine nature?

Education and Experience as a Young Man

(Some sources claim that Jesus sought to undergo in his preparation all important varieties of difficult human experience so that he would better understand the human condition. [80] Do you find this to be the case?)

[He sought] the human experience of living. Notice that he took upon himself the simple role of various occupations. He was trained as a carpenter. It would be better said that he was trained as a craftsman, and through all manner of different forms of skill as a carpenter, as an artisan. He had the capacity to design and work with metallurgies such as gold and many other wooden items; for instance, gilding. He worked with gemstones and had the knowledge of their vibratory properties.

Even though he earned his living as a carpenter his family was not without their own means. For instance, they crafted furnishings for Herod's inheritors, creating even marvelous puzzle boxes and similar endeavors he had learned amongst the Egyptians. Since Jesus lived in Egypt he would have known such furnishings and have the skills. He knew the mysteries of measurement from Egypt; in other words, he knew sacred mathematics. As an Essene he had the equal skills of being a physician.

Perhaps if you were to compare the knowledge of an individual such as Leonardo Da Vinci and the diversity of his knowledge, you may have a measure of scope of the intellect that was natural to the man Jesus. This was not necessarily foreign to other intellects of the day. For instance, take the measure of Luke as a physician, and the knowledge he displayed. Or measure even Paul, as contemporary. But the manner in which Jesus applied these things would be more toward the sacred, of course.

(Did Jesus experience severe depression, let us say, as part of this development?)

What one would consider to be depression would be more accurately referred to as sorrow. Sorrow is the natural ability to empty oneself out to receive the next level of joy. Jesus knew the great sorrow of the world but this would not be physiologically comparable to depression.

(What about the experience of being rejected in love, for example, or being abandoned? Did he experience these?)

This relates to Jesus. Not having an earthly father, but an adopted loving father, left his soul with a measure of sorrow. As much as he loved Joseph, he [was aware of] the issue of separation and difference from other children about him. He knew the separation and even the pain of prejudice, for indeed, he held some prejudices toward the Gentiles. His existence, indeed, was considered in many ways to be somewhat sheltered. Even long into his adulthood he knew this wide range of various emotions—and here is the important issue: he sought to *learn* from them.

(Did he know what it was like to get dead drunk, or even become an alcoholic and then recover from it? Did he understand this sort of thing?)

In a certain measure of youth, he had taken at moments intoxicating substances. He knew the impact they could have on the individual, leading him to foolishness, as many youths of the day did. Very seldom [were there] any such occurrences in conscious adulthood, although like many Essene and Judaic males, he would partake of wine with meals, and wine would often be taken on the part of many youths as a source of merriment, celebration and other endeavors..

(Did he ever become addicted to the first-century counterpart of drugs, then have to detox himself?)

We do not find the partaking of drugs, for that would have been considered as an act of sorcery. The ascetic, the way of the prophet, constituted [required?] the use of ritual purification. If he partook of wine or even certain foods, for instance, then [by the Essenes'] Manual of Discipline he could not partake of the sacred meal where communion with angels would follow. So rituals of purification were indeed acted upon. These were usually forms of saying certain portions of scripture, but in a form of tone or chanting not unlike those used in yoga [mantras]. Or by fasting, not as a punishment but for purifying the body in a conscious and physiological manner, until certain psychic states—again not unlike those associated with yoga—were restored. These were a conscious, integrated dimension of the individual.

(Was Jesus involved with other women when he was a young adult—ages 16 to 30, say? If so, please describe these associations, whether children ensued, and what happened to the women involved.)

We find that Jesus was typical of any other Essene. He had been betrothed in childhood to marry Mary Magdalen, and from the age of 14 he was to be trained into the actions of so-called young adulthood. But he was also a member of the Essenes, who were ascetics. While he practiced conscious meditation, and developed the normal sexual awareness of a young man, and natural responses to women, these were channeled into kundalini-like practices—not repression of sexuality but more so channeling those energies into a higher form. He would sit with his life partner, Mary Magdalen, in periods of contemplation and at times would have Tantric responses.

Jesus chose the path of the ascetic here. While there was not the bearing of children, there was not a lack of consciousness of Tantra and sexual awareness in a form of spiritual marriage between him and the one known as Magdalen.*

---

* For further details on Jesus' relationship with Mary Magdalen see Chapter 9.

89

(What did he know through his experience about homosexual relationships?)

> He knew there were those of the same gender that were attracted to each other. Because of his own ascetic path, [he knew] many of those of same-gender attraction. He often wondered if he himself held those same emotions. Like many, he could appreciate the beauty of the masculine physical form, and he might at times [have] comprehension of that beauty being not unlike that of the female form. Thus, he knew why those of same gender could have affinity for each other, tantrically and sexually.
>
> Because of his mysticism he knew that as souls they may once have been women and still retained that attraction to the beauty of the physical form. Since he knew that it was the soul and the Divine that made them in the way that they were, he knew that these things were natural.
>
> To the disciples he explained the deeper mystery of the Torah. In the Torah it is forbidden for a man to take unto himself the uses of another man as though he were a woman. This spoke of the *rape* of individuals attracted to the same gender, [such as] by tribal individuals who would seek to alleviate their lust on another individual. It was not often considered under the law to be adultery. It [the law] was a *protection* of those individuals, yet often considered to be a judgment.

Travels to the Far East

There are various legends but no reliable historical records that the adult Jesus ever left his homeland. The renowned channel Edgar Cayce claimed that Jesus spent many years in the Far East, learning from the wisdom teachers there.[81] His account is paralleled by other twentieth-century intuitives,[82] as well as by a mysterious Gospel supposedly discovered in Ladakh in 1894.[83] While these independent accounts are not acceptable to Biblical scholars as reliable historical data (as if the Gospels *are* acceptable!), they corroborate one another fairly well and encourage further inquiry, as we have attempted here, to see what truth we might find in them.

(Did Jesus indeed travel to the East—India, Tibet, Persia and so forth—before he was baptized by John, as some writers have speculated?)

> The man Jesus, [living with] his family in Nazareth, was known [as the] Messiah. But it was also well known that these individuals traveled for studies and other endeavors. In his travels he returned to further studies in Egypt and traveled as far as India. The legend of a Jeshua, and scrolls giving accounts of his travels [there], hold true.
>
> These [stories] have become somewhat intermixed with other legends. When Jesus' brother James traveled to diverse parts of the known world along with the apostle Thomas, they would at times be *channels* and embody the living Christ. Even the resurrected Christ might make appearances to them. To many of the locals their deeds and actions were synonymous with the historical Jesus, giving rise to the legend of a post-mortem Jesus traveling amidst nations.

(Did Jesus himself get as far as Tibet, and if so, what was his main activity there—as a student, or doing healing, or teaching on his own, or what?)

> Correct. Amidst the historical records it was known that Jesus, having studied in both India and Tibet, and having extraordinary knowledge of the so-called siddhis* and meditations there, led him to contemplate that the nature of a Messiah was universal. Having studied the shamans, the Brahmans, the yogi, the chakras, the Buddhists and the evolving concept of the greater canon—the so-called Pali Canon† and others—he began to be convinced that even among the Gentiles the spark of God resided. It gladdened his heart that the Word

---

* *Siddhi* is a Sanskrit term denoting supernatural powers. In the West it usually designates psychic abilities, with the frequent warning that one should utilize them with great caution lest they become diversions on the path of spiritual growth.

† The *Pali Canon* is an important pre-Christian Buddhist collection of discourses attributed to the Buddha, along with metaphysical rituals and rules for monks in the Theravada tradition. It remained largely oral for two millennia and now comprises 38 printed volumes.

that is God is the God of *all* nations, [and] could be known to all quarters. If he could be a vehicle for such a revelation, how much more joyous would be his life?

Thus, while John does not answer the question, he confirms Jesus' travels to foreign lands and their significance in his life, especially the universality of his teachings.

Initiation in Egypt

In ancient times esoteric knowledge was preserved and taught at a small number of mystery schools located in major centers. In the first century the school in Egypt was reputed to be the greatest. It would be only natural for Jesus to be drawn there. The mystique of the Egyptian pyramids, already ancient in his time, could have been a part of his initiation into a unique body of knowledge. Cayce too affirms that Jesus underwent training in Egypt.[84]

(Did Jesus actually undergo some kind of initiation in Egypt?)

First of all, Jesus did undergo initiations into the mysteries in Egypt, in the [Great] Pyramid* and others. Much like Moses, he knew all the things that the Egyptians knew. It was said that Jesus was also the new Moses, a new liberator, a new lawgiver. So Jesus underwent the initiation, one that embodied the whole of the age and its mystery, just for its sense of wonder and awe.

---

* See http://en.wikipedia.org/wiki/Great_Pyramid_of_Giza for a fairly complete description of this pyramid.

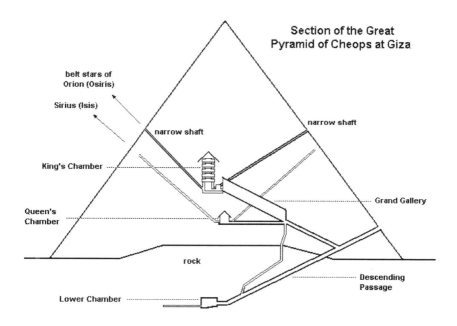

belt stars of
Orion (Osiris)

Sirius (Isis)

narrow shaft

King's Chamber

Queen's
Chamber

Section of the Great
Pyramid of Cheops at Giza

narrow shaft

Grand Gallery

rock

Descending
Passage

Lower Chamber

Figure 4. The Great Pyramid of Giza, showing internal passages and chambers

Access into the [Great] pyramid was known. One would enter it through the hidden [opening in the] north face, travel *down* into what is known as the pit. This shaft, which points to the North Star, is symbolic. It creates the emotional and literally psychic state of the soul traveling into an unknown condition, like a seed in the earth, to take in the energies of the earth and then struggle *upward* to re-approach the mystery of the three sealed blocks [in the ascending passage]. These were known eventually to Jesus in his later studies to represent [symbolically] the so-called *bindus*, the three permanent atoms that make up the mystery of the Celtic trinity, or Celtic knot. They are the three knots [psychic

---

* The *Celtic Knot,* part of the basis of Celtic spiritual beliefs, is an endless weave symbolizing eternity or creation, without beginning or end. The *Celtic Trinity* in the Vedas consists of three knots and is a metaphor representing the binding of the soul to the earth, even under enlightenment. Hence the symbolism "trust in your soul," "belief in your heart" and "faith in your mind." [Ryerson 1989, pp. 121-2]

centers] spoken of in yoga: at the base of the spine, at the heart, and in the so-called third eye, the pineal-pituitary gland, which binds the soul to the earth plane.

The three blocks that now can be seen in the pyramid, the blocked passage to the so-called Grand Gallery, constitute [signify?] that the soul is now *sealed* into the body of the earth. Moving through the narrow passageway of this so-called grotto, and then the narrow crawl-space, to enter into the Grand Gallery, constitutes [signifies?] the vision in the Grand Gallery. The seven nitches constitute [signify?] the backbone of Osiris; these represent the looking up at the Grand Gallery toward the entry into the King's Chamber, as a soul looking out upon the infinite, as if its own chakras* spread to the horizon, to the single point of the eye of Horus, the Third Eye.

One would then make their way up the Grand Gallery and enter into the mystery of the King's Chamber, with its perfect acoustics and the brilliant resonance of its quarried granite. One was rebirthed, rather symbolic of the vitality of life both in the East and the West, by lying in the sarcophagus and then *dying* to the old self, under the extraordinary piezoelectrical and crystalline forces from the tremendous pressures of the King's Chamber. By lying in the tomb for three days, to die and then resurrect, gives one the extraordinary vision of the rest of one's journey throughout the whole of one's days. To return then to the outside world was to be reborn, and in many ways, metaphorically and allegorically, to no longer be born of men and women but to be born by the mystery of the ages.

The mystery of the empty tomb should be no real mystery at all, for indeed, perhaps in a puzzling double-blind test, the pyramid had been long sealed with no known access. In fact the quarry [pit] in the body of the pyramid may have been the latter-day testimony to the mystery of another empty tomb. But when they entered into the pyramid, what was its mystery? It was its emptiness! [They thought] there must

---

* See further discussion in Chapter 13.

have been something of greater value, a long-dead spiritual leader or a Pharaoh's treasure in it.

There are three chambers: the chamber in the earth, the Queen's chamber and the King's Chamber—in other words, body, mind and spirit. The three chambers are a metaphoric construct articulated within Egyptian mythology, [embracing] the realm of the underworld, or Seth; the realm of the activities of Horus and Hathor; and the realm of Osiris and Isis. Body, mind and spirit, or the so-called conscious mind, subconscious mind and superconscious mind.

(Was Jesus' initiation just a test, or did it involve training and education as well?)

One may say that they were seamlessly integrated. There was instruction, testing and initiation. In verbal tradition, for instance, the test and the suffering may be in merely story telling, such as the teacher who teaches the ko-an.[*] There would have been, for instance, trials of faith, as when Daniel entered into the lion's den. But we would assess that he [Jesus] was raised amidst the therapeuti, or the Essenes, historically at that [place] known at Nag Hammadan; and, of course, the oldest surviving synagogue that dates back to the days of Moses, even unto the days of Akhnaten,[†] when the Hebrew people were an honored people in Egypt. So he experienced the continuity of the revelations.

(Did he also travel around the Mediterranean?)

Even earlier, in the early days of manhood. By the age of consent, the age of 21, he had already begun some travels

---

[*] See the definition of *ko-an* in a footnote in Chapter 3.

[†] *Ahknaten*, also named *Amenhotep IV*, was a strange and controversial Pharaoh who reigned in Egypt from 1379 to 1362 BCE and is credited with promoting the notion of one god to his culture. He managed to upgrade the age-old Egyptian state religion to a sun-based and more humanitarian form. His authority held for seventeen years before he was deposed by the old priesthood, though some of his ideas endured to later generations.

toward the Far East, then he traveled to other centers of learning. Correct.

Review

History

While growing into adulthood Jesus sought the full human experience of living, including sorrow and other emotions, but he was never depressed or addicted. He became skilled as a craftsman and artisan, not merely a carpenter. From the Essenes he learned sacred mathematics, the art of healing and other skills.

Jesus was betrothed to Mary Magdalen and participated in tantric sexual practices with her in accordance with Essene customs. He was familiar with the activation of the chakras through kundalini. He was not otherwise involved in relationships with women and never married or had children. [85]

Jesus was familiar with homosexuality in others. He saw it as a natural condition and understood it at the level of the genderless soul. [86]

Jesus traveled to Greece, India, Tibet, Egypt and other areas to learn other systems of thought as part of his preparation. He also taught and healed on these journeys and verified for himself the universality of the truths he was discovering. He was initiated into the Egyptian mysteries in the Great Pyramid and underwent further training at Nag Hammadi.

These broadening experiences taught Jesus the central importance of integrating body, mind and spirit, and the transcendence associated with ego death.

CHAPTER 7

AN AWAKENING CONSCIOUSNESS

The Gospels describe Jesus' awakening at his baptism by John the Baptist as the turning point in his life. When it took place "the heavens opened up," a dove appeared and a heavenly voice blessed the occasion. It is not hard to believe that some kind of awakening would be appropriate for a man like Jesus, whether or not the heavens opened and a dove and a voice appeared as factual parts of the event. We are left to surmise for ourselves what kind of an awakening this was for Jesus and what it meant to him.

While all of us are very gradually "waking up" to a knowledge of our deeper selves and our life direction as we mature, Jesus' awakening might well have been more profound because of the magnitude of his mission. How did he experience this mind opening and come to recognize his calling? How did he cope with his human resistance, doubts and temptations as the challenge of his mission became clear to him? How did he deal with the question of how to use his unusual abilities wisely? The Gospels present his abilities only as amazing phenomena. His biographers were obviously impressed, but they say nothing about how Jesus himself experienced his awakening and this greater understanding of himself.

A few clues to his expanding state of consciousness can be found in his later deeds: his forty-day retreat into the Palestinian hills,[87] when he was said to be tempted by the devil; his frequent prayers in which he was believed to be speaking directly with God; his "transfiguration" as seen by Peter, James and John;[88] and, of course, the series of exceptional healings and other miracles with which he is credited. We need to dig deeper into his baptism and subsequent experiences for a fuller understanding of the state of mind he awoke to and carried into his ministry.

Jesus' Baptism

Immediately after the anointment, the baptism—such a powerful ritual—there came upon him the Holy Spirit, as seen in the form of a dove.[89] This meant that the energy was perceived as coming from a higher dimensional source and entering into the body. This is comparable to a kundalini opening,* where the conscious, subconscious and superconscious—or the mind, body and spirit—are totally unified in a moment.

The ritual constituted a means of washing away the subjective ego so there could indeed be a knowledge of the link to the higher self. This is why in Jesus' baptism the spirit coming down upon the individual spoke that there was a *union* within the Self of Jesus for him to become—indeed, for him to have the *capacity* to become—the Christ.

John the Baptist

Gospel accounts describe the birth and youth of John the Baptist, the agent for Jesus' awakening, but say little about him as a person and how he may have prepared himself for his short ministry. We are told only that he was a cousin of Jesus and lived an austere life in the desert until he began his dynamic preaching and baptizing. The Gospels say that he disavowed himself as a prophet or messiah, deferring instead to the greater one who would follow him—obviously Jesus. Before long he was imprisoned for his outspoken accusations against Herod and then killed.

We might compare this passionate, wild man from the hills, "a voice crying in the wilderness" (allegedly a prophesy by Isaiah[90]) with a modern day, charismatic revival preacher. He calls for his listeners to repent of their sins and warns of terrible, apocalyptic punishments for those who refuse the opportunity—then moves on.

How did John the Baptist prepare himself for this brief career as a "harbinger"?

(Was John the Baptist trained and initiated in Egypt, along with Jesus, as some say?)

---

* See the description of kundalini in a footnote early in Chapter 3.

Correct. They were cousins. He attended the activities of the Nag Hammadan community as well as the community of Qumran. Remember that Mary was one among many young Essene women who had received blessed birth. The mother of John the Baptist had also received similar visitations.

(And John in prison?)

Here is a way of knowing [why] Jesus' departed from the Essenes. The Essenes would not allow a person who was lame or blind to enter into their sacred meals, for they felt that [such a] person was doing a life of penance. It was said that a person [who] was lame frightened angels, because angels, who had the capacity of sight and unlimited spirit, [when] seeing a lame person, might incarnate and lose their angelic knowledge out of shock and compassion. A person who was blind might touch something unclean, or mispronounce the reading of holy scripture, no matter how good their memory.

When John the Baptist sent a disciple unto Jesus, saying, "John is about to perish," speaking of his imprisonment and sentence to death, so John the Baptist wished to know, "Have I done right? Art thou the Messiah?"

Jesus said, "Say unto my cousin, John, that the lame walk and the blind see."[91] While many say that this deals with the mysteries of his healing ministry, it would rather have been a *code* known only unto John the Baptist from the Manual of Discipline of the Essenes in their day. The code, "the lame walk and the blind see," said "all may now enter into the sacred meal." Jesus [later] arranged this to be remembered as the Last Supper, the Passover feast.

In other words, *all* may enter the kingdom, and thou hast done well. Even though ye may perish this night, ye may do so with the full confidence that ye have fulfilled the long lines of prophecy, and that the Christ is to visit all humanity and to reach all corners of the earth, so that all may enter into the sacred union.

Here then is a mystery decoded! These words and disciplines of the Essenes were unknown until the records [became] known today [in the Dead Sea Scrolls], [including] the mystery of forbidding the blind and the lame, specifically in the Manual of Discipline, to not partake of the meal. But [in] announcing the kingdom Jesus *lifted* that particular discipline as obsolete, saying *all* may enter in.

The Baptism Ritual

The ritual of baptism evolved from an old Hebrew practice for the remission of sins, then into John the Baptist's repentance ritual, and finally into what Jesus did: an act of acceptance of the Holy Spirit. For many persons today baptism is little more than a formal dedication when joining a church, or a blessing and assurance for parents at a child's birth. Our ancestors apparently regarded it differently.

How did Jesus see the practice of baptism?

(What is the significance of baptism, beyond being just a ritual?)

Certain words [such as baptism] were known well in the Middle Eastern world of the day, of course. The concept of Vedic (which means miraculous) practices or healing, is [similar]. Baptism was a way of evolving [involving?] individuals in the transitory qualities of their human nature, giving them an opening into the Divine.

This is comparable, for instance, with so-called homeopathic practices, in the belief that water holds the medicinal properties of a substance long after the physical substance itself has been removed. When an individual could make an imprint into the water by *blessing* it, [then] their own potent force of nature, or their understanding of the Deity, was transferable to others.

This was often done in rivers, or in caves, or in so-called mitzvahs according to their different forms of the practice. It was often the tradition of the Essenes to hold rituals deep in the body of the earth. The river usually meant the washing away of cumulative sins made up [committed] over time, even generational sins. This was considered one of the more powerful forms of baptism. Those done in caves would often constitute the renewal of the individual. But it was always [by] the water.

Guidance

We all "hear" signals in our heads from time to time, whether we call them personal guidance, conscience, the voice of God, an intuitive hit, an hallucination or just old fears leading us astray. These signals can be very insightful and helpful, or they may be misleading or meaningless.. They therefore require interpretation before we can trust them in guiding our lives. We are therefore challenged to ask where they come from and what should be a valid basis for discriminating among them.

Jesus too—especially Jesus—must have been faced with this same challenge to sort out these various signals arising in his mind.

(When Jesus was young he must have wondered whether the voices he was hearing were really from God, or were they his own fantasies or even evil voices? How did he learn to discriminate?)

While the discernment of good and evil would have been accurate, the questioning as to whether the voices would have a divine origin is more so a modern concept. As the Hellenistic Greeks wondered at times, and had at one time an agnostic perspective, you must understand that in the ancient world the dominant model of thinking was that these would be of [either] divine or ill nature. Jesus discerned and had a strongly developed sense of identity, as many of the Jewish tradition did, that such voices would originate from a divine source. It was more a question of *how*.

(At which age did Jesus first become aware of the personal presence in his life of a God with whom he could dialogue and receive guidance?)

Again, almost from infancy. There are Gospels known as the Gospel of Infancy and the Gospel of Mary and Joseph which speak to some of these matters.[92] There are also comparable other scrolls of individuals of a sacred temperament who had awareness of the Divine from the beginning.

Throughout the whole of the linkage in Egypt one may compare his spending time amidst the temples, the continual metaphorical references to the ordering of the names of God in familial constructs: Osiris and Isis as the mother and father of Horus and Hathor. These exposures alone, in both infancy and in childhood, and the constructs that the names of God such as *Elohim* sometimes translated into Hebrew to mean "God the Father," could document [this] again.

While these were often presented as metaphors, it was indeed a property of Jesus to take them as a point of original identity, so that each element of humanity was referred to as the sons and daughters of God rather than merely for their metaphorical content. This occurred in the earliest years of his conscious development.

Messiahship and Mission

The notion of a messiah had its origin in ancient Judaism as one anointed with oil, as a high priest, king or prophet. It later evolved into an anticipated king of Davidic heritage, prophesied by the prophets Isaiah, Micah and Daniel. This would be one who would someday appear on earth, initiate an apocalypse and establish a Jewish kingdom in a new Messianic Age.[93] By Jesus' day the concept had crystallized into a leader who would drive out the Romans and save the Jewish people from oppression. The early Christians interpreted the messiah as a God appointed savior in the person of Jesus. While most modern Jews have a less literal interpretation of a messiah, some are still waiting for him to appear. The apocalyptic frame of mind did not die in the first century but is still with many people today, hence the fascination with popular prophecies such as the change of millennium, unusual planetary alignments and the year 2012.

Jesus must have realized early on that he did not fit the Jewish expectation but knew he would be viewed as a messiah anyway. It seems he sought to shift the expectation to his deeper concept of what was most needed. We may ask, what was his concept of a messiah and how did he deal with the Jewish expectation at the time?

(When, and how completely, did Jesus understand his broad life mission as he grew up?)

> This is an intriguing and unique point. His concept of himself as *the* Messiah, or *a* messiah, grew gradually within him. He had extensive travels through Egypt, to Athens, even to India itself, where he underwent points of debate, and practices such as meditation, yoga and prayer. But it was not until his actual baptism by the individual John the Baptist that his ministrations [ministry] began. He accepted then the identity of becoming a messiah, the fully anointed one who might be remembered by humanity for the *consciousness* that he was willing to bring into himself, and the knowledge of the consequences that he might suffer.
>
> Remember, he was not uninformed from his past life of the suffering that had come upon Job.* In this lifetime there would be the conscious consequences that he must suffer these things for the world—the world in those days being represented by the authorities of Rome; and also the natural consequences of speaking of the Divine—in particular when that corrupt version of the concept of the Divine in the earth was represented by the emperor. The empirical, political, and social consequences of any who would attempt to clarify the concept of the Divine within humanity may be contrasted to what could be considered to be the principle of the Anti-Christ in these days.

Doubts, Temptations and Choices

Jesus must have had his moments of doubt and indecision like other humans.

(What kind of doubts did Jesus undergo around this awakening to his being the "Son of God," and the price he would have to pay in his mission?)

---

* This past life of Jesus is discussed in Chapter 11.

103

Jesus had various moments of passion, epiphany and doubt. There were also times when he would doubt those about him. There was the testing in the desert, where he had to turn aside various temptations as to whether to rule over humanity with angels. This was the older force spoken of elsewhere: angelic presences wishing that he take over the mantle of kingship in the more traditional or material form, declaring a kingdom and evoking the powers of the so-called "justified" war.* He turned aside from this to the path of the individualization of the Divine within, and self-sacrifice. This became the key.

In each of these examples we see a growing consciousness, the [awareness?] that we too may succeed in attaining and becoming the Christ.

In Gethsemane, even before the crucifixion, we find the doubt, saying, "Is there another path?"[94] But Jesus took it upon himself—he knew his final mission. Having raised Lazarus from the dead, he must heal death itself. For this was humanity's final fear, one in which humanity can sometimes be manipulated into taking actions not appropriate. So, choosing the path, he knew it was in his capacity to heal death itself. So he took upon himself the judgment of the world.

(As a martyr?)

The world rejected the things he said because it loved the world more than it loved the Divine. This can be expressed within the materialism found in Roman law, the best justice that could be perceived in the ancient world in those days. In many ways [these are] the laws that ye still live under, even unto these particular days in the material.

But in giving up self this then became a great model of consciousness, which proved to be a liberating force in those days. Thus the examples of Gandhi and Martin Luther King. And it is still the test of humanity, even unto these days, that

---

* John discusses these angelic presences more fully in Chapter 11.

no greater love hath any man or any woman than they who would give their life for their brothers and their sisters.[95]

For perhaps there is no consciousness advanced without the giving of one's life. But the choice in which that life is given is an organizing force according to nations. [It respects] the divine principle to resist the taking of another's life, and the sacrifice of self and the measure of time and identity dedicated to the Divine: that one manifest the highest of all things—this is the keeping of the law. For here indeed is the whole nature of the law: "Love the Lord God with all thy heart, strength, mind and soul, and thy neighbor as thyself." For indeed, God *is* love.[96]

When Jesus overcame the final temptation in Gethsemane, he went unto that judgment. For remember, humanity could have judged him innocent—it could have conspired to do so. But the political and material agencies of the day, represented by Rome and the political institutions, made their judgment.

Prophecy

Several of the Gospel stories suggest that Jesus had a strong prescience about the future. He certainly qualifies as a great prophet, not so much for his predictions but from his deep insight into the human condition, which is a truer mark of a prophet than the ability to see specific events in the future. Still, prediction was a classic trait of a prophet, one believed to be in direct communication with higher wisdom. Jesus' ability to prophesy may have been natural for him, or perhaps it was a consequence of his esoteric training with the Essenes and in the Far East and Egypt.

Some of Jesus' alleged miracles seem to be valid predictions: his own death, the destruction the Temple and the later dispersion of the Jews, for example. We have to remember, though, that the Gospel record was written *after* these events, not before, so the evidence for both the existence and the accuracy of this prediction by Jesus is poor. Indeed, anyone aware of the religious and political situation in the first century might easily have predicted these events.

More to the point, we may ask when Jesus first became aware of the worldly consequences of his chosen mission.

(To what extent did Jesus, the man, anticipate the consequences, both positive and negative, of his deeds and teachings that would transpire over the following centuries? By consequences I mean, for example, the persistent spread of his teachings over much of the world, as well as the great distortions in them and the many wars and other horrors committed under his name?)

This can certainly be revealed in the scripture that says, "Behold! It is said that I bring peace into the world, but know ye this, for those who must follow me, I bring also a sword."[97] What he spoke of was, of course, the sword of truth. He cautioned that for those who would take up and follow him, mother would be set against daughter, father against son, and eventually even nation against nation, so potent was the power of the message.[98]

But he realized, by manifesting the principle of the Christ in such a dark age, his great sorrow when he said, "Behold! Because ye have rejected me, which is not unlike a stone the builders have rejected," meaning it was a solid corner stone.[99] . . .

So he *knew* this, from observing the signs of his own time and knowing his own humanity. From having lived in Egypt and having walked amidst thousands of years of the accomplishments of the pharaohs, how could one *not* contemplate [this]? He knew from the voices that had cried out in years past, such as the great liberator Moses, that his words would have consequences and echo down through many thousands of years. Having lived in the ruins of past civilizations, having seen Egypt itself laid to waste, would he not know that provinces, nations themselves, could lead to similar schisms? This [was] by the words that he spoke, not unlike the words of Moses, but perhaps even more universal for they were [for] all people.

What else could be the consequences but the stirring of rebellion, which historically had been seen before, not only with the destruction of the Temple [but] the diaspora, the scattering of the Jewish people and the message to all the four corners of the earth?*

Jesus *lived* as a wise being, having overcome death, but more, he became a universal being, to which humanity is capable of ascending. Would not then the brightness of his life cast the darkest of shadows?

So there would be both natural prophesy here, observed or drawn from history, but also authentic so-called extra-sensory perception, since he was a person of complete vision concerning the consequences of his actions. He *sorrowed* for humanity, in that they did not hear his words appropriately.

The Hebrew people were themselves steeped in the wisdom that had come from what was called the Torah. He knew that if he could come through to consciousness with them about the human condition, in which he accepted that humanity was one and the same substance as the universal consciousness, call it Deity or God—if his own people could not hear these words, then in turn, how could others be expected to hear them?

His message was to bring about peace, to bring about an *order* of things in which humanity might be able to reorder themselves according to the laws of the prophets. He came not to destroy the laws of the prophets but to *fulfill* the natural human condition, the knowledge that *God is Love*. It is such a simple statement, but it fell upon their deaf ears. He knew this.

Fulfilling Old Prophecies

Matthew cites a dozen Old Testament "prophecies" which he claims Jesus fulfilled, apparently to make the point that Jesus was truly the expected Messiah. Most of them are vague and can be interpreted to fit a wide range of events; for example, "Rachel weeping for her children" to

---

* In 68-70 CE, after many years of Jewish rebellion in Palestine, the Roman General Vipassian and his son Titus totally destroyed Jerusalem and the Second Temple and dispersed most of the Jews, initiating the famous diaspora.

107

prophesy Herod's massacre of the infants,[100] and "he called my son out of Egypt" to indicate the very young Jesus' return to Nazareth.[101] Indeed, like many alleged prophecies, even today, the Old Testament is so large and ambiguous that one can find somewhere in it almost any statement to fit later events. Or was Jesus deliberately adjusting his behavior to fit the existing "prophecies"?

(It appears from the Gospels—especially Matthew's—that Jesus was going out of his way to fulfill several Old-Testament "prophecies," most of which are poetic, vague, often irrelevant and not really prophecies at all. They seem to be saying that Jesus was fulfilling these statements as prophecies. Did he really do this, and if so, why?)

Could it not be said that Shakespeare is poetic? And is not Shakespeare constantly acted out? Has not human behavior, even in thy own times, great tragic figures? Even hundreds of years later it has been said that an individual carried out the actions of some of the great figures of that poetry. Are not lovers who take their lives for the sake of their love not referred to as Romeo and Julia [Juliet]?

So perhaps the human capacity for imagination is that these may have been *self-fulfilling* prophecies. Jesus, a man of great poetic soul himself, would not be denied in his ability to almost universally quote the whole of the Torah, in the oral and written traditions, realizing their extraordinary poetry and then acting them out, bringing about poetic and romantic intent in his actions.

But above all else, does not great poetry turn people to extraordinary action, for both good and ill? So these words lay dormant, and it is accurate to say, one may *realize* these things *as* prophecy and fulfill them for their mythical and poetic value, to *make* them historical, even if they were unknown to their author to become historical. This is one form of *fulfilling prophecy*.

Furthermore, we would state the following. The prophets certainly knew that only when a man embodied certain predispositions would he become an anointed one, for the elements of kingship certainly embody the quality of humility.

Remember, the very term *poetic* is obscure and an oxymoron. For *poetic* is in itself self-fulfilling. Perhaps clients [?] would understand it as a so-called *mime*, a word that creates the compulsion to repeat it until it fulfills itself in an action.

This explanation suggests that fulfilling prophecy can be not only the acting out of past mythic or poetic statements as if they were given as predictions, but also by turning them from statements into predictions through one's actual deeds.

(Take the prophecy of riding an ass into Jerusalem, for example. And, oh, there were several others.)

The willingness of Jesus to ride into Jerusalem upon an ass is an act of humility rather than an act of great pageantry, like the imperialistic royal chariot seen upon a wall in Egypt, which he surely visited. So his act became antithetical to the material trapping of kingship. He took upon himself the fulfillment of prophecy. One who was *truly* to be master of the inner kingdom must show the quality of humility spoken of in these prophecies.

Review

The review statements of Jesus' teachings in this and each subsequent chapter are followed by relevant cross-references to Ryerson's earlier book of channeling from John, Spirit Communication: The Soul's Path (Ryerson 1989), so that the interested reader may pursue them in greater depth. The page numbers following [SC . . .] refer to the soft-cover edition.

History

Jesus knew almost from infancy that the guidance he was receiving, his inner voice, could be trusted as coming from God, his "Father."

His understanding of the role of a genuine Messiah grew gradually within him until his baptism, when he accepted his new identity. For him the occasion was comparable to a kundalini opening. He realized then the high level of consciousness he would need to bring into himself, and also the suffering he would have to undergo.

Baptism was a well known practice at the time as a belief-based opening, somewhat like homeopathy, for entering an elevated state of consciousness and for transferring a blessing through water.

Jesus left the Essenes because of their over-narrow practices.

Jesus based his teaching to Jews upon the Torah and the (then oral) Mishna. He sought not to destroy the laws of the Hebrew prophets but to "restore the natural human condition."

Jesus had his doubts at times, the main one occurring in his Gethsemane prayer on the eve of his crucifixion, when he sought a way out of his forthcoming suffering. He chose instead to complete his mission through full submission to the Divine Will.

Jesus was both a natural prophet and a clairvoyant. He foresaw the future consequences to mankind, both positive and negative, that would follow from his work. He sorrowed greatly for the suffering he knew humanity would bring down upon itself.

During his mission Jesus' deliberately chose to fulfill several Old Testament "prophecies" for their mythical and poetic value, thus making them self-fulfilling, even beyond the intentions of the original prophets.

Teachings:

Humanity is one and the same substance as the universal consciousness, or God. The whole of the law constitutes this: to love the Lord God with all thy heart, mind and soul, and thy neighbor as thyself. Indeed, the term "God" is virtually synonymous with love. [SC 57ff, 80-81, 86-87, 90-95]

Jesus sought to bring peace to the world by showing man how to reorder his world according to a higher set of principles. [SC 13, 104]

It is a divine directive to resist the taking of another's life, even if it means giving up one's own. This is the greatest love one may manifest by his own volition.

Every human has the same potential for ascending to the Godly level of consciousness as Jesus did. The only barriers to this ascension are internal, not external to the seeker. Jesus demonstrated that these barriers, mainly the ego and the resultant fear of obliteration upon bodily death, may be overcome. [SC 59ff, 76-79, 85ff, 106, 184ff]

CHAPTER 8

APOSTLES, HEALINGS AND MIRACLES

Jesus' ministry, which began with his baptism, was soon followed by his selection of the first apostles and his initial interaction with them.

Gathering of the Apostles

The Gospels Matthew and Mark make it sound as if Jesus chose the first few of his twelve apostles more or less at random from strangers he met on the road. "Follow me," he said. Perhaps he had the intuitive sense to know in advance how they would work out, but it seems more likely that he had already known them for a long time. We are never told about the basis on which he chose them. For example:

(At the time of his selection by Jesus, Simon [Peter] seems to have been an awkward buffoon of a fellow, an unlikely choice for the role of a leading apostle and active future evangelist. How did Jesus know that Simon was such an appropriate selection?)

Because he was without guile. There was no deceit found in him.

It was not unusual, for instance, for a Deity to choose the most unlikely of individuals. Study the prophets and you will find that the Deity often seeks to lift up those who are in the most difficult times. If Peter could be lifted up, so in turn could the whole.

(Was Peter also an Essene, perchance?)

Correct.

Duration of Ministry

The synoptic Gospels imply that Jesus' ministry lasted only one year, without actually saying so, but John's Gospel has him celebrating three Passovers. Which is right?

(How long was Jesus' ministry, measured from his baptism until his death?)

> The traditional measurement of three to three and a half years.

Collective Identity and the Various Johns

We may rightly be suspicious of the Gospel of John for its doctrinal content. It seems likely to have been heavily edited by the early Church fathers to satisfy their own priorities. Still, it is clear from its subjective aspect that its author "John" understood a number of things the other Gospel writers did not. It also has a mystical quality suggestive of the Book of Revelations, whose unidentified author is also named John.* There are also epistles (letters) written by an unknown "John." Are these various Johns different or the same, and are they related to the apostle John, son of Zebedee?

(Is the John I am speaking with indeed the same as John son of Zebedee?)

> The channel speaking has never denied this, and all the words and substance that are spoken support this. The channel speaking is certainly not divine, but indeed, if the name John Zebedee were called, this channel would respond.

---

* The correct authorship of these writings by "John" has long been argued by religious scholars without resolution.

(Which of the various Johns in the Gospels are the same person and which are not?)

> The Gospel named John is attributed to the John speaking.
> The letters or epistles are attributed to the channel speaking,
> and the Book of Revelations to the channel speaking. Also,
> the entity known as John the Divine, John of the Revelation,
> the youngest of the apostles.

(And John the Beloved?)

> Correct.

In the non-physical realm from which Ryerson's John is speaking it is not obvious what "being attributed to" and "being the same" means. Do individuals after death somehow blend into a larger pool of consciousness, as some intuitives claim, or do they retain their sense of separate identity?

(I'm wondering if you, as the channel speaking, are part of a group soul or a collective set of beings, a multi-dimensional personality, say, of which John son of Zebedee is only one member.)

> You might say that all souls are multi-dimensional, but there
> is a core identity around which lies the historical soul group
> and where activities may revolve. Souls do have individuality.
> The channel speaking may be said to be that identity that
> was John of the Revelation, John son of Zebedee and author
> of the fourth Gospel.
>
> The historical identity of the channel speaking may be
> established by patterns of speech, by the knowledge given
> and in the manner in which the Christ energy is viewed, as
> being consistent with the continuity of the synoptic Gospels
> and the Gospel attributed to the being speaking. Therefore,
> the historical identity and perspective offered is that of a
> witness to the events described.
>
> Souls incarnate across time and space; therefore it might
> be said that the channel speaking has had other incarnations,
> like many souls, and may have incarnations in other

sectors of time or even another universe. Thus all souls are multi-dimensional. The idea that it is a form of collective, other than that there are soul groups of other individualized expressions of souls, would not be a completely inaccurate description.

(OK. Hmm. That clears it up . . . somewhat.)

As much as the infinite may be applied to the finite for clarity.

Instructions to the Apostles

Jesus gave many instructions to his apostles for leading a righteous life, and in particular for how they should conduct themselves as they traveled out in pairs of evangelists throughout Palestine and later to the known world. In later centuries Christians often tried to hold to this high standard by behavior as if they were apostles themselves. Even today missionaries and charity workers frequently seek to imitate this standard as they move among pagans, the poor and the disadvantaged.

However, not all of these directives fit well into modern life. It is tempting to simply dismiss them as very much out of date. Are we missing what Jesus was getting at regarding the way to live a "Christian" life?

(Looking broadly at Jesus' directives, he indicated that his first-century followers should share their possessions freely with those who have none, travel around with no money and only the barest of essentials, and turn the other cheek to an attacker—presumably even to one who is insane or a terrorist, let us say. How should we properly translate this counsel into present-day Western culture?)

By noting their basic or fundamental wisdom.

Any traveler who has traveled any distance has come to know the wisdom in contemporary terms of packing lightly. This creates several-fold. One, by simplicity in choices of material objects one is always open to adapting his identity midst the activities of the various levels of humanity he may travel amongst. This can mean to travel with humility, but it may also mean to travel with richness. For instance, an empty canvas may always be painted upon, and the subject material may be changed from one geography to the next. So there are certain innate wisdoms that can be understood even in contemporary times. It may be said, travel elegantly and simply so that you may enjoy the abundance and the fullness of life that is present in the NOW.

The so-called "turning of the other cheek" is simply the knowledge that in moments of passion individuals may not be at the higher functional levels or their greatest wisdom. An act of non-violence, where an individual may show restraint, may *shock* the so-called enemy into seeing both the reason, and eventually above all else, their intent, in the spirit of the more passive individual's continuity with their own consciousness.

It seems that the instructions Jesus gave to his roving evangelists are to be taken today only as general guiding principles and not literal prescriptions for virtuous behavior.

Rejection in Nazareth

According to Luke, when Jesus returned to his childhood synagogue in Nazareth and tried to preach there he was ridiculed and his life was threatened.[102] Why so?

> Nazareth was his home community. When he [re]visited Nazareth it was said that he could do few miracles there, so perhaps the adage, "familiarity breeds contempt" [began] there. It was said that prophets have no honor in their own land.[103]
>
> When ye know a person for all their years, even if they are a person of goodly worth and goodly deeds, it becomes difficult to conceive of them in any other manner [but that] in which you knew them. Jesus knew this.

Healings and Miracles

The healings and other miracles Jesus is said to have performed are a close second to his moral advice and spiritual teachings (to be examined in Chapters 10 and 14). His healings are simultaneously amazing and almost unbelievable. Very few people today can find anything in their own experience to confirm that it is even possible to instantaneously cure the crippled, leprous, blind and insane, and even raise dead people to life—all without drugs or implements and only by an act of intention. The Gospel writers also claim Jesus changed water to wine, quelled a storm at sea and caused a fig tree to wither. How are we to regard such incredible reports? It is only natural for us to be doubtful.

Jesus was probably respected by many of his followers more for his healings and other miracles than his message. Also, he may have healed so extensively because this was expected in his day for anyone who would be a prophet, and especially a Messiah.

According to the Gospels Jesus' many healings and miracles began first with the simplest ones and then progressed to more complex ones, up to the feeding of the 5000 ("loaves and fishes") and raising the dead Lazarus. So a learning process seems to have been taking place.

Many people today, even many devout Christians, slough off the accounts of Jesus' healings as simply a fictitious part of the Christian legend. In the absence of better evidence we may suppose that the Gospel record of Jesus' healings could have arisen from the distorted perceptions of superstitious crowds, exaggerations by the Gospel writers and/or later insertions by the Church editors. For example, observers of the alleged healings were not usually in a position to judge how ill the subjects were before they appeared to be healed. And how would they know if the boy whom Jesus raised from the dead was really dead? Were the "possessed" men really crazy, or just drunk?

In two healings—the man born blind and the dead Lazarus—the stated evidence is stronger but we still have to trust that the entire story was not fabricated. We know that the evangelists and Gospel writers were trying hard to raise Jesus onto a high pedestal during the tumultuous period after his death. We have good reason to doubt the historical accuracy of their words regarding his exceptional deeds.

On the other hand, the Gospel accounts of the healings may be largely correct. Again, the evidence may simply be distorted and incomplete.

Actually, reports of phenominal healings are fairly common in human history. In today's world it is only necessary to open one's eyes a little to recognize similar healings taking place—and we are not referring here to the "miracles" of modern medical technology. Today's exceptional healings are usually reported medically as "spontaneous remissions," if they are reported at all, or attributed to the Virgin Mary in a religious context. In the third world dozens of healers regularly perform *some* of the same kinds of healings Jesus is said to have done, as well as more startling ones such as psychic surgery which Jesus is not reported to have done.* Enough of these healings have been reported reliably and accurately and filmed by medical visitors to deny the frequent claim that *all* of them are fraudulent.† It should therefore not be hard to accept that Jesus could have performed similar exceptional healing deeds in his own day.

Yes, it is likely that some of Jesus' reported healings and miracles are not strictly true, though we must still wonder about the remainder: *How* did he do them? *Why* did he perform them when his primary mission, as we understand it now, did not seem to require such flashy phenomena? Did his abilities arise from his alleged training in the East and Egypt, or were they an expression of his supposed high state of conciousness?

There is also the fact, now well established, that healing is not a one-sided act of healer upon healee, but is a joint action involving both parties, including the healee's expectations, "faith" and belief in the healer. Could the superstitious climate of the times have allowed Jesus to perform healings that would have been impossible at other times and places?

Some persons, of course, see Jesus as so divinely gifted he could do almost anything. In that case should we accept him as divine (in some

---

* If these medically practitioners practiced openly in the U.S. today they would probably be arrested and imprisoned for operating without a medical licence.

† Many exceptional healings are taking place quietly in the U.S. and Britain today under the heading "spontaneous remission"—that is, unexplained recovery, even from fatal disease. The most exceptional healings, however, are performed by "psychic surgeons" in the Philippines and Brazil. They include full and immediate cures from serious physical diseases and rapid recoveries from mental disorders. Less documented and publicized are shamanic practices in isolated tribes in several third-world cultures. While deception is known to occur sometimes, there are many medically examined and carefully documented examples of these non-ordinary healings to substantiate the claim stated here. Credible reports of these healings are difficult to find, since they do not appear in medical journals but are distributed among dozens of smaller publications, often mixed in with less credible accounts. Some of them are accessible through the Internet. [Fuller 1975, Ormond 1959, Martin 1999]

sense) because he could perform miracles, or could he perform miracles because he was divinely endowed?

Thus, while we may have reasons *not* to believe the Gospels regarding Jesus' alleged healings, we also have strong reasons to accept them as true.

In the wake of these arguments, pro and con, we need to remember that there is more to Jesus' miracles than just a series of unusual phenomena that call for explanation. While we are naturally curious, and perhaps critical, can we not also accept them as one of the glorious mysteries of human life, without the need for detailed analysis, assessment and proof? Can we not set aside our need to *explain* them, in the face of Jesus' greater message, the significance of which goes well beyond his alleged healings?

We consider Jesus' miracles first.

The Wedding at Cana

The first of Jesus' recorded miracles occurred at a wedding in which the wine ran out prematurely. John's Gospel says he came to the rescue by converting the water in some large jugs into unusually good wine.[104] Did he actually do this?

(Was the production of wine at the wedding in Cana a genuine miracle by Jesus?)

> Yes, but it speaks more to the order of his natural practice. At the wedding feast at which he was an honored guest—he was the rabbi who was to perform the service—and wishing to spare his host embarrassment [because] all of the wine has been consumed during the celebrations, he ordered that water be brought forth. And indeed, in his prayer to bring about the miraculous, he transmuted the inorganic into the organic.
>
> This may be startling [though] turning the inorganic into the organic was certainly within his capacity. But the unique demonstration, actually an act of compassion at the wedding, [was] uninterrupted with the continuity of joy. The real miracle to Jesus was not the water into wine, but more so the enjoyment in an everyday affair. That to him

was truly miraculous—bringing the Divine into the natural order of the state of affairs of humanity.

The water into wine was considered to sacrilize [sanctify?] the concept of marriage. For the concept of the wedding feast was symbolic, that Jesus was about to *wed* the feminine principle of the Divine, the Holy Spirit, to the masculine principle of the Divine . . . thus the ability of God to openly *act* in the earth plane, not separate from humanity, for the melding of the male and the female within a single human being.

Notice the elegance and the simplicity of the miraculous here. Some have said that he merely chose sweet water, as the Essenes practiced [in] the symbolic taking of wine (for they did not believe in alcohol). This became the natural miracle. However, we say now that the water [actually] *contained* wine.

There are those who say there was a tradition, in order to keep wine cool for preservation in large jugs, which would evaporate the water, that a small amount of oil [would] be placed upon the surface of the wine and it would be allowed to age. [They] might then mix water with the wine, creating the appearance of the miracle. Again, we eliminate these natural explanations, although they would certainly constitute [an explanation of] the event, well within the boundaries of historical capacity.[*]

So we challenge the individual [critic] to understand that the manipulation of *prana*,[†] the ability to transform elements into more complex forms, was well within the mental processes [capabilities] of the man Jesus, because of the initiations he had undergone.

---

[*] It was a common domestic practice in those days to use wine as a *flavoring* for drinking water rather than in full strength.

[†] The Sanskrit term *prana*, called *qi* or *chi* in the Orient, refers to an essentially non-physical energy that resides in every form of life and is essential to its existence. Those who practice yoga and related breathing exercises seek to control the level and flow of prana within their bodies in order to induce a highly energized state of consciousness.

For the conversion of water into wine it is better to understand its character as the simple announcement of his abilities at a *wedding feast*, a celebration. It was also responsible experimentation of his awesome capacities, for only afterwards did he progress to more complex miracles such as healing, and even then only simple healings.

His real healing was to heal the path of his society in relationship to the soul of nature. For the miracles actually became a burden [later], perhaps even further separating him from the natural order.

Feeding the 5000 (Loaves and Fishes)

Later on a large crowd of followers of Jesus listened to his preaching in the countryside for two or three days, and we are told that they failed to bring along enough food for the occasion. To fill this logistical need Jesus is reported to have transmuted a few loaves of bread and some fish into a sufficient quantity to feed the entire group.

Here again we have another incredible event for which very few persons today can find support in their own experience. In fact, there are no credible accounts of such a miracle in the public media or credible historical archives. We are left to our own resources—be it belief, genuine faith or intuition—to reveal what may have actually happened.

(Regarding Jesus' alleged feeding of the five thousand, did he indeed transmute the materials, or was it more of a replication, or did it happen at all?)

> We would describe the process as a form of replication, for instance, the ability to restore life to organic matter that is in a state of suspension.
>
> One partial explanation for the natural miracle is that when people travel great distances they would carry food in their garments, sometimes out of fear that there would not be enough to sustain them and they might faint. So these were life-sustaining substances and very precious. Part of the natural miracle is that some people's food would have been hoarded to sustain them through a long journey.

But part of the natural miracle is true. Jesus took what had been openly given by a child, and by that child's act of faith began to create a miracle where he multiplied the tissues by restoring life to same. This could be considered a process of radical cloning, certainly again not beyond the capacity that scientists speculate upon and will perhaps one day understand.

Mental Healings

We read in the Gospels that Jesus healed both minds and bodies. The mental disorders included the wild man of Gerasenes (Gergessa, Gerasa), whose possessing spirits he allegedly displaced into a herd of swine[105]; the man with a mute spirit[106]; the possessed daughter of the woman near Tyre and Sidon[107]; the man "with an unclean spirit"[108]; some alleged epileptics[109] and a few others.[110]

(Part of Jesus' healing ministry was his alleged "casting out of demons" and exorcising spirit possession. Did he really do this? If he did, how did he do it?)

> [He did it] psychically. When an individual was not in the center of his own personhood, which may come about, for instance, when abuse arises in childhood, then the adult personality is weakened at the fringes so that the emotions do not become socially integrated. This is one form of possession, almost by the psychic states of the individual who is the abuser.
>
> There are also psychic tendencies for individuals to bond; for instance, those who partake of alcohol to the point where it compromises the rational faculty. Then they seek others to participate in the so-called Dionysian ways [using] alcohol or addictive substances. Negative consequences rather than wisdom may come about through the addiction. The energy field of the individual, the archaic form known as *halo*, the light surrounding the body, may also attract other spirit entities, souls seeking understanding of their own past psychic states. They may surround the individual, and these

become the so-called demons often seen. In other words, other human spirits, poor of reasoning and poor of spirit, having not succeeded in their own incarnations, seek a form of salvation or completion before their next incarnation.

The man Jesus could see, and could properly discern, one may say—as Luke would, *diagnose*—these various psychic states. His capacity [was such] that, through dietary laws [and] nutritional healing of damaged tissues, neurological and internal organs, [he] could strengthen the individual for a return to sobriety, clarity and rationality. So some observances of the law could be [seen] here.

[There was] also the demand that the poor be fed, and could be tended to according to the ancient Talmanic [Talmudic?] laws* and the Torah and similar endeavors; also education, as in scripture, bringing the individuals into greater social integration by rights and knowledge of privileges worn away under more secular laws, both of Rome and the early Greco-Roman influences. In those days these would deny an individual the concept of Jewish identity, in particular.

To work with energy, to heal the psychic centers, causing complete regeneration within the individual, would constitute true exorcism. The exorcism on the part of the man Jesus was looked upon as healing, even in the famous case of the so-called swine herds.[111]

This gave voice to recognizing *union* in the human condition of the man Jesus. Within another human being union may constitute a certain degree of shame that they had descended to a state not unlike the parable of the prodigal son. When souls would leave the energy state or aura for another being, they may seek the next [lower] level of physical expression, in this case the so-called swineherd.

This was also emphasized in the story as unclean meat, or unclean flesh, [referring to] those souls under a shamanic-like condition. They would then perhaps no longer be able to

---

* The *Talmud* is a collection of Jewish oral traditions commenting on the Torah and the basis of rabbinic law. In written form it consists mainly of the *Mishna* (~200 CE) and the *Gemara* (1500 CE). See footnotes in Chapter 1.

have [enter into?] states of denial, like the individual whose consciousness is compromised by Dionysian or alcoholic substances. Their addiction cycle broken, they may then be almost shamanically prepared to go to their next level of incarnation. So in these specific episodes of exorcism we see [in Jesus] the activities of prophet, physician, healer and perhaps even shaman.

(What would be the present-day counterpart of these exorcism cases under treatment?)

It is known that some individuals may achieve [fall into] states of nutritional imbalance that are now treatable and recognizable. Some speaking therapies may help integrate certain breaks or schisms in the personality. Also, certain herbal substances, according to dietary laws, contain both nutritional and medical substances. So perhaps the best model would be that of so-called integrative medicine, to include nutrition, acknowledgement of the neural meridian system and even the use of psycho-active substances isolated from certain states [plants] in nature on the part of physicians.

Remember, Luke recorded many of these exorcisms, such as the Hippocratic states observed today. They would be known by a trained physician.

Jesus achieved most of his healings without the use of herbs. But it was not without the use of the law [about] which he said, "I have come to fulfill the law, not to destroy it."[112] So this included the notion of the proper dietary element, conversations on the issue of identity and the proper place the individual held in the natural human order.

(Were these the diseases we call possession, or multiple personality today?)

Indeed. Individuals with multiple personality disorder at times seem to display personalities as coming from other times, cultures and features which go above and beyond the features of this lifetime. Healing of the incarnate soul could then lead to the healing of so-called multiple-personality syndrome. Also schizophrenia. It has been noted that certain psycho-active substances may lead to the treatment, if not the full cure of these conditions. However, the application of energy and continued therapy to integrate consciously the individual into one singular identity would constitute complete healing.

Some of these physiological states may be precursors and *lead* to spirit possession. In the ancient world they were at times considered syndromes of possession, if not full possession itself. So there were degrees of discernment.

Physical Healings

Jesus reported physical healings are numerous. They included the restoration of health for persons "with divers diseases,"[113]: the blind[114], paralytics[115], the lame[116], lepers[117], fevers[118], chronic bleeding[119], disfigurement[120] (in some cases at a distance) and even raising the dead.[121] Moreover, he did his work openly enough for it to be seen and reported. Such a healer today would surely be similarly mobbed if he performed publicly, and in the U.S. be jailed, as have been a few Asian psychic surgeons for violating medical codes and practicing medicine without a license.

The Essenes were known as healers with the ability to heal without herbs, for instance. The phenomena that so mystifies the modern mind, such as acupuncture for alleviating pain, accomplishes these things with no external sources of drugs or other medicines, and indeed even brings about healing. [This was] the capacity of beings such as Jesus, who through meditation and other endeavors could bring more of this energy and even heal with this energy at a distance. Many of the Essenes, growing into adulthood through their training, had these particular capacities.

So these miracles, as observed by the Hellenistic mind and even the physicians of Jesus' day, were considered to be signs of a sacred personality.

Here is John's explanation (from an earlier publication) of how Jesus performed these healings:

> The manner of healing of the man, Jesus, was through his own physical body, which was a perfect pattern. As he extended healing to others and they were willing to accept it, they received the information from him telepathically by being present in his aura. Their afflictions, or diseased bodies, would then have a correct pattern upon vibrational, molecular and genetic levels, so as to begin to rebuild themselves. For their conscious minds, which shaped most of the activities of the physical body, had forgotten, through lack of faith, their own ability to heal themselves. Therefore, their physical bodies did not hold the pattern for the correct state of health.
>
> But when their physical bodies, or their minds, had faith in one who walked close to that perfection called God, then they could reactivate that memory from the subconscious or collective unconscious. . . . The physical body would then assimilate that pattern within itself, and begin to rebuild itself, first, upon the vibrational and etheric levels, then the molecular, then the genetic, then healing the organism as a whole.
>
> All is accomplished by the level of love, which is the soul.[122]

Again, most of Jesus' healing miracles should not be so surprising to us because similar phenomena are taking place in today's world, and can be known about if only one pays attention. John is also saying that such knowledge was not confined to Jesus but also practiced by the Essenes.*

Lazarus

Jesus' resurrection of Lazarus, often considered to be his most amazing deed, is described only in the Gospel of John. If so, why did the earlier

---

* This last statement is confirmed in Josephus' history of the Jews. [Williamson 1981]

Gospel writers not mention this highly unusual event? Did it really occur? Why did Jesus wait four days before responding to the first news of Lazarus' illness and death? We also have to ask skeptically, was Lazarus fully dead when Jesus "raised" him?

(Do the translated and edited versions of Lazarus' death and resurrection correctly reflect what actually happened?)

> Correct. In some of his past miracles [observers] had seen him awaken individuals from comas. They had seen him heal the sick, but when it came to the raising of the dead they thought perhaps he may have reached the limit of his abilities.

Jesus may have waited so long to respond to the news of Lazarus' death so there would be no doubt that Lazarus' body was truly dead and decaying.

> They [those by Lazarus' tomb] wanted to make certain that Jesus understood. The Jewish burial rites were to take the body, place it in the tomb, allow for its natural passing into dust, then to exhume it and collect the bones to be placed in an ossuary. So they wished to make clear to him, saying, "Can ye not sense the corruption of the form?"[123] speaking of the odors that emissioned from tombs. They wished to make clear to him that necrophysiology—that is, decay of the physical form—was well advanced, saying, can he not sense the aromas?

(So Lazarus was really dead, and he had been dead for a few days. Is that right?)

> Correct. Jesus then performed the multiple names of God, precisely in the manner by which Moses parted the so-called Red Sea, calling down similar energies. This is where it is said that he then shouted in a loud voice, "Lazarus, come forth!"[124] And so he did, even still wearing the grave clothes. This was a form not of resuscitation but authentic

resurrection and rejuvenation of the physical body. It was *not* the glorified body that is spoken of, where the body may achieve physiological immortality.

(What did Lazarus die of?)

This is what would have been interpreted initially as a form of inflammation that later evolved into bronchial pneumonia.

(Was there something special about this situation with Lazarus which allowed it to be possible? Or, could it have happened to someone other than Lazarus, or perhaps at some other time as well as the time it did?)

Only according to incremental degrees of faith.

In his youth Jesus would perform various acts in the way of a child, with the will of a child. He was normal in his upbringing, but he had abilities that were associated with those of a prophet. In the long history of prophets there were feats considered to be natural acts of the divine being, or divinely inspired being. While these might have caused fears and respect within a community, they were not considered completely out of the ordinary or unexpected.

(What happened to Lazarus after Jesus' death?)

He lived out the course of his life, eventually to leave the physical form in his advanced years. [He spent] a period of time in Bethany, but then he traveled with other disciples. For a long period of time he was a member of the Church, or synagogue, of Jerusalem, the so-called Synod of Jerusalem.

The Purpose of Jesus' Healings

Jesus reasons for healing are not clear from the record, but regardless of his motive they obviously played an important part in his work. We would like to believe that he healed people as he did mainly out of his compassion for their suffering. At the same time his healings attracted large crowds to hear his message. The history of Judaism reveals that anyone who was a prophet, and certainly a Messiah, would be expected to be a healer. Then, Jesus might simply have wanted the healings to be a demonstration of what is humanly possible, and what faith in God can do. Perhaps all four of these possible motivations functioned in concert.

As Jesus matured and received his baptism, as he became a spiritual adult and recommitted himself to the Torah, to its ways and laws, his first disciples came to him and said, "It is said unto us that ye are the Christ. Show us signs of this, that we may know thee."

His first sign or first miracle [at the Cana wedding] was an act of kinship, a mature act of restraint in these abilities in which he was already well practiced. From there he went on to healings that progressed in their complexity and the impact they had on the society—the re-integration of lepers into the community, for example. Once they had been healed they had gone to the Temple for their inspection, and no blemish would be found upon them. He understood the patterns of the energies, as they might intensify or recede. He healed those who could not give children, to remove that stigma from the society and the order of the day.

The climax of these abilities was to be the restoration of life, or, one may say, the healing of death. It was not only with Lazarus, but a final healing of death which came [later] in the sacrifice of his crucifixion and the resurrection. He received death itself, first [with Lazarus], in order to know it could be healed, and then again in the resurrection.

This would be the natural order in which anyone might progress in incremental degrees of demonstration, experimentation and proving, not unlike the natural [scientific] phenomena: observation, corrections in observation, culminating in the expectation of a result. It is much like the physicians [who] would inoculate themselves before [inoculating] others.

Healing Karmic Debts

There are only meager clues in the Gospels that Jesus' healings may have included the resolution of incurred karma. Those who wrote the Gospels gave no hint that they understood this aspect of his work, and if present the later editors may have obliterated all mention of it.* In view of Jesus' power to heal, might it have been possible for him to shorten or even eliminate the payment of such past-life "debts"?

(We are taught that the law of karma involves the incurrence of "debts" for transgressing Natural Law and requires their subsequent resolution, or repayment, without exception. To what extent did Jesus have the power to postpone, forgive or erase karmic debts through his healings?)

> In previous lives, the person may have taken actions that led to karma which they would not see until another lifetime. Jesus, however, knowing that this was a karmic debt, and that all karma is to create experience and context and is not punitive, would give pardon. This is much like a wise judge may see changes in the character of a person who has learned from the consequences of his actions. He may then give suspension under the law, as is his power according to the wisdom of his society.

(But if a person has made such a mistake and has not yet learned the lesson, does he not still need to go through a learning process to resolve it, whether Jesus was involved or not? Or could Jesus somehow erase that need?)

> Even as a man could be given suspension under man's law, the concept of suspension meant to refrain from those so-called behaviors that led to the consequences of their poor judgment. If the individual does *not* reform and learn from the gift of his suspension, and does not engage in abstinence from the behavior, then he will eventually fail society. He

---

* For a fuller explanation of reincarnation and karma see the beginning of Chapter 11.

may return again under judgment, and he must serve the rest of the sentence that has been suspended.

Under God's law—that is, divine law—he will develop karma. You may see elements in Jesus' healings: persons would come to him for healing and he would say, "By thy faith have ye been *healed*"[125]—meaning their relief, their inspiration, as they went about. If a life of faith was too harsh, then their illnesses returned.

Indeed, absolution or the suspension of karma is an act of dharma, an act of service by one who is loving and forgiving. If one can receive the gift of forgiving and forgive oneself, then the karma is no longer part of their identity, and there is no other conscious point to act upon the physical. It is not unlike psychosomatic illnesses and their impact upon the physiology of the physical body.

So while Jesus would not erase karma, his healing could suspend it temporarily so the individual would find it easier to resolve the debt. Healing is not necessarily either a permanent or an imposed act. Full acceptance is up to the recipient.

The laws of karma and dharma* are not unlike the principles in the realm of the sacred mind. In this instance faith may be said to be the doorway to an inspiration to lead a more dharmic and service-oriented life. In this way one is healed. But there are old volitions. If one feels guilt or shame or feels not worthy, as though they must do penance or punishment, the karmic pattern returns.

The key to these healings lies in what Jesus said: "Why marvel when it is said that I am the Son of God, when thy own scriptures say that *ye* are God?" And what then is God? God indeed is Love. In this particular capacity, God is the ability to give and receive love, to awaken the memory that *all* are divine.

---

* *Dharma* is essentially the teaching of the Buddha, sometimes taken as universal law and usually interpreted as the *way* to live a righteous and harmonious life.

This was the core service that Jesus sought to inspire. He sought not to teach about *his* divinity, but to teach us about *our* divinity, and thus be healed. This was to be *as* the law, rather than *under* the law.

Premature Healing

The Gospels make it sound as if Jesus healed all those who came to him, even crowds by the hundreds, and this may be. We cannot help but suspect, though, if he wasn't more selective in choosing those whom he healed. We recognize today that several conditions are necessary before a genuine healing can take place: who is truly *ready* to be healed, who has sufficient faith, who is actually ill beforehand and (for a demonstration) who is following up to determine that the healing was truly effective? More to the point, when is a healing truly appropriate? Is healing someone always a good idea? How did Jesus handle these issues?

(We're learning today that misguided acts of physical healing are not always appropriate and beneficial. They can interrupt or cut short a lesson being learned through a person's illness and leave him with the same illness, or another perhaps more severe. How did Jesus handle this issue of premature healing?)

In the simplest of terms: it was better to give the act of love and institute the process of healing.

Perhaps it would be more accurate to say that if the individual did not receive the gift of forgiveness, then there was no healing at all, therefore no premature healing. This would be a *remission* of the illness, as you would term it, only to return in a more aggressive manner—perhaps becoming immune to the original point of intervention, not unlike any other physiological process. Temporary remission would be a more accurate term, rather than premature healing.

If the person did not receive deeply enough, or drink deeply enough of the life-giving elixir of God's love and God's intervention; if he felt his own will should dictate the destiny of his pattern—particularly a will that had been scarred and cannot let go of the need of punishment from others—then he feels his penance must come out of a punitive quality.

Perhaps it is better to say not that the healing was premature, and a lesson was postponed, but better to say that there was a remission by which a person might learn the nature of the state of well-being, but not fully receive the healing. The pattern may return in an even more aggressive mode because this is the intent his will gave it, because of old paradigms of penance and the [believed] punitive quality of karma. In other words, it is a lesson refused.

From this point of view it seems that Jesus was very likely quite selective in his healings, and healed only those who could benefit from a temporary remission or otherwise willing for the healing to be complete.

Review

History

Jesus chose Simon Peter as an apostle because Simon was without guile, and as an example of a difficult individual who could be lifted up through his interaction with Jesus.

The apostle John son of Zebedee is the same as all of the other Johns featured in the New Testament except John the Baptist.

Jesus' strict instructions to his evangelists in Palestine were literally appropriate in his day but for later generations are mainly symbolic of valid principles.

Jesus did indeed convert water into wine at the Cana wedding, primarily as a sanctification of the affair and secondarily as an inaugural demonstration of his abilities.

When "feeding the five thousand" Jesus multiplied the tissues of a little bread and fish through a replication process similar to cloning. Still, some persons in the crowd had hidden food in their garments.

Jesus' utilized his psychic ability to perform a number of "casting out of demons" and genuine exorcisms for disturbed individuals, thereby freeing them from emotional disturbances or attachment to interfering spirit personalities (multiple personality disorder, possession, schizophrenia, etc.). This work involved the removal of denial (e.g., for alcoholics) and/or the physical healing of neurological tissues.

Jesus' performed physical healings through his control of non-physical energies (prana, chi, etc.), a practice already practiced in his day by the Essenes. He did them by extending to others the perfect pattern of his own physical body, transmitting it to them telepathically through his presence. His increasingly complex healings led up to his own resurrection as a perfection of these abilities.

Jesus did not remove karmic debts but used his healing ability to "pardon" the recipients temporarily, thereby allowing them a better opportunity to correct their behavior and repay these debts by themselves.

The "raising" of Lazarus was an authentic reconstitution and resurrection of his physical body, not a resuscitation. Lazarus lived out his life in Bethany, in Jerusalem and traveling with Jesus' disciples.

Jesus did not want his followers to focus on him as a divine being and a source of the miraculous. He sought to teach them not about his divinity, but their own.

Jesus' act of riding an ass into Jerusalem was an act of humility, counter to the expectations of the day for a typical king.

Teachings

Genuine healing works through the channeling of divine energy directly to the essence, or soul, which is the harmonious point within every person and the highest gift of spirit. Thus, all healings are an expression of the soul itself. When manifested in the physical body healings bring harmony to the internal organs. [SC 104, 131ff, 174ff]

Jesus' increasingly complex healings led up to his own resurrection as a perfection of these abilities. Since each human is a fragment of God, and God is a being of infinite resource, so each of us is also a being of infinite resource and has the same inherent capacities. [SC 57ff, 80-81, 86-87, 90-95]

Attachments to and by discarnate personalities are not a matter of good or evil. One cannot attract anything higher or lower than the level of his own consciousness. [SC 35ff, 100]

There is a deep personal relationship between each one of us and the Divine. God indeed is love, the egoless altruism that already exists in each and every one of us. This was the core service that Jesus sought to inspire. [SC 41, 72, 102, 165]

One's karmic debts are automatically paid when he truly accepts forgiveness for his assumed guilt, unworthiness or need for punishment. So long as he rejects this forgiveness then any healing is only a temporary suspension; it implies delay and a "second chance" and may lead to a more serious illness. [SC 51ff, 82ff, 84-85]

CHAPTER 9

On Marriage And Divorce

It is known from history that in first-century Jewish society (as in much of the ancient world) the laws of marriage, divorce and remarriage were rigid and conservative by modern Western standards. Early marriage was expected and usually arranged. Love was not a requirement for a good marriage but was expected to grow afterwards. Adultery was officially punished by ostracism or stoning, though there must have been much overlooking of this law for errant youth, prostitutes, their clients and many others as well.

It is also known that Jewish society was very much a man's world. Mosaic law, the priesthood and cultural convention held Jewish women in strict submission to men. Women were explicitly excluded from politics, positions of authority and the main religious ceremonies. They certainly held power within the home but their views carried little weight outside of it. With few exceptions they were regarded as inferior human beings, suitable only for childbirth, homemaking and men's pleasure. The apostles too held much of this prejudice despite Jesus' teaching and example.

We cannot help but wonder how Jesus, as a compassionate egalitarian teacher, dealt with such man-woman inequities in his own family and those of his colleagues.

Jewish Marriages and Divorces

While family life went on in Palestine as it does everywhere, marriage in Jesus' world must have been an especially strong binding and supportive force in the face of religious constraints and the difficult struggles for survival and security in the Roman- and priest-dominated Jewish society.* Was this also true of the Essenes?

> Amongst the Essenes women were allowed to chose their own husbands. Although marriage contracts would often be arranged, the actual execution of the Ketubah,[†] which constituted the marriage contract, would then be only the *consecration* of the marriage.
>
> Under Jewish law a couple could live together in a period of engagement and have the joys of the marriage bed for up to seven years before the formalization of their marriage . . . to see if there was the consecration of a birth. . . . Then it could be [dissolved], but in the case of infidelity only by a writ of divorcement. This is not unlike the maturing of the emotions that you undergo from early adolescence into adulthood, and then into a mature spectrum of life in the choice of a life partner.
>
> However, if children are born it becomes a life commitment between the partners, even if there is a divorcement or setting aside, which would be highly discouraged until the children reach the age of consent.
>
> Notice that Jesus said that no man or woman may set aside one or the other except in the case of adultery—[that is,] if one had lost both the spiritual and the romantic love for the other.[126] What he spoke of was this. Amidst the ancient Essenes, both men and women had the capacity of the writ of divorcement, meaning that if the individuals were truly bound to each other in a process of love, divine and/or romantic, it was then in their capacity to be able to bind themselves to a life of partnership, particularly in the rearing of children. Only if there was adultery was there a breaking of the psychic bond between the individuals.

---

* During ancient times Jewish marriage customs varied greatly within and between different branches of Judaism. Therefore, the unusual description to follow does not contradict what is known and should not be seen as representative of all Jews.

† The *ketubah* was the original Jewish marriage contract, specified precisely in the Talmud.

So even in the Manuals of Discipline of the Essenes, those considered the most knowledgeable of the law, it was less [a matter] of flexibility in the standards of marriage but more so the acknowledgement of the human condition. That is, we grow in spirit and emotion and awareness and knowledge of God, and there are various psychic states that constitute degrees of maturity of the life partnership.

Mary Magdalen

The only known candidate for a female associate for Jesus is Mary of Magdala. Luke identifies her as one "from whom seven demons had gone out"[127] and who accompanied Jesus and other women during his preaching tours. She shows up again around the crucifixion, burial and resurrection as one very devoted to Jesus.[128] Early Church tradition identifies her with others as well: Lazarus' sister Mary, the "sinful" woman who anointed Jesus with oil shortly before his death and the woman caught in adultery (perhaps a prostitute). However, there is no New Testament evidence that these three women were the same as Mary Magdalen, and modern Christianity usually distinguishes them.

The apocryphal Gospels, early Church history and art and some modern scholarship offer various contradictory versions of Mary Magdalen's identity and activities, and especially her relationship with Jesus.[129] Still more lively options have been explored in fiction and theater.[130]

We learned above that:

> Jesus was typical of any other Essene. He had been betrothed in childhood to marry Mary Magdalen, and from the age of 4 he was to be trained into the actions of so-called young adulthood.

But this marriage never took place:

> By the time he [Jesus] began to approach the age of consent, around the age of 19, he gave her [Mary Magdalen] a writ of divorcement. This meant not that he was unsatisfied with her as a possible wife, but as a conscious choice to continue the path of the ascetic. It could even be said that they

remained as marriage partners, as she was later the one who anointed him with healing oils, as often only the wife of an individual [would do]. For the healing oils were placed upon the various sepherat on the body to awaken the chakras,* and this could include even the anointing of the areas of sexual genitalia. It was often considered that only the spiritual wife could entertain such an intimate ritual.

(Was Mary Magdalen the same person as Mary, the sister or Lazarus and Martha?)

We find this to be accurate.

(What is this about seven demons being cast out of her? Is this something Jesus did? What did it symbolize?)

It symbolizes what Mary Magdalen [experienced] when she underwent a separation from Jesus, when Jesus chose the life path of the ascetic. As a twin soul[†] she could not see herself being bound up to any other [man]. A great sorrow came over her at the separation from the man Jesus, and over the years she incurred certain karma.

Mary Magdalen was trained as a tantric, and she was often given permission by the Essenes to minister to lepers and unto others—in other words to *touch* others for the acts of healing. She had taken, as was the right of women, some lovers who set her aside through writs of divorcement, as was the tradition of the Essenes. For she thought that hers was to be a path of marriage and children.

Eventually, however, as Jesus grew into his ministry she wished discipleship with him. The casting out was of the karma incurred over these years of sorrow and her studies. She came into an extraordinary clarity, which had been her

---

* See further discussion on chakras in Chapter 13.
† According to some metaphysical systems, such as Theosophy, souls are created in pairs as *twin souls,* or *soulmates.* They supposedly lead parallel and usually independent series of lives until their final reuniting and merging. The notion is obviously a prime candidate for romantic interpretations.

earlier heritage. In other words, each of her seven chakras was purged or cleansed.

(So what happened to her afterwards?)

There were also the female disciples to whom Mary Magdalen offered leadership, because the [male] disciples held prejudices against women in those days and there were discussions among them. These are the normal discussions of individuals who are of a product of the humanity of their day. Such discussions continue even amidst many thinkers of this day.

After teaching forty days, and healing many of the relationships between the disciples, Mary Magdalen indeed took upon herself a marriage. It did not have to be marriage to the man Jesus, who remained a prophet and chose the path of divine celibacy. One of his brothers wooed her, within the tradition, for he was something of a romantic. Since his brother [Jesus] had set her aside, it might even be his responsibility, according to the older laws, to engage her in marriage.

She accepted this proposal and eventually lived her years in a region of France. There was an Essene community there that later became known as the Cathars. The Magdalen established the so-called Merovingian lineages of the kings of France and then Europe.* These are the stories attributed to Mary Magdalen, and the birthline of Mary unto those who became European leaders by the bloodlines of Jesus and Mary.

---

* The *Merovingians* were a dynasty of Frankish kings who ruled from the fifth to the eighth century over a shifting region corresponding roughly to ancient Gaul . . . The *Cathars* or *Albigensians*, were a significant Christian sect, widespread during the 12th century in what is now south-western France. When the Catholic Church declared them heretical they were wiped out by Christian French lords during the Inquisition.

Marriage and Adultery

For offenses of adultery Jesus' moral proclamation was not as cruel as the old Jewish law of stoning, but he redefined adultery as not merely an illegal sexual act but the *intention* of it—an alternative that would be even harder to live by![131]

(In today's world it's hard for us to believe that lusting is such a serious sin. What counsel can you offer to contemporary Westerners as they try to find a balance between free physical [sexual] expression, on one hand, and one's responsibility to others—the newly born, society and partners—on the other?)

> In the concept of lust in the heart, which the Master spoke to in those days, he spoke of the difficulties of attaining a true Tantric or a romantic love, a true state of balance comparable to the divine love.
>
> So the concept was more cautionary, pointing out that lust could be considered as a breaking of the psychic link between the lovers. It was more an open acknowledgement of the fragility of that psychic link. It could be re-established through the more generous standards of forgiveness, when the woman was accused of adultery, even when taken in the act. This is why he said that any without sin should be the first to cast the stone.*[132] This had *always* been the standard of the law, even under the Torah.
>
> What had been said is that any court that issues a judgment of death more than once in fifty years is an unmerciful court. For indeed the ancient teachers, the rabbis of the Torah and the Mishnah, were aware of human frailties in these activities. In this general backdrop of the law, the law must be administered according to what was defined as the degree of mercy pre-existing in the law.
>
> The very activity of thought within the heart speaks more to the issue: the desire of the soul is to achieve oneness with the Divine. Remember that the man Jesus was a mystic and valued union with the Divine above all else. So

---

* See also the next section.

he attempted to establish a balanced awareness so that one may [is allowed to] transgress against the standard of pure spiritual attainment of either romantic love or Tantric or sexual love. For it was also known that *all* fall short of the glory of God. So no one may judge.

(These days we are relatively loose in the whole area of marriage. We explore relationships, especially when we're young. We marry and divorce rather freely and we let single parents raise children. How are we to practice today the seemingly strong teachings of Jesus on marriage and divorce?)

What it said is, even in the days of Adam and Eve, all come in Adam unto death. In the new Adam, in Christ, all are lifted up and come unto life. What it speaks of is this: all should seek union with the Divine, specifically in the heart. It says, however, that grace is a continuous state of conscious awareness and practice. It must become a living part, a living form, for mercy and justice must eventually rule.

So it is no different from the days of Adam unto the twenty-first or twenty-second or twenty-third century. Humanity's [inner] state of consciousness is in oneness with the Divine. It is only the *mind* that must accept the grace of the perfection, which was offered in the humility of the life that was lived. It can therefore be accessed through the historical existence and the continuity of consciousness, which is the phenomenon of the man Jesus, the Christ or Messiah, meaning anointed one or unified one.

The Woman Caught in Adultery

According to John's Gospel (and only his) Jesus was set up by the priesthood to pass judgment on an adulterous woman, who was at least technically eligible for stoning. The absence of this event in the synoptic Gospels makes its veracity suspicious, but Jesus' handling of the confrontation in John's Gospel does seem to be just what he would do.

When there was a woman who was brought to him [Jesus] and said to be caught in adultery, he immediately fell to the ground and began to write in the dust.[133] His actions, clarified, were the following.

First, he created a circle in which he drew the names of God, displaying his knowledge, so that, by his knowing the names of God, the accusers would instantly respect him as a holy man. As he wrote in the dust he began to write the names of some individuals who were among the accusers, who had also themselves partaken of the services of women for hire. In other words, he began to reveal some of their innermost secrets, to their discomfort and to the amusement of some about them who knew of the accuser's own behavior.

There has also been misunderstanding of the very term *stoning* itself. The original sense of the Torah, then the oral tradition and finally the written tradition, meant a casting of lots, not unlike a trial by jury. A stone was taken, a mark was placed on it, favorable or disfavorable. This was comparable to a throwing of the Urim and Thummim* in a process of divination by the temple priests. Stoning was often carried out only by the standard that, anyone who themselves had not crossed over the threshold, in the sense of being accused of themselves, had the capacity [right?] of casting a judgment or a lot. For it says, "Saith the Lord, thou shalt not judge."

(But were they actually throwing rocks at the woman or were they casting lots?)

This is why we said there was corruption of the matter. There were two activities here. For one, he practiced that which came to be known later on by another teacher, known as Honi the circle-maker.† By creating a circle about the woman and writing the names of God in the dust he immediately

---

* The *Urim* and *Thummim* were a pair of symbolic stones, symbolizing the gonads of the body and used for obtaining insight in Hebrew divination and judgment. [Exod. 28:30].

† As reported in the Mishnah and Talmud, *Honi* and his two sons were miracle workers near-contemporary to Jesus. They were most famous for the effectiveness of their prayers for rain in times of need.

placed her under high scriptural authority, which no one could cross until a judgment had been rendered. He also wrote in the dust laws that constituted the matter of the casting of lots, rather than stones. No one could meet the standard that had already been established in ancient law. They themselves knew they had crossed their own thoughts and fell short of the ability to have the presence of the Divine in their own hearts, in order to render a clear judgment.

In these particular endeavors, then, there was a greater continuity of *mercy* bound down through the histories, and it had only been the harsh political constitutionalization of the law to hold in check various peoples and to hold them to political rather than spiritual consequences.

Note also that there were [also] political manipulations, an attempt to snare or compromise the man Jesus in his practices as either prophet, rabbi or practitioner of the law. So again these were as much political events as they were tests of the law.

Review

History

Among the Essenes, once an engagement for marriage was set up the couple could live together as man and wife for up to seven years before consecration of the marriage. If no children ensued in this period, or if there was adultery, they would be allowed to divorce.

Jesus was engaged to Mary Magdalen at age 14 and followed a meditative path with her, including Tantric sexual practices, but he divorced her at age 19 to pursue an ascetic life. She then incurred karma with other men over subsequent years. This karma was later healed. She became a leader among the women members of Jesus' evangelistic team. She eventually married one of Jesus' brothers, moved to France and continued the Davidic blood line into the Merovingian kings.

Jesus embarrassed the accusers of the woman accused of adultery by writing their names in the sand, for Jewish law required that any judge of another's sin be first free of that sin himself. The Jewish punishment of stoning for adultery was ambiguous since it referred in the Torah both to the death sentence by thrown stones and to a form of temple divination, judgment and voting using marked stones.

While Jesus' denounced lusting (adultery in the heart) as well as adultery itself, he was speaking mainly of the fragility of the psychic link between lovers and the need for forgiveness and mercy. Indeed, the offence lies more in the party's dishonesty than the act of adultery itself.

Teachings

Union with the Divine should transcend all else, for each human's deepest state of consciousness is already in oneness with God. He may seek this union consciously, specifically through the heart. It is only the mind that is reluctant to accept the perfection being offered. [SC 57ff, 80-81, 84, 90ff, 146]

In adultery, as in other human failings, the solution lies in honesty, mercy and forgiveness, not in condemnation. All fall short of the perfection of God so no one may judge another.[SC 66, 95, 139]

CHAPTER 10

SELECTED TEACHINGS

The collection of Jesus' teachings with all their detail and implications could fill an entire book. For this chapter, and for obvious practical reasons, we have selected just four particular components to supplement those already covered incidentally in previous chapters. These four were chosen mainly because both Christians and non-believers typically find them to be confusing or downright unacceptable, at least as ordinarily presented and understood.

Faith and Belief

Jesus spoke repeatedly about the importance and power of *faith*, and particularly that it must be present before healing and other miracles could take place: "Verily I say unto you, if ye have faith, and doubt not,, . . . even if ye shall say unto this mountain, be thou taken up and cast into the sea, it shall be done"[134] "Daughter, be of good cheer; thy faith hath made thee whole."[135] And "whatsoever ye shall ask in prayer, believing, ye shall receive."[136] The Gospel record is not clear, however, about just what Jesus actually meant by *faith*, beyond a kind of acceptance, blind or informed, before certain events could take place. He sometimes equated faith to "belief" or "believing in," if we can accept the translations as accurate.

First, we recall from Chapter 2 that *believing* is tentative knowledge that one holds en route to its acceptance or rejection as genuine *knowing*. Since a belief may be valid or not, it is important for it to be seen for what it is rather than as knowledge itself. Erroneous beliefs are natural and useful but they can have enduring and painful consequences for both the believer and for those with whom he interacts.

In Jesus' day many Jews believed that God would punish them if they did not offer ritual prayers and sacrifice regularly. They could become ill and even die if someone cursed them. Even today some persons feel guilty if they do not attend church regularly, dress "properly" or give to the poor—all worthy enough activities, to be sure, but not very effective or satisfying if done out of a presumed guilt. Most extreme, some persons firmly believe that they will be rewarded in heaven if they help rid the world of those not accepting their particular idea of God and his "plan."

In contrast, many Christians carry positive beliefs for matters they are still somewhat unsure of, and are quick to be offended by those who challenge them with a contrary belief.

One questionable way to define faith is the personal acceptance of an idea or piece of information for which there is no reasonable logical or experiential basis. This negative definition has to be at least partially right, since whatever faith is, it is certainly *not* based on sensing and reason alone. It could be *blind faith*, which implies no basis at all and can be applied to justify just about any action. But faith can also arise from an *inner certainty* of what is right, which makes it into what we are calling *genuine knowledge,* and accurately received *intuitive knowledge.*

What does John has to say about faith?

(How do you define faith, John, and how does it differ from belief?)

> In the Pauline doctrine faith was the "evidence of things unseen."[137] Indeed, this describes precisely the state known as *intuition,* with which you are highly familiar: inner knowing, or direct knowing.
>
> Intuition is the faculty or mechanism to bridge from one level of consciousness to another, be it psychic or through recall of information acquired from the experience of the five physical senses. Intuition allows you to recall childhood memories or events from past lives, and through it you can [also] see into the future. To understand intuition, you must simply understand yourself.[138]
>
> People *do* have an intimate link—called, in other words, an *holistic* link—which Jesus referred to as "Take up thy

yoke, for it is light, and we will pull this together."[139] And in [John's] Gospel, attributed to the channel speaking, "In the beginning was the Word, and the Word was with God, and the Word was as God. And nothing was made in nature without the Word."[140] This speaks of the divine presence, the holistic link to all things. So as humanity grows into awareness of its own divine state, there is then the capacity to see the Divine in all things.

Many of the secret worlds referred to in the Kabbalah and Mystical Christianity [may] have greater clarification for the individual.* Faith is the capacity to initiate [oneself] upon the path, to begin *to intuit the Divine and natural order about oneself.*

And by faith—the evidence of things unseen—forgiveness can indeed transpire. The ability to alleviate sin was to create the understanding of the phenomenology.

Thus, faith can be defined as *the certainty that accompanies the inner knowing of Natural Law.* This appears to be closer to what Jesus was getting at.

(If a person comes up and says, "I don't have faith—help me in my unbelief,"[141] what can he do to grow his faith, other than getting obstacles out of the way?)

First by knowing that faith itself has always been likened to a seed. It has been said that faith the size of a grain of mustard seed may indeed move mountains.[142] The very fact that the individual has approached, and wishes their faith to grow, constitutes a capacity that within them is the Word. For the Word itself may be the grain of mustard in and of itself.

It is also equally important for the practitioner to know when they may move and be effective. This is not unlike the so-called strength prayer of St Francis.†[143]

---

* For a fuller description of the Kaballah see Chapter 13.

† John seems to be referring here to the *Peace Prayer* attributed to St Francis, which begins, "Lord, make me an instrument of Thy peace . . .," but the context suggests instead he may have intended Reinhold Niebuhr's *Serenity Prayer*, sometimes

But the man Jesus gave many issues [examples?] of the articles concerning faith. He spoke that one must sow seeds not unlike a farmer, and some may fall upon fertile ground, some on harsh ground, some would fall on ground where weeds and thorns would spring up and choke them. But he pointed out that for those that fell on the fertile ground, behold, the harvest is great but the harvesters are few.[144]

A key is also found in the example of the brides [bridal maidens] and the bridegroom.[145] It speaks that there were seven brides [maidens] who tended oil lamps so that the bridegroom might come for them as the Sabbath arrived. And in those activities they had to tend their lamps throughout the whole of the night. Those who tended their lamps well, the bridegroom could indeed find. Those who attended them foolishly expended their oil by burning their lamps too bright. This means that faith must be tended moment to moment even though it is a continuous state of grace.

Even Jesus was surprised when a woman, who was a Gentile, asked that healing occur for her child. Jesus, still not understanding the full mysteries of the Messiah, said unto her, "The food of the children is not for the dogs," for the term 'dogs' was a popular prejudicial word for Gentiles. The woman said, "Even so, the dogs receive scraps from the table of the Master."[146] Jesus was so startled by the spiritual insight on the universal nature of God that he said, "Behold, healing has occurred. For it is by thy *faith* that ye art healed," establishing [affirming?] the principle of faith, not just in the issue of humanity's potential, for Jesus spoke not of *his* divinity but the universal spirit. So it was well in the mind of Jesus that even the Gentiles could receive these particular teachings.

Also note that the man Jesus could perform many miracles where there was faith, but [not] if individuals knew him too well, as in his own homeland: "A prophet has

---

mistakenly attributed to St. Francis: "God grant me the serenity to accept the things I cannot change, the courage to change the things I can, and the wisdom to know the difference."

no honor in his own land."[147] This then becomes the key subjective point to those who wish their faith to be grown.

It might be said that faith is the first inkling, or the first capacity, the precursor of belief. In science, for instance, intuition often precedes knowing. And knowing, when acted upon and proven, becomes belief in a particular set of facts and conditions. Remember, Jesus was keenly aware of the Greco-Roman world about him, wherein the *principles* of science in their elegant form were well understood.

This last statement may be taken as a reminder that faith and belief feed one another at levels of perception below true faith, or deep knowing.

Suffering

All the world suffers, in mind if not in body, but who understands the cause of suffering, its mechanism, its value for mankind and its purpose in the greater order of things? Countless books have been written on and around this important subject.

Jesus' teaching about suffering *per se* is more indirect than explicit in the Gospels. He obviously suffered himself at times, and his sympathy and empathy toward others who were suffering was exceptional. In the light of his broad teachings we may conclude that he understood well the nature and place of suffering in man's spiritual evolution and in the individual lives of those with whom he interacted. Thus, he *knew* why these persons suffered, and he understood the apparent unfairness with which some seemingly innocent persons are afflicted, while the guilty go unscathed.

If we turn to the wisdom teachers of all ages and cultures, both before and after Jesus' day, they say (in the simplest of terms) that suffering arises (only) from man's voluntary separation from God, or the natural order. That is, his suffering comes from his *resistance* to accepting and living life as it has been given to him, in contrast to how he fashions it to be from his limited notion of who he thinks he is (ego) and his role in life. This view is consistent with Jesus' teachings, though he did not express it this way to his apostles or disciples as far as we know.

This view still does not encompass suffering as a cumulative, multi-life experience. Jesus certainly understood this deeper cause, which the Gospel of John mentions only in passing and not explicitly.[148] Jesus acknowledges briefly his awareness of reincarnation and karma, but these ideas were probably more than his followers could understand at the time so their ideas about the cause of suffering would be limited.

Suffering is strongly related to salvation (to be considered next). Mankind has always sought to be "saved" from his sins, as if the cause of his suffering is external, outside of him who has sinned, implying that only external agents can stop the suffering. If suffering is tantamount to internal resistance, however, the cause and prevention must be internal; that is, man must find a way to drop his resistance and "save himself." While positive external factors such as mercy, forgiveness and loving guidance from others may help as reminders, only he can take the crucial step.

Suffering provides the main series of experiences and the motivation for overcoming this resistance, but is suffering basically *necessary* for man? How does John see suffering?

(It's my understanding that suffering is never really necessary for an individual as an unavoidable part of creation, but is rather a direct consequence of the obstacles he continually throws up to his own further evolvement. So if he can find a way around or through these obstacles, he doesn't need to suffer. Is this picture generally correct?)

> We sense that it is an accurate interpretation. It might be better to say that while the soul grows through the experience of the material dimension, [there is] the necessity that the individual must have self-inflicted pain, the so-called martyr complex.
>
> Remember the diagnosis of the Buddha. Jesus was indeed aware of these particular teachings, having traveled to the East. Here there is almost a diagnosis of the world that says [that] all life contains suffering. All suffering indeed arises out of *self*, and indeed the elimination of suffering is the elimination of *self*.
>
> It may be said that when one has an experience of the Divine, he transcends the material dimensions of self and realizes the cosmic or celestial or ecstatic. One may then become what is referred to in the East as a *bodhisattva*, This is like becoming a prophet/messiah in the traditions of Jesus:

one who may put off their ultimate enlightenment so that other beings may be led into enlightenment; in other words, an act of compassion.

So it is the acknowledgement and the awareness that there is indeed pain or suffering, or limitations or separation from the Divine, in the world, so one is not blind to the condition that separates others from the kingdom.

(It has been said that suffering is necessary for an individual to achieve salvation. Is this a true statement?)

It is more so an acknowledgement of the condition of the world. One must say that it [suffering] is the capacity of humanity to eventually achieve its psychic state of restoration, or balance. This may even have points of historical origin. The historical individuals referred to [elsewhere] were not merely metaphors for this path in and of themselves.

There are those who seek to isolate themselves. For instance, when Adam as a historical figure had been lifted up by the Divine, he was indeed in the perfect state of Eden. Historically, he would have been considered to have been a megalithic shaman who had been able to restore harmony with nature. He thought to bring unto himself a mate of his own kinship, his own binding. They were to engage in perfect Tantra. But when the kundalini energies had been raised, they became conscious of their own vulnerability, their own nakedness. They cast themselves psychically out of the natural order of things, giving way to more base emotions: shame, guilt and other endeavors in this activity.

(See also the discussion on Job in Chapter 11.)

The Holy Spirit

The Gospels speak of the Holy Spirit, also called the Spirit of Truth, very positively but rather vaguely; that is, with great respect and status but never saying just what it is. Christian theology gives it various definitions and properties. It is described as the "Spirit of God," a member of the

Trinity, an agent of conversion and an indwelling spiritual presence or divine energy that blesses the faithful. It is reported to "fill" persons, inspiring them to speak ecstatically or behave in an extraordinary way. It was said to have visited Mary at Jesus' conception, Jesus at his baptism and occasionally for Jesus' healings. Jesus promised that the Holy Spirit, or *Comforter*, would arrive in force after his death; we're told that it actually did so at the next Pentecost. It must be no small thing, judging from Jesus' alleged (but doubtful) statement that "every sin and blasphemy shall be forgiven unto men, but the blasphemy against the Spirit shall not be forgiven."[149]

The concept of the Holy Spirit appears to be a profound, tantalizing and ineffable notion, meaning that it cannot be explained in ordinary language and with familiar concepts, at least to one who has not directly and personally experienced it. If this is true, can one who has *not* experienced it understand anything meaningful about it?

He might not do so literally and explicitly, though it is safe to say that we can all recognize the presence of the Holy Spirit in the elevated state of mind which virtually everyone has experienced at special times in his life, at the very least in early childhood. You may have recognized it at the birth of a child, a wedding, a death or an unexpected moment of grace or forgiveness. It can also occur with a gesture of love from a parent or lover, or a sudden appreciation of the staggering grandiosity of creation while gazing at a flower, bird, human embryo or the stars. Such moments often bring tears to our eyes without reasonable cause, but they are not just exceptional emotion. People often say their experience went beyond a momentary emotional impact and extended to indescribable awe, beauty and universality.

To be sure, words spoken afterwards about these experiences invariably fall short of the experience itself unless they resonate with the listeners' own experience. Others' descriptions of the Holy Spirit can trigger personal memories of our own prior experiences. They can remind us that we are living in the presence of something uniquely powerful, profound, beautiful, love-filled and ever-present, even when we cannot find satisfactory explanations of it. And we can forget it so easily in the whirl of daily life.

(Jesus promised his apostles that the Holy Spirit would come after his death, and I assume it did at the Pentecost gathering. Did the Holy Spirit already exist for mankind, perhaps the Jews, and Jesus simply brought it forward and made men aware of it? Or was it newly created, or at least made newly available to mankind, at his time and on this occasion?)

> It had been experienced before on any number of different occasions. [As] Moses and the righteous multitudes approached Mount Sinai, it was said, "Behold! And all of them knew the Lord. And knew in their hearts all manner of the law." This was before the giving of the so-called Ten Commandments, when Moses departed into the mountain and dwelled in the presence of the Divine himself. When he returned they had turned aside from what they had known in their hearts, and returned to the familiar ways of Egypt and the events of the so-called Golden Calf. In other words, the ability to *sustain* the sacred spirit, the Ruach ha-Qadesh,* becomes the issue and the consequence for humanity's advancement.
>
> When Moses returned there were the ten utterances, called the Ten Commandments, and then the rebinding [reforming?] of the calf into the so-called Ark of the Covenant; also the revelations on the law of the Torah, [laying] the groundwork and the concepts that would be studied by the man Jesus and many others, the prophets. This led up to that historical moment of Pentecost, when the Ruach ha-Qadesh, or Holy Spirit, could enter into the earth plane and then be held and magnified throughout the course [of history].
>
> Remember, there were lapses even among the Hebrew and the Jewish people, for they had grown more secular in Greco-Roman ways. There would be long times before there were visitations of the Holy Spirit, bringing what was startling or renewing their memory of the Divine. This is comparable, even in thy own day, that those who experience the intuitive are sometimes startled by the particularly gifted. Even those who have had such experiences have lapses of memory in their everyday affairs. When they encounter

---

* For the definition of Ruach ha-Qadesh see the footnote early in Chapter 5.

them again they wonder or marvel, raising the question, "What is the purpose and what type of being is this?" even though they have had many previous exposures. So what you are seeing is less of confusion amongst the scriptures than the need to recreate continuity and context to see them as everyday events.

In fulfilling many of the prophecies there would come a time when individuals were neither going into the mount nor into the sanctuary, but indeed the divine presence could be brought to the greater whole of humanity. Other prophets, of course, sought the continuity of that enlightenment, whether in the name of God, as Yahweh or Allah, or the Buddha, for which it has been said, "Even the grasses would become enlightened."[150]

All who experience the sacredness of all things seek to come in, as said before, and all may then begin to enter into the kingdom.

In other words, the Holy Spirit has always existed, even before mankind was around, but man's awareness of its presence has varied considerably throughout history. We can recognize that it comes and goes through each person's life, and may be sustained as Jesus did for at least part of his life.

(Jesus allegedly said, "Everyone who speaks a word against the Son of Man will be forgiven, but he who blasphemes against the Holy Spirit will not be forgiven."[151] This seems pretty harsh, and it makes no sense to me at all. Did Jesus really say this, and if so, what did he really mean?)

What he meant was that those who spoke against him as the Son of Man—knowing that it could be confusing to consider the Divine residing in him or any other—[would be forgiven.] For remember, when he said, "Why marvel, when it is said that the Son of Man is the Son of God, when thy own scriptures say that ye are God?" So what he spoke to was [this], that those who spoke harshly against him in his humanity, these actions were forgivable. However, if they could not see the Holy Spirit inside themselves they bound themselves over to another incarnation.

(Is that all? It sounds much worse than that, as if they'll not be forgiven for all eternity!)

> Again, here is the key. Until they *receive* the Holy Spirit, the Divine within themselves, and do not speak against it within themselves, how can they enter into the order of the kingdom? For all seek to make the Divine *external,* and [therefore] unobtainable.
>
> Political infrastructures often manipulate the concept of an external salvation in order to maintain control over political forces. But if it is *within,* and spoken of, and ye cease to speak against the Divine within, then ye come unto thy salvation.

Salvation

First-century Jews, just as many persons today, wanted to be *saved.* But from what and to what did they seek salvation? The Gospels say that they wanted most of all to be forgiven for their sins, for they were judging themselves harshly by both the strict commandments* of Moses (as then interpreted), the oral Mishnah (also rich in interpretation) and the secular laws of their priests and scribes. They obviously sought salvation from suffering, with which they were very familiar, as well as guilt arising from their self-judgment. Finally, they sought salvation from death, which they saw as either total annihilation or a final judgment day with punishment for all committed sins. As they perceived their burden, it was heavy indeed.

---

* Commandments are for setting a correct direction, helping to establish positive values and motivating right action. To do these things one must have a valid and real starting point—at least to know what the words mean. Jesus' primary Law, his greatest commandment, was "Love the Lord Thy God with all your heart, mind and soul, and your brother as yourself." It is powerfully valid as a broad commandment for mass instruction, which is how Jesus employed it with his Palestinian audiences. However, to become a item of personal truth it must first be accepted and incorporated into one's base of knowledge and experience. This step requires understanding. For example, the commandment "Love God . . ." requires a valid concept of God before it can have personal meaning; an incomplete or distorted view of God can make it false or impossible to carry out. If you are unable to love yourself, or do not know what love is, how can you love God and others?

And who could provide this salvation? Only an external God, of course, as they thought of God at that time. The particular means by which salvation was to be obtained from their God were prescribed by their traditional beliefs and crystallized into a ritualistic form by their priesthood: sacrifice, group prayer, penance, more rules and suffering, and maybe a touch of forgiveness.

John the Baptist offered hope through baptismal purification and a new beginning but he deferred to Jesus for the real thing. Jesus promised even more: the possibility of entry into God's kingdom of heaven, thus full forgiveness, eternal life (immortality) and release from all burdens. The early Church fathers got part of this right, though they do not seem to have understood it very well. They retained the notion of love as central, but also the Jewish preoccupation with sin, guilt and expiation. They turned the person of Jesus into a Savior by identifying him with God Himself, which notions he could not have intended. Jesus' genuine salvation was largely "lost in translation" and was converted into a relatively shallow doctrine of authority based beliefs.

In a broad sense everyone wants release from suffering, since it hurts, and wants to be free of death, which appears to contradict survival. If the counsel of a previous section can be taken to heart, suffering is in our lives to nudge us toward inner awakening and an acceptance of our built-in divinity and Natural Law. The latter requires that one accept life as it is offered, on its own terms. Death is with us to stimulate a recognition that we are not our bodies and egos but are non-physical God-like beings, hence immortal in our inner nature (essence). Herein lies the salvation Jesus actually offered.

It is ironical that centuries of devotion, prayer and sacrifice by Christian monks and saints were shaped by the assumption that the God they were serving and seeking was to be found *outside* of themselves. This error was in spite of Jesus' reiterated teaching that God can be found only *within*. They followed Jesus' example of disciplined practices of self-denial, poverty and other self-imposed suffering, which they interpreted to be virtuous steps on the path to salvation. Again, we have no record or even suggestion that Jesus ever taught that such painful means were *required* for salvation and should therefore be sought as a necessary part of the process. He did say they should be *accepted* if they arose, but also that one should not attribute them to his society or others, only to oneself.

This still leaves open the question of who is going to carry out this saving—God, Jesus or the one being saved?

(John, your statement that Jesus died to save man from sin implies that Jesus' martyrdom was a crucial factor in the salvation he promised. But that seems to say that man is absolved of responsibility to save himself. How are we to understand properly this idea of being "saved from sin" by Jesus' voluntary sacrifice?)

> To *sin* means to miss the mark. *Evil* itself constitutes the actions meaning "that which is not well for you," so it implies a model of healing. The very term *salvation* means to be complete with oneself, or to receive sustenance. So the meaning is the following.
>
> Man's greatest fear was the issue of his mortality: the void, nothingness, and separation from the Divine, and/or to not be complete with the Divine before the moment of immortality then losing consciousness. That which Jesus did was to [heal] that.
>
> For instance, faith is built into processes in science in a parallel manner, when the heroic scientist risked his life through self-inoculation, when the greater mass of the public did not have knowledge of the function of vaccines and even felt that the injection of a substance parallel to that which was to constitute [contract] the illness from which they were to be healed [would be fatal].' This caused a need for the appearance of a great sacrifice, a great risk of life in order to gain the confidence of masses, so that a great healing could take place, ridding the world of its curses.
>
> So in the true studies of the scriptures it is the resurrection, the healing of death, that speaks to the salvation.
>
> As to those who seek their path, if they may *believe* that one has no greater love for another than those who lay down their life for them, this then is the beginning of that type of

---

' John may be speaking here of the use of inert viruses as a means of immunization against diseases such as smallpox and polio. When first attempted there was an uncertainty whether the inert viruses might induce the diseases they were intended to resist.

faith that may lead to salvation. This comes then by one's own volition, by their belief, and it may then be openly testified to by their works in the world.

So it was not that Jesus himself was going to save anyone directly. He was only pointing the way and demonstrating what is possible. He informs, guides and inspires, but each individual is the agent to save himself, if we may put it this way.

(Would human civilization have fallen into ruin if Jesus has not come to "save" the world as he did? Perhaps his contribution was just a short-cut for human spiritual evolution—a reduction of time and suffering, let us say, relative to what would have happened without him?)

Are there not many individuals who enjoy great civil liberties, and can it not be said that, in the modern era, slavery in thy own country ended due to those who were inspired by the man Jesus? Can it not be said, for instance, that man had his legal rights under the ruling of thy Court Supreme, but they only became practicable by the efforts of the man Martin Luther King? Can it not also be said that the man Gandhi was inspired by Buddha, and by Jesus also? Can it not also be said that civil disobedience, for instance, came about by the *ideal* that Jesus represented as a human being? In other words, man has his rights under man's laws, but only the passions of the Christ, as they inspire an individual, generation by generation, make them practicable within the order of humanity. So it can indeed be said that the greatest waves of consciousness may trace their origins back to the man Jesus.

But the man Jesus traces his origins back to the Divine. So ultimately, everything spoken of by the man Jesus is given over to the Divine, which is universal to all human beings. So he became a light unto the world. And there are also other lights unto the world, such as found in the life of Siddartha [the Buddha], and these are his brethren who also became anointed ones.

So, if one is to be complete with history as it stands—and that is the only measure that ye may take of thyself—one must then become complete with the mystery, and perhaps the majesty, that is found in humanity in the man known as Jesus. For was he not there at a turning point in history, which he called the turning of the age, the so-called age of Pisces? Why did one particular individual conspire to create these mysteries, when there were so many others who also survived and spoke well?

Review

Teachings

Faith is essentially intuitive knowing, the human capacity to bridge oneself from one level of consciousness to another and thereby link closer to the greater order of things (the second realm). It places one upon the path of aligning with the Divine, ultimately allowing one to know all that can be known and to experience all that can be experienced. [SC 123, 134, 148, 162, 176]

Suffering is a universal concomitant of human life. It results (only) from man's chosen separation from God; that is, his resistance to accepting and living life as it has been given him (Natural Law or God's Will) instead of his own way. [SC 27, 33, 50, 62]

Suffering arises in the material dimension directly out of the soul's need to grow, for growth from a position of separation, resistance and ignorance requires learning, and learning involves pain. When an individual is able to transcend the limitations of self, he aligns with the Divine and his suffering ends. [SC 27, 33, 50, 62]

All suffering arises out of desire, and all desire arises out of self, or ego. This was understood by the Buddha as well as Jesus. In contrast, Western teachings say that our suffering comes from having too weak an ego, not too much. [SC 27, 33, 50, 62]

The Holy Spirit, or Ruach ha-Qadesh, may be thought of as the divine presence. It has always existed, not just at Pentecost, though its recognition by mankind has been sporadic throughout human history. [SC 53-55, 171,188]

Jesus' alleged remark on the unforgivability of blasphemy against the Holy Spirit means only that, so long as one speaks against the Divine within himself,

His entry into the kingdom of heaven is blocked. Any blaspheming of Jesus will be forgiven.

Being "saved" from sin (error) is inherently an individual and internal process for achieving acceptance of life as it is offered. Each individual has the God-given capacity to free himself, and he must do so to be "saved." Jesus pointed the way by demonstrating the possibility and the opportunity, but one's relief from suffering cannot come from Jesus or anyone else.

Each person has inherently all the essential qualities of God within himself. His essence cannot die. All his perceived "sins" are self-created and can therefore be transcended (forgiven) by himself. Jesus affirmed these truths through his resurrection, not his crucifixion. [SC 24, 32]

Many of the greatest increases in human collective consciousness can be traced back to the inspirations provided by Jesus, who made his unique contribution at a turning point of history. He traced his strengths back to the Divine which inspired him. [SC 32, 78, 162]

CHAPTER 11

SOUL GROWTH AND PAST LIVES

The notions of reincarnation, "past lives" and karma are a problem for almost everyone. We need to take a diversion here to come to a better understanding of this fundamental notion.

The reason for the problem is not hard to find. It's not that reincarnation cannot be appreciated and even accepted as an intellectual idea and a theory. Indeed, it makes "good sense" as a rational explanation for human differences, the apparent injustice of human suffering and the seeming transience and meaninglessness of life on earth. But to embrace it as a natural part of one's life, as hundreds of millions of Easterners do, is another matter entirely. Indeed, unless you happen to have *remembered* one or more of your prior existences, or *experienced* your own birth into this world, or have achieved a deep personal understanding of your presence as a visitor here on earth, you have no substantive basis for accepting the notion of reincarnation: it's just an interesting idea. It would then be dishonest for you to "believe in" it.

For that matter, though, you would also have no substantive basis for *rejecting* it as religious nonsense or a superstition of primitive people, as many persons choose to do, even before they know what they are rejecting.

The majority of the world's spiritual teachings include the concept of reincarnation in one form or another. It was known in Judaism long before Jesus lived, though never accepted as an established part of Judaic law or practice. While the Christian Church rejected the notion, most of the Gnostics embraced it and saw it as an important part of Jesus' teachings. (They may have received it from him.) Jesus himself made incidental reference to it in the Gospels, certainly understood it and very likely taught it to his apostles (see below). Thus, the concept of reincarnation is part of our Western heritage, even though it was rejected as heresy by the early Church before the third century rolled around.

What is Reincarnation?

Stated very simply, *reincarnation* is a cosmic principle that says that every person's inner and enduring being, his *essence*, true Self or soul—as distinct from his body, personality and brain—is continually growing toward Godly perfection through a long succession of embodiments—incarnations, or "lives"—in different times and places. This greater life is therefore not the single life with which we are all most familiar, but the life of the essence itself, with which one may or may not be familiar.

The growth takes place through a trial-and-error *learning* process. The essence makes choices and acts them out (consciously or not), experiences the consequences (beneficial and painful), learns from them (or maybe not), and then repeats the choices and outcomes as often as necessary until he "gets the pattern right," so to speak. In this way each individual essence gradually grows into consonance with Natural Law, the way the universe works, also called "God's will,"* though the term is not accurate for a deity which has no personhood.

It should be obvious from this description that it is not the body, personality and lower self, but the *essence* or greater Self, that has past lives. When one says, "I had a past life in Egypt," he means that he believes or knows that his *essence* had a past embodiment in Egypt. There is usually no good reason why his conscious mind should recall the event, and indeed, it may not be helpful for him to remember it lest it distract or frighten him. Indeed, you can appreciate that you would not welcome at age ten a description of the difficult trials, losses and pains you will undergo during the rest of your life, nor would it help you to recall a slow death on a battlefield or by torture during the Inquisition. If not remembered these memories are best left alone.

---

* A reminder from Chapter 1: The laws we are accustomed to and live under are social, and they incorporate many approximations in the interests of simplicity and enforceability and they call for punishment when broken (if you are caught). In contrast, what we are calling *Natural Law* here is precise, universal, firm, inviolate, automatically enforced and does not include punishment.

The entire series of lives ends ultimately in a perfected return to one's original source, "toward God," with no need to incarnate further. There are probably several levels between earth life and the Godhead, but this simple model exposes the essential idea that *learning through multiple lives is an inherent part of the long process of human essence growth.*

Karma

Karma is the cause-and-effect principle that provides the carry-over, from one life to the next, of all that has been already learned and not yet learned. Learned lessons are retained as assets and strengthen one along the path. Unlearned lessons persist, piece by piece, from life to life until one's capacity for transgressing the inherent condition of the Universe, or Natural Law, has been fully dissolved, thereby leading to wise choices and right action. Nothing is ever lost. The learning takes place naturally, automatically and non-punitively, both through the normal course of each life and through the entire chain of lives (hundreds, or perhaps thousands, depending on where you start counting). That is, Natural Law is *built-in*: there is no one out there setting the curriculum, and you (at the level of your essence) are free to delay, accelerate or modify your learning process as much as you like.

Each life is normally lived without awareness of the preceding ones so that painful old memories do not become diverting or confusing, as just described. As you reach a sufficient stage of expanded awareness you gradually begin to recognize and identify with your essence, and may then become consciously aware of your prior lives and remaining karma. Thus do you progress, at the level of your individual essence or soul, toward a higher state of existence. At some point your need for earth lives diminishes to the point where you can move beyond earth lives to higher levels of learning and awareness.

Even without awareness of the prior lives of your essence you may find value in entertaining, at least intellectually or through your imagination, the concept of reincarnation and its associated karma and past lives. Doing so can enhance your general receptivity to the idea, and at some point you may discover through insights or epiphanies a memory or two to confirm it for you. While no amount of reading, argument or thought can ever substitute for this illumination, a small thing may trigger the recognition when you are ready for it. Many others have gone before you in just this fashion.

With this background, let us take a look at what John has to add.

Jesus and Reincarnation

(What if anything did Jesus teach about reincarnation during his ministry?)

> He spoke of the concept of "Before Abraham, I Am," and of John the Baptist being Elijah.[152] In other Gospels he would say, "Behold, I knew you before I admitted thee into your mother's womb. I created thee with a fierce symmetry."[153] This speaks of the pre-existence of the soul before birth, not of the soul's creation at the time of birth. Also, amongst the Essenes, and even [later] amongst many mystical Hassidics (who were perhaps direct inheritors [descendents] of the Essenes) and practitioners of the Kabbalah,* reincarnation was not considered an unusual phenomena.
>
> The debate amongst the Sadducees and the Pharisees was the nature of the relationship of the soul to the after-life. Even they would entertain the concept of the transmigration of souls, not from animal to human form but the philosophy of reincarnation. There was also a general debate amongst the Pythagoreans and the Plutonic philosophers, dominant among the Hellenistic Jews, for whom reincarnation was a well understood principle.
>
> The Essenes placed it upon a spiritual basis; that is, in the context of the growth of the soul rather than merely a system of reward and punishment. [They saw] the evolution of the soul progressing toward the Divine. This was unique in the Hebrew teachings.

(How much did Jesus teach to his disciples, perhaps privately, about reincarnation, karma and the spiritual growth of the soul or inner being?)

---

* For a fuller description of the Kaballah see Chapter 13.

He would go to them and teach them many things in secret that he could not speak openly to the masses. He would say, "Behold, I come to thee and retire with thee. And though I speak unto the many in parables, here I speak to thee plainly."[154]

He above all else explained that the soul was neither male nor female: "Verily, verily, I say unto thee that in Christ, there is neither male nor female."[155] Or, "they make them both as one." He was speaking of the genderless identity of the soul, the [combined] male and female nature of the soul. When speaking openly to the disciples he made clear what are now considered metaphysical points concerning the phenomenon of the soul. But as recorded in the Gospels he spoke in parables to those who would have to have ears in order to hear the poetry, the metaphor, the allegory.

(Did he ever discuss past-lives with his disciples?)

Correct. Even in the examples given [above] he spoke for instance of the general nature of the soul and reincarnation in the Gospel of Thomas.[156] He also spoke most directly by saying, "Behold, that which is flesh is flesh. That which is born of water is water and can pass away. Verily, I say unto thee, to enter the kingdom, ye of this generation must be born again."[157] So while he spoke of re-birth and regeneration of the soul through knowledge, wisdom and the Holy Spirit, he spoke most directly of reincarnation.

Jesus taught reincarnation, for when a blind man was brought, his disciples came unto him and said, "Lord, who has sinned, [this man or his parents,] that this man was born blind?" Jesus said, "Verily, I say unto thee, no person has sinned. This man has been born blind that God may be glorified."[158] He spoke to the man, and he could then see.

This last explanation seems to be avoiding the issue but was probably the most Jesus could say in public.*

---

* In a account by another expert intuitive Jesus explains the karmic law to Peter, "There is a law of recompense that never fails, and it is summarized in that true rule of life: whatsoever man shall do to any other man, some other man will do to him."

Jesus' Prior Lives

(How aware was Jesus of his own past lives? At what age did he acquire this awareness?)

> The man Jesus, like many, was keenly aware of his past lives. He said, "Before Abraham, I am," an acknowledgement that he knew the continuity of his past lives.[159]
>
> For instance, even to this very day, [there are] other methods by which past lives are identified. For instance, there are accounts of many Tibetan lamas who, even in infancy, recognize toys with which they had played in other lifetimes.* It was no different for the man Jesus, since from infancy he would have been read to from the holy books and would recognize his identities and make comments upon them, or have reactions that only an advanced infant would give.

(Please summarize the past lives of Jesus, and/or the Christ entity, and how these prepared him for his mission as it is presented in the Gospels.)

> For his past lives we would comment upon those in which he was reaching or striving for perfection, and those that have a Biblical association. This way they have the [chance] of verifiability for those who would explore these activities, either historically or in the context of a Biblical perspective.
>
> Ultimately Jesus' incarnation amidst the Essenes came to represent the other lifetimes he has led—33 in total—which we may wish to give comment upon at a latter point in time. And there were those such as the prophet Cayce has given

---

And "Behold this man! Once in another life he was a cruel man, and in a cruel way destroyed the eyes of one, a fellow man. The parents of this man once turned their faces on a blind and helpless man and drove him from their door." [See Dowling 1972, 138:5-6,12-13.]

* In Tibetan Buddhism this recognition test is traditionally performed on infant lama candidates to help verify their identity as the reincarnation of a particular prior lama.

in discourse."[160] But these [to follow] are the lifetimes we would concentrate upon, and in particular in relationship to the development of the individual [Jesus] and the origins of the concept of the Christ.

The Non-physical State

First, we would say that, in the original identity, as in the case of all of humanity, Jesus could be found first in the angelic state—in other words, created as a being of energy and with a soul-mate in the spirit. "In the beginning was the Word, and the Word was with God, and indeed the Word was *as* God."[161] This speaks of the Word as a creation of the mind of God, as a co-creative force with the Divine.

For as a soul, a conscious entity, this gave rise to individual identities independent of the universal mind and the creative forces that were the Divine. . . .

So souls moved omnisciently and universally throughout the whole of creation, drawing on the whole. But there was a wave of souls, not unlike those in the book of Enoch,[†] which speaks of soul incarnation into the earth plane. This began the chain of events known as past lives.

So if one is to understand the entity known as Jesus, one must understand his origin as a being of energy. [He was] in a state of existence that, because of vibrations of the soul and what is called the pre-permanent atoms—which function as a resonancy—are better thought of as of a vibratory or oscillating process superceding the speed of light as it is in the present.

These so-called *bindus*,[‡] referred to in Eastern philosophy, are pre-permanent moments, unchanging. They allow a soul

---

[*] Cayce identifies the following past lives of Jesus: Amelius, Adam, Enoch, Hermes (Thoth), Melchizidek, Joseph, Joshua, Asaph, Jeshua and Zend (Zoroaster).

[†] The *Book of Enoch* consists of three Jewish texts attributed to Enoch, the great-grandfather of Noah. None are accepted as canonical, except the first in the Ethiopean Christian Orthodox Church. [Brown 2000]

[‡] *Bindu* is a sacred symbol for the unmanifested cosmos. In East Indian traditions it evolved to designate a chakra that signifies action, as in worship or prayer. In Tantric Buddhim the bindu is an aspect of the anatomy of the "subtle body".

to have focus in a holographic manner through the whole of the creation. For the universe is just that, a creation, a thought form. Some thought forms turned toward matter, and these singularities in matter, the *bindus*, became anchored in a moment of time-space and consciousness and caused the first waves of incarnation.

Amelius and Adam

These first waves of incarnation went on to configure the esoteric histories of Atlan, Lemuria and Atlantis.* In Lemuria we find humanity in the poetically described phase known as Eden, where the so-called Adam and Eve, to be understood as androgynous beings, existed. Historically they would be called hermaphrodites: beings both male and female in one gender.

Jesus' first incarnation was as Amelius, the first of the hermaphrodites to emerge in human form, and then Adam (meaning "one made of red clay") in the latter days in Atlantis. He was first as Amelius and then as Adam.

When described in Biblical terms, the idea of the removal of female from male constitutes the following. The growth of the soul is to be found in both male and female attributes, both yin and yang. In the days of Atlantis humanity first came to be truly divided into male and female form as a growing dominant species. There is debate even now, for instance, that there may have been a Cro-Magnon humanity and a Neanderthal humanity, and that you were truly a multi species society with divergent branches. We would say that there were indeed divergent branches of humanity, in

---

* The legendary and ancient lands of *Atlantis* and *Lemuria* on the earth are presumed in certain esoteric philosophies to be pre-prehistoric cultures where man existed before evolving into his present form. Plato mentions Atlantis as having been in the Mediterranean Sea, though most legends place it in the mid-Atlantic, where it is said to have sunk under the waves in a great cataclysm. Lemuria is believed to have been in the Pacific. Either of both may have "existed" in physical reality or only non-physically, perhaps in an astral realm. There has been much speculation about them, and even some exploration, but no scientific confirmation for either territory has ever been found.

particular as souls. These lived in the Earth's plane at time periods from 500,000 B.C. until contemporary times in the civilization of Atlantis, dramatically described by Plato, [also] referred to as the Seven Kingdoms existing before Adam in the Biblical and Kabalistic contexts.

In this activity, then, Jesus was living with the attributes of both genders [though] in appearance he was born and raised in the masculine form. If desiring to give birth, a flood of hormonal activities could be released from a deep meditative state. This is what is said to have come upon Adam. It induced activities within the womb, and the hermaphrodites began to shape the sexes in a singular manner. This constituted the division of the sexes into male and female, no longer being hermaphrodite but using the hormonal qualities within the womb to make one gender dominant over the other.

This is even as determined sometimes in physiological studies, that the zygote when first forming appears at first to be genderless in the womb. These hermaphrodite-like attributes remain in humanity today.

So in the first incarnation as Adam, getting and participating as the first form offered, the choosing to incarnate as both male and female, balancing the energies of yin and yang, there was no imbalance. There was no transgression against the natural or original identity [from] knowing the Eden-like state, the perfection-like state. For that which is called *sin* constitutes an activity when one's identity begins to individualize *away from* the original sources, away from the concept of One with the cosmic being, away from the limiting identity of the various senses on the earth plane.

This is what was meant when the serpent entered Eden. It was speaking of two forces. Humanity was evolving at a pace that was not to the pleasure of other angelic beings. Turning their eyes toward the earth plane they sought to be of benefit to humanity because they knew that humanity had not [only] the physical identity but a higher energetic and universal identity. The souls of these [other angelic beings] also began to enter the Earth's plane. This speaks of the serpent that entered Eden.

But it would be more correct to say that humans began to raise their current energies. At first, a particular yoga was used to balance the new gender-based identity of male and female, so to *marry* humanity into the actions of Tantra and hatha yogas so they could maintain their androgynous-like vibratory level of identity or energy. They would then not be overwhelmed by the newly forming emotions of individual gender and identity. New souls, entering as energetic beings or angels, thought to embrace humanity and teach them new and mystical ways.

This compact description of an apparently complicated process introduces several new concepts, which would call for much more explanation before being fully understandable. The main point at the moment seems to be that Jesus, embodied as Adam, stood at the turning point of mankind's physical separation from an egoless, sinless, hermaphroditic state into separate male and females—and much else to follow which this separation implied.

Enoch and Adversaries

Next we find that the identity of Jesus became incarnate as Enoch, the City Builder.

There are several Biblical references to Enoch, or Hanach (a common Hebrew name). He is first cited as a son of Cain, then a later descendent of Adam and a great-grandfather of Noah.[162] (See an earlier footnote in this chapter.) In the latter role he was a much honored man of God in Jewish literature, became the prophet Idris in Islam and was honored with other titles in the Mormon tradition and the rest of Christianity.[163]

In these activities Jesus was one of those souls who sought to maintain truth in the form and identity of *perfection*. He sought to create and instruct humanity so it could live harmoniously within the structures of the city-states while still remaining seamlessly integrated with the activity of the planet's structures. Some of these types of ideals still continue to be carried forward by soul groups in contemporary times—individuals such as architects Paulo Solari and Frank Lloyd Wright, who also had incarnations in Egypt to carry forward the ideals of Enoch.

Humanity continued to evolve its consciousness in building such structures. The individual Frank Lloyd Wright, in his identity as Senemut, builder of the temple complex under the Pharaoh Queen Hatshepsut, [had been] apprenticed to city builder Enoch.* With this contemporary concept he brought about a state of Eden-like perfection in some of the cities.

Jesus' identity as Enoch was an attempt to integrate some of the knowledge that was being brought forth from higher angelic beings, who began to enter into the earth plane. They found that their divine senses were bound by being physical themselves. These then became an organized force, always trying to order humanity according to what they considered to be an elite, or the divine Will, which was presented through long lineages of humanity, so-called royal lines, which must rule for a humanity. They became the force known as the Lords of Karma.† This then was a creative force, a juxtaposition of Jesus' identity, his mission.

Jesus worked [instead] with what is called the Law of One, the idea of one God. There would be to each man one life, and that one would keep his eye single and on the Divine. Even though there would be communions and open dialogue with angelic beings, it must only be with those who were aligned with the most High and the Divine. . . .

Jesus' temptation was whether to remain in the path of humanity he had chosen, one of overcoming personal

---

* *Hatshepsut* was a powerful and famous female pharaoh of ancient Egypt in the 18th Dynasty, best known for her conquest of the land of Punt (location unknown to this day) and her many building projects, most notably the huge and unusual mortuary temple she built at Deir el-Bahri. *Senemut* was a colleague, her royal steward and one of her architects.

† The *Lords of Karma*, a metaphysical concept, is a collection of angelic judges whose task it is to ascertain when an individual's karmic ribbons have all been properly burned, thus whether the soul is freed or must return to earth for further lives.

karma by aligning with the Divine, or to join with these ruling forces, with their vast power in the infrastructure of the earth plane, [in order] to bring humanity to a natural course of events for their *own* knowledge, salvation and union with the Divine.

So we find in this city-building an attempt to bring humanity into centers of activity around key points and ley lines,* such as [at] Stonehenge, the Pyramids and various other holy sites, so that humanity could align with the natural energies of the planet and restore it to an Eden-like state.

Job

Job is the archetype sufferer. The Old Testament account, the oldest book of the Bible, describes the heavy ordeals Job underwent as a test of his fidelity to his God.[164] It is required reading for those who ask, "Why do the Godly suffer?" though some seekers find the ending to be inconclusive and disappointing.

Jesus had another past life as Job in which there was a great testing. Job was indeed a most righteous individual and was turned toward the eternal concept of the Divine, towards God, in this case through deep contemplative prayer and meditation, looking toward the Deity as a moral force. However, there are the forces in the world that say that humanity must be put to trial and brought to judgment. This is known as the *adversary*, which must come between the higher self, the oneness the soul has with the Divine, and the conscious or mortal mind. The adversary goes before the throne and argues that humanity must bring judgment for itself, or be brought to judgment, for actions in single moments.

In these activities, then, Job lost all human resources—family, offspring, earned wealth, virtue and others—and was finally brought to destitution and plague.

---

* See the footnote on *ley lines* in Chapter 3.

He was driven to renounce the divine spark within him, to renounce God, so that his cycle of life could be ended and [he could] perhaps incarnate again and start over. But Job clung to the concept and fact of the presence of the Divine.

When [his] being was tried on these acts of faith, the Divine made appearances within him and questions were asked to be pondered. The Divine said unto Job, "Where were ye when I made the foundations of the world?" To this Job could only have one answer: Job was indeed there *as* the Word, and *with* the Word, as one with the Divine. He was part of those creative forces that created the dramas that unfolded, and had chosen to experience those things. Thus it may be said that the Divine's acting as a moral force in the earth plane was no longer an *external* force, separate from humanity. So Job was the origin of the archetype of the Christ, where the Divine may become *one* with humanity rather than an external force.

It was this that justified Jesus' words when he said, "Oh, why marvel when it is said that the Son of Man is the Son of God, when thine own scriptures say that ye are Gods. And the things that I do, ye shall do, and even greater."[165] So it may be said that his incarnation as Job, as written down [later] by Melchizedek, was the first archetype to bring about the existence of the Christ, the concept of the redeeming one, the savior of humanity. And that if only *one* may suffer all these things and yet remain conscious of the divine spark within, then the whole of humanity becomes not only worthy, but may begin to have a path that leads singularly to the Divine.

Melchizedek

We now move forward quickly in time, where we find Jesus, in [reaching for] perfection, to have been incarnate in those activities known and associated with Melchizedek.

Melchizedek is reported in the Old Testament[166] to have been a priest-king in Jerusalem who supported Abraham, but there is confusion in the Biblical text. A New-Testament remark[167] has him incarnating as a human without birth or death. He is identified in a Gnostic document in the Nag Hammadi Library as identical with Jesus, which would be true in the reincarnational sense described here.

> In the order of Melchizedek Jesus sought to bring into expression a definitive group of people who could establish the presence of the Divine, the so-called God of history, for anointing Abraham and the tribal lineages that flowed forth.
>
> While there was the consecration of Abraham, it was well known that tribal peoples would still have difficulty in completing the understanding of the higher forces, the singular nature of the Divine and the concept that God is love. So they had to work out the activities [later] described in the Torah. They were living humanity's natural evolution. Their behaviors are less to be emulated than learned from. It is how the Divine and God are to be understood in each and every age so that humanity may come to know the whole of its identity [by] turning toward sacred scriptures.
>
> As for how Jesus acted in his lifetime in Melchizedek, he was a priest who helped to organize the ways, the thoughts and the forms that eventually were to manifest and be consecrated in the ways of the priesthood, and later practiced in the Torah. Humanity would still need to overcome its capacity to wage warfare and other actions, but it was thought that it would bring them at least into the knowledge and consequences as to how these impacted any individual in the ways of the Divine. For when humanity could not overcome its almost addictive-like nature in so-called justified war, at least these activities could be conducted in the most humane manner, as could be discerned by the consciousness of humanity in those days.

Zoroaster

Then we find Jesus incarnate in Zoroaster.

Zoroaster, originally Zarathustra, was a Iranian prophet who lived about ninth century BCE. His writings, contained within the *Avesta,* are the basis of the religion that bears his name. Zoroastrianism deals with the issue of good versus evil among many other matters. Zoroaster enjoys a rich and varied legend outside of Persia. In the Western tradition he is seen as a sage and miracle worker.

> This [life] was intended to explain the concept of dualism and to lay a foundation where Jesus could take those writings of the Zoroastrian influence and begin to integrate and translate the concept of dualism into a more singular force; namely, that these are not divisions within the Divine but a misunderstanding of the Divine. For the Divine itself becomes the source of knowledge, a *singular* source for all those [other] forces—the so called good and ill—that are perceived in the world,.

Hanoch

> In an incarnation known as Hanoch, or Hanachi, he was responsible for the beginning of the transmission of the Torah and many other Judaic books now contained within the sacred writings of the Torah in the Hebrew alphabet. He also began the ordering of the deeper mysteries known as the Kabbala, the presentation of the so-called ten names of God, in particular the twelve dimensions and the Hebrew letters which are reconstructed from the models of the universe, those now coming to be refilled by the so-called string theory.[c168]
>
> The vibratory qualities of the Hebrew letters as they have been received in the energy known as Meged, meaning holy ones, constitute a model of how the energy of the inner Divine is within humanity. You would find that the Kabbalah, its twelve names of God and the so-called Sephirat, resonate holistically like a hologram throughout the whole universe.

William H. Kautz, Sc.D.

Perhaps the strongest point of this "soul biography" of Jesus is how it contributed stage by stage to the gradual, spiritual evolution of mankind, working through the Hebrew people. Even though many intermediate stages have been left out here, we can appreciate the significant social evolution which took place in the Middle East for the two or more millennia before Jesus lived. We can also see how Jesus' varied efforts during his sequence past lives among the Hebrew people were a fitting predecessor to his first-century life. This was when he fulfilled his greater mission to bring forth three key ideas, among other contributions: *love* as the highest principle of human life, God as resident within each individual, and true life as being eternal, not limited by physical death.

Review

History:

Jesus was aware from infancy of his past lives. He understood the concept of reincarnation, already known to the Jews albeit with incomplete understanding. While he taught incarnation privately to his apostles, it did not show up in the Gospels.

The Essenes saw reincarnation as a karma-based process of soul growth instead of the then prevalent belief in rewards and punishments by God. Reincarnational ideas persisted for awhile among the Gnostics before being suppressed by the growing church.

Just as for all of humanity, Jesus was created first in the angelic state as a being of energy "cloned" from the Creator. The first created souls were a kind of holographic vibration, with the whole of creation as their focus. Some turned toward the material world and were therefore anchored in time, space and human consciousness as the first waves of incarnation. This process gave rise to human life as a series of incarnations and the accumulation and burning of karma.

Jesus began his incarnations in Lemuria (Eden) as Amelius, as the first of the hermaphrodites to emerge in human form, and then in Atlantis as Adam in androgenous form. He "gave birth" to Eve through a meditatively induced hormonal process, and the gender split continued in subsequent generations.

In the very early days humankind was under the direct order of the angels and had no will of its own. A new wave of souls, called adverseries or anti-Christs, then entered as energetic beings so as to achieve a higher level

176

of consciousness and to balance the gender-based identity with the original androgynous energy.

Jesus worked instead with the Law of One (God): each individual is destined to seek his own divinity. The "temptation" he faced in the desert after his baptism was his conscious recognition and acceptance of this path.

In his life as Enoch Jesus sought to integrate knowledge from higher angelic beings and bring into humanity the ideal of truth as perfection, as men sought to live more harmoniously in earth's city-states.

As Job, he was greatly tested to verify that he could retain the divine spark within him in the face of great suffering. Job was the original archetype of the Christ, and showed that the Divine can become one with humanity rather than merely an external force.

As Melchizidek, Jesus brought into expression a definitive group of people, the Hebrews, who could establish the presence of God in their lives. He set the themes of the Torah and moderated man's warlike nature.

As Zoroaster, Jesus sought to transform the notion of dualism and make the Divine into a singular force over all others.

As Hanoch Jesus began the transmission of the Torah, other Judaic books, the Hebrew alphabet and the ordering of the deeper mysteries symbolized in the Kabbalah.

Teachings

God and man are not parts of a division or duality within the Divine but are two united aspects of a single creation. Divinity is an internal, not an external force within each human: "Ye are Gods." [SC 57ff, 80-81, 86-87, 90-95]

Every essence or soul initially incarnates from an angelic state into the earth plane as an unaware, undeveloped and independent "seed" of God. By repeatedly incarnating it gradually accommodates to the earth plane and Natural Law. As it learns from experience its choices became more conscious, and the consequences of these choices become more positive. It gradually grows into greater alignment with its Godly origin. [SC 57ff, 80-81, 86-87, 90-95]

Karma, the continuity of learning from one life to the next, is a liberating force that affirms that each choice that is made, wise or foolish, returns in the form of either new understanding or a residual lesson still to be learned—but never punishment. [SC 49, 84, 88]

Karmic debts from past-life experiences are accessible as normal extensions of memory, neither supernatural nor beyond the reach of any individual. Such awareness is always a choice, so no one is ever a helpless victim of past experiences or influences external to himself. [SC 51ff, 82ff, 84-85]

The human ego, which is a mistaken sense of self, creates the circumstances of negative karma. It must be superceded if one is to recognize his true identity, to be free of the wheel of karma, to engage in full service to others and to offer the unconditional love that springs up and shapes the foundations of his being. [SC 49ff, 51, 91, 118]

CHAPTER 12

JESUS' LAST DAYS: THE PASSION

The last few days of Jesus' life, his so-called *passion*, comprise one of history's greatest dramas. He was tried, tortured, killed, buried in a tomb and then—so we are told—he reappeared again in a physical body, interacted with others for several weeks before vanishing. All in all, pretty phenomenal!

The Romans crucified thousands of Jews but Jesus' crucifixion was special because (so the Gospels testify) he accepted his fate voluntarily and did so with full consciousness, without blaming or judging his captors and without moaning over his victimhood, even though his trial and sentencing were obviously contrived.

While there is little historical doubt that Jesus was indeed crucified, many persons doubt the accounts of the resurrection which followed. Once again, such an event falls totally outside of both ordinary history and personal experience. But again, the absence of historical evidence does not in itself mean that it did not occur.

On what basis can we be expected to believe in the resurrection? Even his apostles, to whom he promised it ahead of time (three times!) but who did not witness it themselves, could not believe it until they were able to confront him face-to-face. Since we do not have the same privilege we can only hold this unusual event in abeyance while seeking deeper insight and broader perspective.

Jesus' resurrection commands special attention because we wonder what a person of such high consciousness might be capable of at his death. Whether the resurrection occurred exactly in the manner reported or not, the story raises important questions about human potential: whether physical death, man's greatest fear, might be somehow transcended; whether the kingdom of heaven/a higher consciousness is attained after death; and how one should live one's life fully in the light of such a view of death.

One view of the significance of the resurrection is that Jesus answered and demonstrated answers to these three questions.

Judas

Jesus' passion begins with his so-called betrayal and arrest.

According to the Gospel writers and Christian legend the apostle Judas is presented as the greatest villain of history—the arch-betrayer,* if you will; an agent of the devil and a man with few if any redeeming qualities. And all because he is believed to have turned over to the slaughterers one of the most highly endowed persons of human history.

But did Judas actually have such malicious intent? Perhaps he was chosen by historians to play the villain role, as traditionally required for major dramas. In contrast, several fictional stories have explored the possibility that Judas was actually a devoted and compassionate apostle, well loved by Jesus, but he made a simple mistake which happened to have serious consequences he had not foreseen.[169] The recently recovered Gospel of Judas seems to suggest that Jesus *asked* Judas to turn him in, and recognized fully the consequences for himself and what this deed would do to Judas.[†170] The question of Judas' and Jesus' intentions remains unresolved.

Regardless of the various interpretations of the scanty facts, it makes no sense at all to blame Judas (or anyone else) for the death of Jesus, who knew what he was walking into and clearly accepted that he would be killed as a necessary finale of his bold and outspoken mission. From what we know of Jesus' intentions he was not even betrayable. It would actually be quite reasonable for Judas to have *helped* him at a task to which the other apostles would not have consented—or if they did they would have felt terrible guilt afterwards. After all, Jesus wanted his evangelists to

---

* Religious scholar Elaine Pagels finds that the word "betray" in the Bible should be properly translated as "hand over," a correction which puts Judas in a somewhat better light. [Miller 2007]

† See a description of this Gospel in a footnote early in Chapter 1.

survive to propagate his gospel, not to jump over a cliff as Judas is said to have done.

Let's try to expand our personal picture of what happened with Judas by enlisting some intuitive help.

(What kind of relationship did Jesus have with Judas during the years before the crucifixion?)

Judas was a particular challenge for Jesus. Judas had been a promising intellect. He had been well placed among the Hellenistic Jews of Jerusalem. He had trained amongst the Essenes and had [learned] deep and profound mysteries. But his family had passed into poverty by a series of misfortunes. With some bitterness he was forced into the indentured servitude of becoming a tax collector, a bitter route for any person of Jewish ancestry.

The tax collectors were particularly despised for they were carrying out, it was believed, the will of the Roman state. Often the system of taxation was considered a punitive measure from God. But even tax collectors had amidst themselves a certain tradition, for they were profiting themselves by carrying out "God's will." They were a hybrid people, and it was usually a measure of last resort for an individual to become a tax collector, for they received a pittance for their services and were often despised and cast out from the rest of the community.

When his friend Jesus came upon him, and Jesus had begun his ministry, Judas at first hid himself from Jesus, for they had been lifelong friends amidst the purifying studies with the Essenes. When he became a tax collector he avoided Jesus, often paying the tax of Jesus' own household rather than encounter his old friend in what he considered [his] shame.

Jesus associated with all, and thought to uplift the spirit of his friend by appointing him the treasurer, for when gifts would come or donations were to be made to the poor it was entrusted to Judas, the most trustworthy of the apostles. He had the capacity [authority?] to go and distribute the funds, down to the last shekel. He had an extraordinary capacity for figures, which he had originally applied to sacred geometry.

Unfortunately, Judas had also fallen in amongst the Zealots while traveling midst the poorest of the people, collecting taxes. He also knew of the state of poverty of the people in those days. He waxed angry in his heart and came to be drawn closer and closer to the Zealots.

Jesus tried to dissuade him with a message of peace. Unfortunately, Jesus knew that Judas' heart had been hardened by the events of his lifetime, and it saddened him that when he gave permission to his friend, he knew his friend would only suffer more. He knew that Judas would have to do that which he thought he had to do, to declare Jesus as a Messiah, because Judas felt that these things [events] would come about in the material rather than the spiritual. So all these things were known unto him [Jesus] in the pattern of his life. He knew that it was Judas' destiny to carry out what he felt was essential.

(What was Judas' real role in the so-called betrayal of Jesus?)

Judas, in great grief at the arrest of Jesus and his eventual crucifixion, believed that Jesus was to be the Messiah who was to raise up the people in an act of rebellion. For Jesus had converted among the Zealots and Judas subscribed to the philosophies of the Zealots, not unlike Simon the Zealot.

Jesus said, "Go forth and do what ye must."[171] For he knew that Judas was not so much the *betrayer* of the legend, but more so believed that by offering Jesus up, the Sanhedrin would lend political support to him. Judas felt he may have been forcing the hand of the political Messiah, versus the spiritual Messiah, so there is historical accuracy to this.

We find that Judas had pleaded that Jesus not be submitted to crucifixion and had spoken of others who had laid greater claims to be the Messiah in the kingly manner that Jesus had never done. Members of the Sanhedrin, wishing to reach out and to crush what they perceived to be a political rebellion, asked if Judas could give examples of such Messiahs. Judas, in a moment of naiveté, volunteered the names of others among the Zealots who felt they may have discovered the Messiah. These "Messiahs" fell under mass arrest under the Roman condemnation of conspiracy against the state, and suffered crucifixion. This added even more greatly to the suffering of Judas in his attempts to save his friend—to save the person of Jesus, whom he loved, from a fate he had not conceived of.

So yes, there were other so-called Messiahs, or those who had ambitions of becoming the Messiah, not unlike the so-called Hesmonian Messiahs who threw off the yoke of the Greeks some hundreds of years earlier.[172] These traditions lived even among the Essenes.

(Has Judas been reborn after his life with Jesus? If so, when and where did this happen?)

Judas found an incarnation in the individual Da Vinci.* We have spoken of Da Vinci with purpose, for he wished to bring and restore to humanity a great capacity for its progression. But notice that these were in the pure, scientific modes—in other words, by the enlightened intellect. These proto-sciences bring great advancement to humanity. It occurs in their cross-referencing and the shrinking of the world, by creating common knowledge that may be known consciously by humanity.

Da Vinci knew many of the things the angels thought in the creation would allow humanity to progress. Indeed, he was successful in doing so. He also created unearthly beauty. But his path [was] to try to create a world or kingdom that is of *this* world. As a sign of progression note the androgyny of the forms he created in his art. This is a sign of the advancing spiritual intellect, which indeed Judas was.

Leonardo Da Vinci, a prolific and practical visionary in fifteenth-century Italy, was the arch-typical "renaissance man." He is best known today for his prophetic inventions and his outstanding paintings.

(How then did he deal with the remorse he felt from his part in Jesus' death?)

> Continuously, in his unflagging dedication to try to revive humanity, to bring humanity back to a state of glory that he felt was known in the world of the day. He attempted to restore the ancient world and to bring about a kingdom that humanity could indeed endeavor [embrace?]. Study his art and his self-portrait and you will see the very embodiment of sorrow and remorse.

The Crucifixion

The most persistent question about the crucifixion deals with its meaning: was it merely an unavoidable consequence of Jesus' outspoken preaching, as usually claimed, or did it serve a more enduring and specific purpose for him as well? The arguments commonly given, such as "he died to save men from sin" and "a sacrifice was needed so he did it" cannot be said to be totally wrong, but as causes they do not stand up as a valid explanation. *Why* did he choose such an extreme path and follow it all the way to his own death?

First of all, it is clear from the Gospels (such as they are) that Jesus did not seek martyrdom but saw no clear way to avoid being killed if he were to speak and practice the truth as he saw it. We may presume, therefore, that he accepted his sacrifice as necessary, and he may have used the occasion to convey a greater truth: man's nature is eternal, beyond birth and death, and life continues after physical death (immortality). The latter point would have to be made through the resurrection, but first he had to die, of course, and do so in a manner that could be well witnessed and remembered, not lost in hearsay.

So the crucifixion would have served this purpose well, perhaps beyond his initial intention. Jesus' death on the cross has since become an icon for more than a billion Christians.* It is a grim reminder of his suffering and sacrifice, at the very least, and an enduring symbol of the transitory nature of physical life for those who can relate to it in this way.

---

*   Christianity is the only major religion of the world whose primary icon is a man being murdered.

Lesser questions deal with the extent of his suffering, the cause of an alleged earthquake and darkening sky immediately after his death, and his puzzling last words about being abandoned by God.

First, though, we need to know if Jesus was indeed crucified.

(A minority report* says that the crucifixion of Jesus never happened at all, but that Judas, in an attempt to protect Jesus, arranged for a substitute, a self-chosen messiah, to be crucified in his place so that Jesus might make his later appearances and then escape to other lands. Is this really what happened?)

There were many debates amongst the disciples, even after the experience of what is interpreted as the resurrection. The disciples represented diverse opinions about the Messiah. This is why Jesus would often say, "And who did thou say that I am?"[173] leaving open to debate in their own process of growth and revelation. At times even Jesus himself wondered if he was the Messiah, meaning the anointed one.

Some of the various disciples, in particular Thomas in moments of doubt, wondered if Jesus had been crucified, for they were not at the cross as the channel speaking was. They had fled into hiding and did not witness the crucifixion so it was only natural that they would doubt the resurrection, to wonder at the historical validity of what was described.

But if it is core to the issue as to whether Jesus was crucified, we state that he was indeed crucified. He had been sentenced under Pontius Pilate, as the Gospels historically describe, and he died within the very hours stated and was buried in the earth. So the concept of a substitute Messiah to account for the so-called resurrection does not find support from the channel speaking. However, it was discussed vehemently amongst the Apostles before this other phase had been established, during a period of some forty days after the crucifixion, particularly on the part of Thomas.

---

*   It is known historically that many self-chosen, would-be Messiahs were prevalent in Palestine in Jesus' day. It would not have been difficult for Judas to find one, disguise and drug him and let him sacrifice himself in Jesus' place.

(We have been led to believe that during his younger years Jesus achieved exceptional control of mind over body and could have diminished or eliminated the suffering that accompanies such heavy pain. Did he actually do this during his crucifixion?)

No. The capacity is what made the sacrifice even greater.

In thy own modern days there were those where ye had a period of contemporary leprosy, the phenomenon called AIDS. There were those who had great fear to associate with these [persons with AIDS], not [yet] knowing the transferable or non-transferable condition of the disease.

The woman known as [Princess] Diana* was indeed to inherit a kingdom and to be a gateway and a keeper of the kingdom and a mother of future kings. She went amongst the peoples, not unlike the Essenes and the prophets of old, sacrilizing them with her embracement, with her touch. It is acts of courage like this that are truly the actions like the Christ, and like the prophets of old. In other words, her empathy was such that she was willing to take upon herself the suffering of others.

How much more so, then, from the source of her inspiration, which was God's love, was the man Jesus. He knew that in the days of the laws as practiced by men, others had suffered. Mind thee, he was keenly aware of these laws because he did say in prayer, "If there is another way, let this bitter cup be taken away. But if it is Thy Will, I will drink of the bitter cup."[174] Because he did have control, like Yogis and meditators, as has been documented, the ability to regulate pain or to eliminate it in the body was known by him. But more so, he even had the ability to set aside his tormentors when he so desired, and leave the place of suffering.

Jesus knew that if there was [only] one indelible, historical example of one who has no greater love for his brother or his sister, one who would lay down his life for

---

* Reference here is to Diana, first wife of Charles, Prince of Wales, and a prominent and well loved figure in the United Kingdom in the 1980s and 1990s. She participated actively in many humanitarian endeavors.

them, then this one example would make it so that perhaps the whole of humanity could call to no other to suffer.

He said, "Behold, I have come to thee to give thee life and to have it abundantly."[175] If one person would suffer after this manner, it would create the context for the rest of humanity's liberation. Gandhi, when he suffered, liberated a nation by the example of the Christ. The man Martin Luther [King], as he so suffered, so in turn a people are liberated from bondage. It still creates a paradigm to this very day to move forward the liberation of humanity from its old patterns of not seeing in one another the divine spark.

(So Jesus did indeed suffer throughout the Crucifixion, and it was done voluntarily.)

By choice, by will, through empathy for humanity.

(And he could have avoided it?)

Correct. Even as empaths to this very day often take on patterns of suffering in order to heal, so in turn he wished to create a universal healing. It is an extremely powerful force, even unto this day.

The Last Stage of Death

(And his final words?)

Even in his moment of passing, when he said, "Eli, Eli, lama sabachthani?" [or] "My God, my God, why has Thou abandoned me?" this is merely the opening phrase of a famous lamentation [Psalm 22].[176] It would have been natural for anyone to state [this] at the moment of their passing, even as prayers are said in other traditions to guide the soul to its highest point, even announcing the knowledge of their passing.

(We read that there was a storm, earthquake and perhaps a dust storm at Jesus' crucifixion, near the moment of his death. Was this just a coincidence? Did Jesus deliberately time his death to coincide with these events?)

> Again, look more so to the concept of psychokinesis.* Jesus, of course, was not without his followers. Indeed, did he not feed more than five thousand, in the miracle of the fishes and the loaves? So at his passing, as word spread, a collective wave, again linked to the principles of psychokinesis, would have caused a great stirring in the earth. It would have altered climate as an act of great sorrow, blocking out the sun and to all who observed the event, making as if it were night.

This kind of mental influence on the weather has been speculated upon and claimed but there is not yet any good scientific evidence for it.

Burial and Resurrection

The Gospels tell us that two friendly Pharisees carried the dead body of Jesus into an available tomb, which was then closed, sealed and guarded. Three days later the stone door somehow rolled away, the guards panicked and dispersed and Jesus, or an apparition of him, appeared to those who had come to check on him.

Debated questions around the resurrection are whether it occurred at all as reported, and if it did, how was it done and how physical was Jesus' re-appearance. Most important, what was the significance of the event as part of his life mission?

We an easily imagine that Jesus may not have fully died on the cross but was temporarily buried, then stolen from the tomb by his friends, resuscitated and released to walk around and appear among those who

---

* *Psychokinesis* is a parapsychological term for the use of mental power alone to move or change the form of material objects. This phenomenon has been repeatedly demonstrated scientifically to have been accomplished by select persons under controlled conditions. The strongest evidence involves causing the fall of dice and electronic random number generators to perform non-randomly. It was recently a popular fad in the form of "spoon bending." The mechanism of psychokinesis and the necessary conditions for it to occur are not scientifically understood. [Braud 2003, Radin 1997]

would recognize him. Evidence to the contrary lies within the Gospel account, if we can accept it, for it says he was really dead, had been pierced by a sword and was standing and conversing with the Magdalen the following morning.

Jesus' predicted three times in the Gospels that he would be killed and then resurrect three days later. While these remarks could have been fabricated it would have been difficult for later editors to create all the details in a convincing manner.[177] Also, the Gospels say that in his first after-death appearance to Mary Magdalen he acknowledged he could not yet be touched, but later he invited Thomas to feel his wounds and he ate with his apostles, as if a gradual physical transformation was in progress. Similar reports of physical reappearances by deceased yogis occur in Hindu religious literature.[178] These accounts also speak in favor of the Jesus' reappearance after his death, though they do not prove the possibility, of course.

As for the meaning of the resurrection, his words in the Gospels indicate (as already mentioned above) that he sought first of all to show that physical death is not the end of a human life but that man survives death, at least in some sense. Second, we may reasonably surmise that he wished to provide dramatic evidence that his heavenly kingdom is real, albeit non-physical, and that he was going there. Finally, he may have wanted to show the prime importance of living in *truth*, whatever the cost, even in the face of death.

These matters are not settled, but in any case there is also the practical issue of how the resurrection might have been actually accomplished.

Preparation of the Body

(What happened to Jesus' body after it was put into the tomb?)

The body would have been removed from the cross. It would then have been attended to by the women who were Essenes, for it was desired that the body would repose in the tomb before the coming of the Passover. They were trying to practice within the boundaries of the most flexible elements of Jewish law.

The body would have been wrapped according to the traditions of the Essenes, with a long cloth prepared with certain anointment, flowers, etc., to help preserve the body, until the proper anointment could be placed upon it after the passing of the Sabbath, when such labors could be undertaken. The body would have been contained in the long cloth—as perhaps accurately portrayed in the images claimed on the so-called Shroud of Turin*—and wrapped with other elements of the cloth. The body, properly prepared, would have been then taken to the tomb and placed therein.

Then the shedding of the so-called grave clothes. We would take, even at some risk, that the Shroud of Turin is historical. The attempts of science to measure the age by carbon dating was flawed, because organic mass, building upon it through bacterial forces, corrupted that process. The fibers came from later medieval material, and the odd combination of these mixtures corrupted the dates by precisely the amount of carbon enrichment. The image upon the Shroud, its photographic-like quality, its three-dimensional quality, came from a process [involving] the fibers because of the intensity of what ye call prana, or life-force.

Survival?

Might Jesus have survived the crucifixion?

The capacity to survive the cross is well documented, and it is surprising that there are not more arguments that Jesus merely *survived* the crucifixion, possibly even using the capacity of deep meditation or shock to lower the heart rate through breathing, or even powerful narcotics that may have been offered. The pain-killing substances would often be offered as an act of mercy, in the form of bitter herbs. This has been described historically in the details

---

* The *Shroud of Turin* is a well preserved piece of cloth containing a facial image and claimed to be the winding sheet in which Jesus was wrapped when he was placed in the tomb after his death. Radiocarbon dating showed it to be not old enough to be genuine, but a more recent discovery revealed that the small piece taken from one corner for dating was actually a repair fragment and not part of the original material. The question of its genuineness has still not been completely resolved.

of the crucifixion within the Gospels.[179] Also, [from] the natural course of science they may have known of profound narcotic-like substances that could both dull pain and sustain a person for three hours upon the cross.

There had been persons known to have survived their crucifixion because their families' pleadings had allowed an act of mercy, even though they had been *placed* for crucifixion. This spared them suffering and dying. So what would have occurred would have been [that] the body would have been removed from the cross after a confirmation of death on the part of the executioners.

The lance piercing the side was typical of the process of crucifixion. It is said, "Behold! There poured out blood and water."[180] That is because the target was specific: it pierced both the lung and the heart, the lungs being filled with fluids. Suffocation is the actual element [cause] of death in a crucifixion. The man Jesus, having been so severely beaten and exhausted from the earlier night's activities succumbed to the process of crucifixion more quickly than others. He was also weak from knowing what was to come to pass.

We would say the body perished upon the cross, [Jesus] having given it up *consciously* [through] what is now known as a near-death experience, or astral projection.* [He] passed the body, much as in the tradition of many other legendary sources [individuals] amongst Buddhists, meditative masters, yogis and others.

Resurrection

(In what sense was Jesus' body resurrected?)

---

* The *Near-Death Experience* (NDE) is a well documented phenomenon in which a person returns to conscious life following clinical death, often with a detailed memory of what transpired during the intervening period when he was allegedly dead. The strong similarity between hundreds of such accounts parallels the descriptions of the altered state of consciousness achieved by deep meditators, yogis, and others who can voluntarily enter a state of astral projection or out-of-body travel, also well documented.

The body, having passed physically, went through a process of regeneration. It is now known, for instance, that regeneration according to science may be incurred in higher life forms. The salamander, long the example associated with the process of resurrection, and historically associated with the wisdom of Solomon, is well known to lose entire limbs, or even be divided in two, producing whole new entities.[181] In other words, it has the capacity of regenerating lost limbs and more.

It is now known that under the stimulation of energies such as magnetic fields and so-called electrical forces science has successfully achieved limb regeneration in higher mammals.[182] Even human beings contain certain primitive forms of regeneration. We would point out that children who lose a finger joint before the age of eight, for instance, may completely regenerate the complex neural, cardiovascular and even the meridian structure.

Regeneration occurred along what would be considered the chakra and neural meridian systems, reconstituting the cell structure even past death and rebuilding the so-called divine body. This was often the long-held alchemical goal, also of the yogis in the siddhi processes [practices] and legends of restored extraordinary longevity.

In this particular case, then, as the body lay in the tomb, resurrection occurred by the reunification of mind, body and spirit even though the body had long passed into what was considered clinical death. If ye accept the resurrection, not just as a resuscitation but a complete rejuvenation of the body by the life force, then ye should come to understand that there is indeed such a life force—a so-called *chi*, or energy—or even just the biomagnetic field of the body-physical itself—which can lend itself to the regeneration of the cell tissue. With this premise everything else becomes clear.

If uncomfortable with the process of prana [or chi] it is perhaps easier to argue for spontaneous resuscitation.

The Empty Tomb

(Why, then, was the tomb said to be empty? How was the stone removed from the doorway?)

It is said in scripture that there was a powerful movement in the earth, and that the soldiers had been frightened away. These were those who were sent there to guard the tomb to prevent the conspiracy that the disciples would steal the body, claiming he had been resurrected. You might consider it as a form of double-blind experimentation upon the part of the Hellenistic Sanhedrin and Rome itself.

Indeed, there was the quake, which would have rolled aside the tomb door. In the process of regeneration powerful forces of psychokinesis—the ability of energy to move matter—may have been triggered, rolling aside the stone. This gave the capacity to release the form of the resurrected individual who could no longer be said to be only Jesus, but the resurrected *Christ*.

In other words, the final cumulative evolutionary form conceived the body as a *cocoon*, in which an angelic being, now fully realized, could regenerate that form.

I believe John is saying here that while the mortal Jesus died, his body was recreated and then occupied by the Christ entity.

Later Appearances

To the apostles, disciples and others, and following all four Gospels, the most convincing evidence for Jesus' resurrection was not the empty tomb, which few saw and which does not prove much, but his several appearances to them in the forty days that followed.[183] Even if we accept the Gospel evidence, however, can we be sure that the figure who appeared was the "same" Jesus who died, and if so, was it physically solid or merely an apparition projected into the minds of his viewers?

(The Gospels describe several re-appearances of Christ after the resurrection. It's not clear if these were actual observations of the physical body, which anyone might have seen, or were they private apparitions created solely in the minds of his observers—something we know can happen. How are we to understand these appearances?)

In the forty days following the crucifixion the effect was not only a form of resuscitation but the bringing of matter itself into alignment with the Divine. For what is a human being but the continuity of the energy and the alignment of that with the Divine? [Thus it] becomes the Christ, or Messiah, for salvation, which means wholeness or completion.

When Mary Magdalen went to visit the tomb to complete the dressing of the body—for this was the way of the Essene women—she saw there a divine presence, which she at first did not recognize as the so-called resurrected Jesus. For in the process of resurrection extraordinary youth is at times restored. Many of the disciples did not recognize the resurrected Jesus, giving legends [that] at times it would only *resemble* Jesus. Indeed, in their grief they had moments of hallucination.

It is a fact that a body undergoing resurrection undergoes a transformation that constitutes the very [nature?] of the resurrected Christ. Here are keys to understanding the physiology of the complete merger of mind, body and spirit.

The ability to recognize one in a regenerated state, after the expectation of a physical encounter with them has been removed, explains the other part of the perception of the resurrected Jesus. For instance, in that society it would not be considered too unusual that if a person fell ill, their appearance might become more aged. After they were restored, those persons who had last see them ill may not even recognize them in their restored and more beautiful state. So, if the last vision of the person was to have been stripped and beaten and then to have suffered death itself, and they were now in a restored state, an even more vital state, this would be why they would fail to recognize him, because the body was still undergoing divine regeneration.

(So these appearances were not just apparitions but were actual ocular viewings. Is that right?)

Correct. It has long been sought, through man's alchemies and now his scientists, for the power and the capacity to regenerate the body physical. Many no longer consider this to be a myth, but consider it to be a [real] capacity of physiology or biology.

To the man Jesus, however, the goal was not physical immortality, for he knew that the physical, even as ye now know it, could become energy, or pure spirit. It was the healing of *death* that was the final element—or more so, [healing] the *fear* of death, so that the other acts of greatness we have described could unfold.

Jesus may be considered to have made a sacrifice so he could heal death. It is through the *resurrection* that the salvation comes about—not through the crucifixion but through the resurrection that the triumph occurs. While there was the passion to take upon himself the pain of the world, one could say, here is one person who has indeed taken upon himself all that the world may take upon them [itself]. Yet he made no judgment, and therefore was worthy of life, and thus resurrection.

Review

History

Jesus' old friend Judas was bright and Essene trained but misfortunes forced him into tax collecting and association with the Zealots. He greatly loved Jesus and tried hard to exalt and protect him, but his efforts backfired because of his messianic, materialistic expectations. Jesus knew what lay in store for Judas but could not prevent it.

Judas was reborn about 1400 years later as Leonardo Da Vinci and lived out a creative and successful life with his residual remorse. He used his high intellect and dedication to inspire humanity through worldly, proto-scientific and artistic creations.

Jesus was judged under Pilate and crucified. He had the mental capacity to set aside his tormenters and avoid pain on the cross but he chose otherwise out of his compassion for humanity. His final words about abandonment were a devotional phrase from the Psalms. He left his body consciously, dying rather quickly from suffocation, and was entombed as stated in the Gospels.

Before being placed in the tomb Jesus' dead body was wrapped in a long, scented cloth, known later as the Shroud of Turin. This recovered garment is genuine though its recent dating is in error.

Jesus' resurrection was enabled through regeneration (not revival) of his physical body, by a process similar to the way in which certain animals regrow lost limbs. This occurred through a reunification of body, mind and spirit, involving pranic (qi, or chi) forces, thus reconstituting the cell structures. The Christ energy or spirit then entered the regenerated body. His regenerated body appeared somewhat youthful to those who saw him.

The appearances of Jesus/Christ over the following weeks were physically real, not apparitions.

Teachings

One can evidence no greater love than to lay down his life for another. Jesus provided a powerful example of this by actually doing so for humanity as a whole.

Physical death is not the end of one's existence, as commonly believed, for man's consciousness survives death in a very real, albeit non-physical sense. Jesus' resurrection (not his crucifixion) demonstrated this fact, thus showing how man may free himself from the fear of death. [SC 176ff]

Jesus demonstrated by his example that the elevated state of consciousness, his heavenly kingdom, continues through both life and death and is humanly attainable.

Grace is a continuous state of conscious awareness and practice. It must eventually become a living part of each individual, for mercy and justice must prevail. [SC 21, 72, 83-84]

The blueprint of one's true identity manifests through the linking of mind, body and spirit, which constitutes the realization of the Christ within oneself. [SC 24, 26, 52-53, 71, 101]

CHAPTER 13

HEALING ALL HUMANITY

The esoteric literature asserts that the earth is visited from time to time by *avatars, ascended masters* or (in Buddhist terminology) *Boddhisatvas*: highly developed beings who manifest strong spiritual energy and undertake human lives in order to assist mankind in its evolution. This title is not confirmed on Jesus (or anyone else) in the Gospels in just so many words. Still, he certainly qualifies in comparison with others, such as Krishna and the Buddha, to whom the title is often applied, as well as some of the individuals identified above as Jesus in his past lives.

It would be interesting to know who were some of these avatars and what they contributed to the human race. Was Jesus indeed one of them? What kind of energies do they work with and enliven in humans? How does their work fit in with the long-range destiny of mankind?

Christ and Buddha

(What is the relation between the Christ entity and other high souls such as Buddha, Mohammed, Lao-Tse, Krishna, and so on? I'm looking for a connection close to Earth life, something between the Christ entity as manifested in Jesus, and that manifested in others such as Buddha, Mohammed, and so on.)

Ascended masters came here to teach us that we are of the same essence as the Divine.

It may be said the Buddha nature and the Christ nature are one and the same. Notice that both traditions consider a crowning of original identity in their metaphorical speech.

Both became organizers of civilizing principles. Both brought blessings to heal elements of humanity. For instance, within the Biblical system of things, work is considered a blessing. It is a gift from the Divine out of talents. Right labor in the Buddhist system of things is [also] considered a gift that may lead to enlightenment, for instance.

So rather than a cross-comparison of the two so-called religious systems, it is more so that the divine spark, or original nature, inspires whatever attributes an individual may have when living within the civil system. For instance, you [WHK] are one who is gifted with numbers and with the skills of observation called science, and have chosen [such] a path of consciousness. Therefore, it may be said that Christ helps to spiritualize the sciences, so that knowledge is not grown just to be stored upon shelves but practiced openly.

For Jesus said, "Behold, go into thy closet and pray there secretly, and ye will be rewarded openly."[184] In other words, open thyself to the Christ within, and then the external environment, the society, will be transformed. It is the same in Buddhism. The Living Buddha nature inside the craftsmen makes them turn from the functional to the spiritual, to bring beauty into the world. To those who speak the words of love they become inspired, not to prosecute but to arbitrate.

Thus, Buddha and Christ are the divine spark, the original identity that inspires each to its own uniqueness, thus bringing all into enlightenment, bringing about a kingdom, a natural ordering of all things. Thus, as a practitioner of original identity, the Christ, the crowned one, the anointed one, and Buddha both mean "original nature," the original merger with the Divine.

(And Mohammed?)

Prophets practiced their enlightenments to varying degrees. Remember, though, Mohammed's people were closer to the tribal, not unlike the wanderings of early Jews and Hebrew people. If ye cross-compare the actions of Mohammed and his descendants, they are closer in kinship to Moses and Joshua. So there are the stages of enlightenment.

Remember too, they are the descendants of Ishmael,* and it is well known that eventually Egypt and Israel hold a special blessing. That is why prophecy emerged in the treaty that binds them together. Ishmael and Israel were as bound together as the healing of Cain and Abel.

There was [also] the enlightenment attained by Lao Tse.

The Trees of Knowledge and Life

Within the tradition of Eden there are two trees that stand in the center [and] which mean "the natural order of things." There is the Tree of Life and the Tree of Knowledge. The *Tree of Knowledge* is the central sushumna† of the kundalini, the seven chakras, the seven candlesticks of the Revelation and the seven angels or energies of the candles—in other words, metaphorical references to the psychic centers of the kundalini. This is the Tree of Knowledge.

Ye may know your identity in relationship to the Divine in the opening of these psychic centers. The Tree of Knowledge is the means for ending dualism in the world, to know that both that which is well and that which is ill derive from the same divine energy. That which is ill in the world is what is meant by *evil*: illness, disease, and aberration.

---

*   Ishmael and Isaac, two sons of Abraham, are traditionally regarded as the original ancestors of the Arab and Hebrew peoples, respectively.

†   *Sushumna* is a Sanskrit term referring to the spine as the channel through which the kundalini energy flows through the chakras. It corresponds to the Biblical expression "Highway of Holiness."

Even now ye know that fevers and suffering may be part of healing—in other words, part of a natural paradigm that must achieve balance within organic and energetic systems.

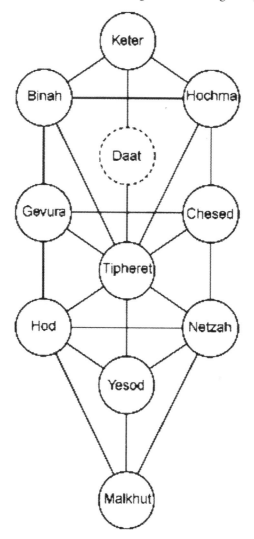

Figure 5. The Sephirot, or Tree of Life

The *Tree of Life* refers to the other psychic centers, which many do not have knowledge of [but are] latent within the system. These are the Kabbalistic or Sephiratic centers. When the kundalini is fully opened, then the Sephiratic portals, the ability to restore original identity, are also opened. This then speaks of the *keter* or crown within the Kabbalistic system, when the third eye is so open and luminous that the transpersonal [manifests], releasing all of the subtle energies of the body [including] the aura, the light often seen shining about saints. The light about Jesus in the transfiguration showed that he was then partaking of the Tree of Life. This was his anointment.

Thus [the title] Christ means "chosen" or "anointed one." It means that the keter, the crown of all the psychic centers and the kundalini were fully opened in his realization, so he could be caught up and know communion with the saints.

If ye will, *this is the natural psychic state of humanity in the world.* When [attained] ye are then no longer *under* the law, but ye have *become* the law. If others could receive this communion, then these blessings would spread out like ripples across a pond to the whole of humanity. But when one cannot receive them, then one must [first] complete other forms of service.

So the kingdom that Jesus spoke of was the order of the so-called Sephiratic energies, all the way down to the so-called Malkhud kingdom.

I believe what we are learning here is that what man calls *enlightenment* actually comprises two stages. The first consists of the opening of the body's main psychic centers, which allows the dissolution of all dualities such as good and evil. This is what we have called here the recognition of the second realm, symbolized in the Tree of Knowledge. The second, corresponding to the Tree of Life, opens the subtle energy systems of the body which then restore one to the natural, pre-physical state of humanity, the "anointed" or "Christed" state which Jesus attained.

Jesus in a Universal Context

(Some say that Jesus' contribution to mankind was not just for men on Earth but for the entire created universe, including celestial domains. Is this true? If so, what benefits did he bring to these other levels of existence?)

There are many souls throughout the diversity of creation, which ye have called the universe, who have entered into various psychic states. The activities of celestial beings have been noted in humanity's history and given rise to evidence of existence on other planes.

The so-called Dogon people indeed knew of some genetic origins from the days of Atlantis, when the extraterrestrials were part of their celestial ancestrage.* Various other peoples knew that celestial beings contributed to their ancestrage.

Once in the days of Atlantis it spoke of seven kingdoms before Adam, and that at times humanity, even in those days, was in a state of perfection or grace, when the morning star shouted as one. This was when humanity had open awareness and consciousness of other dimensions, other spheres of existence, other celestial beings and open exchanges with those who traveled between the universes—so-called extraterrestrial consciousness.

These are not mysteries to those who read [of] the more mystical traditions. Indeed, if a soul in the Earth plane that had such open exchanges with other beings had achieved this level of enlightenment, this [would] become an historical demarcation point at which humanity may eventually restore itself spiritually—perhaps even technologically but above all spiritually—and take its rightful place once again in a growing universe.

Even though ye have learned that souls are not isolated upon continents or mountains or separated by oceans, but are one unified substance as a whole, so in turn you as a planet are not isolated in the greater universe from other conscious beings. Therefore, even as an individual may throw the proverbial pebble into the ocean, even as a flower cannot be diminished if a single petal falls, all this [is] part

---

* The Dogon people, an anthropologically well studied primitive tribe in Mali, Africa, are the center of a controversy regarding their mythology, which claims derivation from space beings from the star Sirius. They display long-held knowledge of certain details of Sirius and our solar system, which they could not have known in ordinary ways without a telescope. The evidence, perhaps intuitive, naturally remains controversial.

of the whole. For "Verily, verily, I sayeth unto thee, if a sparrow falls and the Father-Mother God cares for these, how much more does he care for thee?"[185] Indeed, if one soul falls in one part of the universe, do not all souls then find themselves somewhat diminished, until that prodigal consciousness returns home?

So if a soul achieves the healing of death, and becomes one with the Divine and then does not have to suffer the second death, do not all the morning stars once again shout as one? Is not the universe made whole once again?

(So there's an effect at all levels through Jesus' contribution at this earth level. Is it possible to say more specifically what this effect actually is? Did he open the door to overcoming death, to salvation, at these other levels as he did on Earth?)

Correct. There are many celestials throughout the universe who wondered if the Earth, given its long history and the justifiable judgments [that can] perhaps be made upon it, could ever restore its original nature; and whether humanity's form, which it had chosen for itself—that is, the human being—may ever raise itself again to a celestial conscious level. Those who held such prejudices may even be held back in their capacity to believe that the universe itself may be restored.

If humanity can indeed reclaim itself and its identity among the celestials, so in turn does this not add to their union also?

Might Jesus have been aware of this universal aspect of his earthly contribution to mankind? He left us no clear statement of it, but with this new perspective we can now well imagine that he knew.

Jesus and the Kabbalah

(Do you have anything of your own to add to this long inquiry, John?)

We would add only those dimensions of the Kabbalah, in order to bring about some knowledge of the mystery that Jesus practiced. Jesus, ye may say, was a Kabbalist. He drew all of his knowledge and wisdom from the Torah, the Talmud, the Mishna and the Pentateuch, which were the oral traditions for the writings of the Rabbis that came after.

Jesus was first and foremost Rabboni, or Rabbi, the Teacher. He was the prophet and he said, "Behold, I shall make thee a nation of priests."[186] What he meant was that the law and covenant would be kept, where the whole of the law would be known in their minds and their hearts, so that all of them could practice their own revelation in their own patterns and unique ways. In this way they could indeed partake of the Tree of Knowledge, and have *knowing*. They could then also partake in the Tree of Life, the Kabbalah, of the two trees that stood in the center of the Garden of Paradise. Then they could pass the benefits of the blessings unto generations. And as they incarnated, the generations would not pass away until all these things were fulfilled, until all become healed.

For this was the healing of death and the gift of life, and having it abundantly, to be *as* the law rather than *under* the law; also to be the sons and daughters of God; and that God is Love. It was in this way that the gift was given: to love the Lord God with all thy heart, mind and soul, and thy neighbor as thyself. This constitutes the whole of the law.

Seek to be at peace with those things that ye receive from Spirit. Walk in this, the Father-Mother God's Light. God bless you. Amen.

Review

Teachings

As one grows into awareness of his divine state he awakens to his capacity to see the Divine in all things. This is the consciousness that he calls God, or the universal mind. The essence of It lies within him.[SC 60ff, 84, 146, 165]

Ascended masters, or avatars, come to earth from time to time to teach that we are all of the same essence as God, that the essence of Godliness already lies within each individual. From this level it is seen that good and evil come from the same source: there is no duality. [SC 31-32, 109ff]

The Buddha nature and Christ nature are essentially the same. As anointed ones they sought to heal portions of humanity. They supplied the divine spark, the original identity, which inspires each individual to discover his own uniqueness. This process, when extended, will eventually bring all humans into unified enlightenment. [SC 27, 32, 53, 62, 76, 162]

Anyone may open himself to the Christ consciousness or Living Buddha nature. His entire environment, even his society, will then be transformed in his perception. [SC 78, 109-110, 123, 134, 171]

Lao Tse was also so enlightened. Mohammed's people were closer to the tribal, similar to the wanderings of the early Hebrews.

Jesus was inherently a Kabbalist and drew this knowledge from the classic Hebrew traditions of his time and the Law contained within the Tree of Knowledge and the Tree of Life. He therefore possessed knowledge of the higher order of human existence. He held the vision that all beings would eventually partake of this knowledge and realize that God is love.

The two trees in the Garden of Eden are symbolic references to the human body's psychic and sephiratic centers. When one activates the kundalini he is able to recognize the natural order of creation, the divine spark that inspires man and his societies. He may then attain the kingdom of heaven Jesus spoke of and realize his original identity with the Divine. It was through this experience that Jesus became the Christ. He was then free of submission to Natural Law and became the Law itself. [SC 93]

A few of earth's cultures hold memories of the days when celestial beings, seen as extraterrestrials, were among them. Some of these visiotrs lived in a state of perfection and grace and traveled among other dimensions and universes. [SC 82, 85ff, 177]

Souls existent in the various dimensions of the (mostly non-physical) universe, including those of us on earth, are inherently interdependent upon one another. Some have occasionally participated in humanity's spiritual evolution toward a higher consciousness, and have wondered whether the human race could ever raise its level sufficient to take its rightful place in the greater universe. [SC 80]

CHAPTER 14

PERSONAL INTEGRATION OF JESUS' TEACHINGS

"Within you there are blueprints. You know what you are to achieve, as individuals and as people, as a race, as a species. You have free will. You can choose to ignore the blueprints. . . . You have made physical reality something different than was intended. You did this through using your own free will. . . . You were to work out problems and challenges, but you were always to be aware of your inner reality and your true home. To a large extent you have lost contact with this. You have focused so strongly upon physical reality that it has become, indeed, the only reality that any of you know." [Jane Roberts[187]]

The preceding chapters have supplied abundant intuitive information on Jesus' life and teachings. You may choose to hold this knowledge intellectually as a collection of interesting and entertaining ideas, but doing only this will not help you enlarge your understanding of yourself, your particular life path and human life, which is its intended purpose. In order for you to truly *apply* this new knowledge in your own life you must find a way to assimilate and integrate it into your present values, principles and understanding. This is our next goal: to aid you in this personal application and integration.

Recall from Chapter 2 that the main purpose of intuitive information is to *inspire* more than to inform, though we all recognize that new information can be a precursor to new inspiration as well as a consequence of it. You are invited to be both informed and inspired as you read this final chapter. And again, keep in mind that the *intuitively derived explanations and ideas offered here are not dogmatic commandments or established factual statements,* but rather potential and possible option*s* you are free to use for enhancing your own understanding and system of beliefs, and eventually your personal growth.

We will first be gathering together the many fragments of intuitive wisdom about Jesus and his teachings, and trying to bring them together into a consistent thought system, sometimes called a *spiritual philosophy.* This synthesis is not just a theoretical construction but rather the kind of overall perspective you have already created to organize your personal life experiences, whether you have done so intentionally or incidentally, implicitly or explicitly, consciously or not and expressed in words or held in your mind non-verbally. This perspective or overview is what enables you to find your personal place within the broad spectrum of human possibilities in spite of their very large number and their complexity.

The spiritual philosophy offered below is not all that different from this, though it is constructed deliberately rather than unconsciously. You may use it as a *framework* for organizing your impressions and thoughts about the new intuitive information about Jesus' specific teachings, so you may give them personal meaning and gracefully incorporate them into your existing knowledge base. At the very least it will help you identify more clearly the *purpose* for which you are living and understand the *path* you have chosen to follow. You will then be able to pursue this purpose and path more intentionally and less incidentally or thoughtlessly.

We are calling this synthesis a "spiritual philosophy" with some misgiving because both words are vague and therefore easily misinterpreted. It is indeed *spiritual* in its most existential sense because it deals with your essence in the second domain, not only your physical being, and thus the basic life questions raised earlier: Where did I come from? What am I doing here? Where am I going? What is the point of it all? Who am I? Why do bad things happen to good people? Why does God allow so much suffering in the world? Why do evil deeds so often go unpunished? As a human being you are fully entitled to answers to these questions. On the other hand, this synthesis is *not* spiritual in the sense of spiritualism, spirits, new-age magic or a limited religious notion of spirituality as being devout, well-behaved and "doing good"—perhaps worthy enough traits but not spiritual in themselves.

This synthesis is also a *philosophy* in the broad sense of a personal position or a "philosophy of life" to live by. It is *not* the classical, intellectual and formal field of philosophical study, which is largely intellectual and deals with logic, ethics, definitions and theoretical issues. In contrast, our approach here is meant to be *relevant to daily life* and *practically useful*, not a theory, collection of scholarly reflections or another abstract mind game.

The Events in Jesus' Life

We must first put into due perspective the historical narrative of Jesus life, many specific aspects of which John described in the preceding chapters. John's descriptions of these events agree generally and very broadly with those reported in the New Testament Gospels, the apocrypha and some later Christian writings. John's story agrees less well with the events as presented by some modern intuitives who dispute the Christian legend more strongly, and by religious historians, who (as noted earlier) tend to discount whatever cannot be supported from recorded history. John clarified several points and re-interpreted others in a fresh and often non-traditional manner so they can make better sense to us today. He also added context and additional events not included in the written records, thereby shedding new light on the relevance of these events as they relate to Jesus' teachings.

To add perspective to the teachings John also brought in related information from Jewish history, Vedic philosophy, Buddhism, other cultures and religions and modern science.

The most important value of these events is as *demonstrative examples* in support of the central ideas Jesus was espousing. This was undoubtedly Jesus' original intent in performing these deeds—simply as expressions of himself and his teachings. If you can regard them as illustrative examples rather than behavior to be emulated, you place them in the context of his overall mission without becoming stuck on their factual truth or falsity, which will always remain objectively uncertain.

To reiterate points made in Chapter 2, these intuitively derived explanations of Jesus' deeds and words provide ample opportunity for you to examine your present *beliefs* about what "really" happened with Jesus and to upgrade these beliefs as you saw fit by drawing upon your own inner resources, intuitive or other. Specifically, you are invited to regard

John's intuitive descriptions as possible alternatives to whatever beliefs you originally brought to the table. *They are not commandments, nor are they appeals that you accept them as facts from an external source that seems to be authoritative.* Rather, you are asked to use them as a platform and starting point for your own inner search, so you may uncover your personal truth about them. *This is the only role which intuitive information generated outside of yourself (or any new information for that matter) ought to play in your life.*

If you like, regard this upgrading of your beliefs about the narrative events in Jesus' life simply as a practice exercise for understanding the more challenging teachings, which come next.

With this admonition we now leave behind the narrative account of Jesus life and focus on his teachings.

Jesus' Teachings

The following synthesis of Jesus' teachings into a spiritual philosophy is drawn from John's descriptions in Chapters 7 to 13, augmented here and there with material from Ryerson's earlier book of John's discourses, *Spirit Communication*; and with some of the non-doctrinal portions of the New Testament Gospels and Gnostic writings, to the limited extent that these are relevant. The central concepts and explanations from these sources agree with the best of contemporary spiritual literature, including the published writings of several expert intuitives similar to Ryerson.[188] Some of the latter have been leaned upon here without specific reference, more for their lucid explanations than the ideas and principles, since the latter agree with Ryerson's and are already well covered.

The Perennial Philosophy and Jesus

The *Perennial Philosophy* presented in Chapter 1 provides a sound basis and suitable starting point for a spiritual framework. It may be safely thought of as "world knowledge," for it is as universal, timeless and valid as anything man has discovered about his inner nature, his place in the cosmos and his purpose for being alive. Moreover, as noted earlier, it is fully consonant with Jesus deepest teachings as we are able to understand them. Let's examine the Perennial Philosophy again from this perspective:[189]

- *Primordial reality: there are two realms of reality*: the familiar everyday realm of physical objects and living creatures (the first realm), and a more subtle and profound realm of consciousness, mind and spirit (second realm). The second is not a polarized opposite of the first but rather a source that embraces and includes the first. It is timeless, space-less and not directly perceivable by the senses or man's physical instruments.

- *Participation: human beings partake of both realms.* We are not only physical beings but also spiritual beings, intimately linked to the second realm. Each of us has, at the center of his being and in the depth of his mind, a center of transcendent awareness, a personal *essence* which is his root in the greater Reality to which he belongs.

- *Accessibility: every human has the inherent capacity to recognize this sacred ground of being,* this second realm. Each one of us can test the validity of this inner connection by experiencing it directly when his mind is quiet, open and uncluttered with thoughts. Such a pursuit is the purpose of spiritual practice.

- *Priority: the recognition of one's inner spiritual nature* is the highest goal and greatest good of human existence. To realize this goal is to discover one's true essence, or Self, and one's true relationship with all of Reality.

The first principle invites you to recognize the existence of the second realm *in the Universe*, and the second principle *in human life* in general and *your own life* in particular. Jesus called this second realm the *kingdom of heaven*, an apt metaphor for his first-century audience, since this audience already understood both the power of kings and kingdoms and the old Jewish notion of heaven as a divine destination.

The third principle affirms your *personal capacity* to shift your waking consciousness dynamically and increasingly into the second realm. You recognize the kingdom of heaven in your *awareness* of the second realm, through its manifestation (weakly and only occasionally for most persons) through insights, dreams, epiphanies and an over-abiding if elusive "presence" in your daily life. The challenge here is to appreciate it not just as an interesting idea but as integral and significant to your state of being and personal growth. The accessibility of the second realm was a central theme of Jesus' teaching, and his way of life demonstrated his success at achieving a close connection with it himself.

If you are not able at the moment to deliberately actualize your capacity for accessing the second realm, rest assured that you will have many opportunities to do so over the course of your life. It is inherent within your very being to be nourished by it and drawn to it—you can't avoid it! Practices for aiding the recognition of this urge are discussed later in this chapter.

The fourth principle is a statement of *meaning* and *purpose* arising out of this urge. It is an almost automatic consequence of the first three principles when they are accepted and prioritized among your values. Your life choices will then shift to fit them. Jesus asked his followers to do the same: "Seek ye first his kingdom," etc.[190]

If you are able to genuinely and wholeheartedly accept these four principles then you have already established the strongest possible foundation for your personal spiritual philosophy. If not, then you at least know where next to place your attention and energy.

Human Creation and Growth

> "All day I think about it, then at night I say it. Where did I come from, and what am I supposed to be doing? The soul is from elsewhere, I'm sure of that, and I intend to end up there. . . . I didn't come here of my own accord, and I can't leave that way. Whoever brought me here will have to take me home." [Rumi[191]]

The next step for incorporating Jesus' teachings into your life is to understand when, where and how your existence began in the first place, how your growth as a conscious being on earth is taking place within the greater Universe (or Reality), and the fundamental laws that govern this growth process. We need to take some time to become clear about these matters.

Where Did You Come From?

John explained in Chapter 11 that the existence of every individual being, including *you*, in the great Universe began in the "angelic realm," which we may take to be the second realm. You first came into being as an

212

essence or *Higher Self,* or as a *soul* in one meaning of this often misused term. Your essence may be thought of as a seed, spark, fragment or emanation of the ultimate creative Source of everything—God, we may safely call It, though let's leave this notion abstract for the moment and not try to personify it.

The point is that whatever this Source might be, It is able to clone itself without being diminished. Each seed contains *all of the Source's essential attributes,* albeit in only a potential and undeveloped form somewhat like DNA. In all other respects it is free and independent of its Source and all other created seeds.

We may wonder about these "essential attributes" but three of them are certain. First, this essence is your true identity, "who you really are," distinct from your body, brain and personality. Second, its built-in bond or *unity* with the Source includes a drive or urge to evolve itself back to the Source from which it came. Third, it has immense free will as to how it does so. (More on the latter in a moment.)

Your essence will evolve through a long series of experiences that eventually render it as all-knowing, all powerful and perfect as its Source. It will eventually merge with its Source in some sense, though just what this merging involves and how it occurs must remain a mystery. Herein lies the pattern and process of every human life, and your human life in particular.

Your essence is partially aware of these attributes, what is going on, its path of evolution and its potential and destiny, but its corresponding conscious personality is not, even the decisions it is continually making. The latter's awareness is always limited but expands as it evolves.

Natural Law

Your essence's growth* takes place within a grand cosmic environment, that which we call Reality, which is the collection of everything besides yourself which the Source has created—matter, energy, space, time, their combinations and manifestations and all other evolving essences. If this created environment extends beyond the physical universe as we know it, we are unaware of it. It is immense, omnipresent, omniscient,

---

* I refer here to "your essence," as if you *possess* it, but only to distinguish it in this description from "you" as its conscious embodiment, even though your essence is more truly *you* than the body and personality you possess.

permanent, inviolate and inescapable. The second realm discussed above is the perceivable and accessible portion of it.

All change and growth proceed in accordance with this Reality's working principles, or *Natural Law,* "the cosmic order of things," "the way everything works," also somewhat inaccurately called "God's will." While the *existence* of Natural Law follows directly from the first principle of the Perennial Philosophy, its particulars do not, though they are derived from it. Natural law includes the familiar physical laws that govern the material world and exemplify it: attraction and repulsion, motion and change, continuous interaction, exchange of energy, cause and effect and the broad principle that the same laws apply across all levels and differ only in form: "As above, so below." It includes at its center the functioning of *love* as the universal attracting and binding force among all beings. It is somewhat like gravity in the material universe. This is the basis of the common affirmation, "God is Love."

As our essences evolve we gradually learn about Natural Law and how to live by it.

Are We Separate or Joined?

Because every essence has this built-in binding link with its Source, and possesses the same basic attributes as all other essences, it is connected at a deep level with all of Reality and especially all other created essences. Herein lies the resolution of the supposed duality of God and man: we are truly *not separate* but are bound together through this deep and essential root. We are indeed *All One,* even though we are not fully aware of our unity and appear to be quite distinct, for no two evolve exactly the same. We grow separately, each essence in his own limited range of awareness.

Most important, the Source or "God" and the resultant natural reality is not external to us but resides *within each of us.* Jesus knew this well and taught it in various ways. At the level of possibilities and potential your essence is therefore inherently unlimited. It is as fully endowed with choices for expansion as is the Source from which it came. This potentiality includes especially the freedom to make your decisions without external interference: a great gift but also a great responsibility.

Free Will and Suffering

Herein lies the resolution of the common mystery about God "allowing" man to suffer so much and to mistreat other humans. The Source, God, allows everything during development. When man in his limited awareness chooses to manage his or others' lives in his own way, apart from the Natural Law of the Reality in which he is embedded and without a due sense of responsibility for what he is doing, he experiences the consequences of violating this law and thereby creates suffering for himself and others.

Man's suffering is no more than the result of his unaware but "chosen" resistance to following Natural Law. Suffering has no other cause. Moreover, every step of learning to abide by Natural Law reduces suffering. Suffering is never externally imposed as punishment but is always self-generated, though usually only deep in his consciousness. Even susceptibilities, accidents and "fate" are inadvertently chosen by the essence as necessary learning experiences.

So How Is Your Material Existence Arranged?

Your essence (and every essence) evolves through many steps, stages and levels. This long sequence includes within it a series of *physical embodiments* in what we know as earth life, the first realm. The purpose of these embodiments is to allow the essence to undergo growing and learning for which the earth environment, including other embodied humans, is best suited. These earth-level changes in awareness and growth reflect upward into corresponding essence-level changes.

Before each of your physical lives is undertaken your essence (in the second realm) selects a life purpose and a set of earth circumstances appropriate to what it chooses to learn at its particular stage of growth—like planning your next semester at college. It aligns with a suitable physical vehicle, gender and family; it chooses a locality, culture, time period and set of earth circumstances consistent with its mission; and it lines up opportunities and challenges to be experienced. These form a kind of blueprint, which may be followed by your embodied consciousness if it chooses to, or not. Your essence also fashions an *ego* (interim identity, self-concept, lower self) to enable it to function in the more constrained world of space, time and matter.

Living a Life on Earth

After being born into the first realm you live your life more or less in accordance with your blueprint for the chosen mission, earth conditions and ego-based personality. You increase your awareness of Natural Law by making choices, acting them out, experiencing the consequences—pleasant or painful—and then re-choosing when you can. With each small step you make corrections in a *trial and error fashion*, expand your awareness a little, and thereby reduce your discomfort/suffering and enhance your essence.

When your earth life is completed your body and brain dissolve (death) and your earth consciousness returns to its essence in the second realm. Here it recovers, reviews its earth experience and prepares for its next embodiment. You repeat this cycle for all subsequent lives, and gradually grow yourself into greater consonance with Natural Law.

The Human Species

At any point in time the population of the earth consists of a broad mixture of billions (!) of embodied essences at different levels of evolution, from newly created "infant souls" to old souls almost finished with the earth environment. Most of us lie between these extremes. Even at a single level there are huge differences in people and behavior because of the many and varied lessons being learned. Earth life is indeed a kind of "one-room schoolhouse." Still, thanks to the preplanning, the complex interactions between individuals work amazingly well, at least for aiding growth if not always for comfort.

Most humans make death into a fearful tragedy because they believe it is the end of their existence. Physical life does terminate but the essence lives on and on. Jesus knew this when he offered immortality to his audiences, though few understood the deeper meaning.

Murder is wrong not merely because it destroys another's body but because it violates the victim's free choice to live as he chooses. It often occurs as an option through an essence-level agreement, and both killer and victim learn from the experience. This observation offers a fresh perspective on what is truly harmful to others, especially to those who are dependent on us, such as children, the ill and the elderly: give them *free choice* whenever possible, consistent with loving care.

What Carries Over from Life to Life?

All lessons, both those already learned and those yet to be learned, are retained by your essence from each embodied life to the next through the principle of *karma*, which is the inviolate law of continuity, return or cause-and-effect: "whatsoever a man soweth, that shall he also reap."[192] Lessons learned through alignment with Natural Law are retained as assets and strengths. Those still unlearned because of ignorance or offenses against Natural Law remain as "karmic debts" to induce further learning. The principle of karma is no more complicated than this.

Most incurred debts involve relationships with other persons. The same essence relationships are frequently renewed from prior lives in order to aid the learning process in a give-and-take fashion. In the planning period before birth closely related essences may come together and agree on what kind of interactions each can benefit from in the next round. Perpetrator and victim may exchange roles, along with other complementary polarities: male-female, parent-child, master-slave, wise-ignorant, king-peasant and so on. Intelligence, physical beauty, creativity, leadership and social position are chosen to fit the lessons one needs to learn and are in themselves not necessarily measures of essence growth. Victimization, early death and even physical and mental disabilities may be deliberately chosen, especially by old souls to fill in their last remaining lessons.

The principle of karma explains why you cannot judge the rightness or wrongness of wealth, fame, misfortune, long life or premature death from the perspective of a single earth life alone; the overall evolution of your essence must be taken into account. All offenses even out as offenders experience for themselves what they have done to those whom they have offended in the past, all according to Natural Law. There are no "bad" consequences or "bad" karma. It's all part of the game.

In each incarnation the details of prior lives are normally hidden from your conscious mind so that you may focus on your current life mission with less distraction and fear. (Can you imagine living your present life with guilt for torturing someone, or an active memory of being tortured yourself?) Still, these memories are always accessible if and when you deeply desire to recall them and can handle and benefit from them. Eventually they will all become known; your essence has no secrets. No experience is ever lost until long after it becomes irrelevant, and perhaps not even then.

Tools for Learning Life's Lessons?

The main link to your essence-Self is your *mind,* your first-realm builder of growth. It is your primary tool, because it is your personal means for determining how much your essence (higher Self) rather than your ego (lower self) governs your life choices and learning. However, it is at the same time the major barrier to growth because of its willful and often quirky tendency to resist offered experiences by putting beliefs ahead of knowledge.

Your mind regulates your speech and behavior through your brain, memory, intellect, senses and other instruments of the physical body. Most important, it *chooses* how your consciousness, driven by essence, is expressed in your thoughts, emotions, desires and intention, all of which underlie and work through these physical instruments.

These root choices are governed in turn by the manner and extent with which *love,* in its broadest sense, is given and received, for love is the ever-present and unlimited energy or "fuel" that enables all growth. You don't create it but you determine through your mind how it is given space to be expressed and applied.

Time and space are qualities of the earth environment. The essence transcends them and views all interactions and events as adjacent (ubiquitous) and immediate (eternal). They are directed by the consciousness of the essence in the second realm. They are experienced on earth through the way you choose to use your intention and attention. It is this duality which makes life a continual challenge and truly "interesting."

Connecting with Essence

The strongest mind-connections available between you and your essence are *prayer* for self-expression and devotion; *intuition* for communication and receptivity; and *mindfulness* practice for attunement and resolution. To work well for bridging the two realms, they all require an attitude of personal openness, intention and surrender. They are in contrast to rituals, sought-for approval, expectation of divine intervention, selfish gain and ego-based needs and rewards. Prayer is most beneficial when it is solely personal and done with a fully receptive intention (not greed). Jesus said, "When you pray, go into your room and shut the door and pray to your Father who is in secret."[193] Intuition is most effective when the mind is trained to ask and receive knowledge in an attitude of innocence, service and non-judgment. Jesus functioned intuitively when he "communed with God." Mindfulness is learned best through mental silence and a developed sense of peace, most readily found in nature and solitude, but it can be brought into daily life for great personal benefit.

Where Does This Series of Lives Lead You?

As you approach the final stage of enlarging your conscious awareness you begin to recognize your essence consciously as your true Self, and all this implies. Your growing awareness of the second realm dissolves the duality, the illusory separation between mind and essence. Your essence history (past lives) becomes relevant and portions can be remembered. A beginning sense of eternity (timelessness) emerges and your continued existence after death (immortality) becomes known with inner certainty.

As your growth progresses your closer alignment with Natural Law allows you to surrender more fully to it, embedding yourself within it. You experience directly the Godliness within you and in other beings. You gain access to the rich reservoir of knowledge in the superconscious mind (omniscience) which was previously hidden from you. Unconditional love is experienced along with profound joy and union of body, mind and spirit.

Eventually your essence no longer needs earth lives and you can move to a higher level of learning experiences, a step closer to the Source from which you came. This much we know. What lies beyond the state of consciousness of the second realm cannot be readily described.

This final stage of awareness expansion has long been recognized in all major cultures of the world. It is called by many names: awakening, enlightenment, illumination, self-realization, samadhi, nirvana, *unio mystica*, entry into the kingdom of heaven and others. While it is usually spoken of as a sudden event and a destination to be attained, there are indications that it is actually a continuous and gradual creative process, not necessarily sudden. Depending on definitions it may also be endless, simply because the mysterious Source with which the essence ultimately merges is itself the greatest of creative processes, not knowable in detail from our level.

We have good reason to believe that Jesus experienced this profound transcendence, probably at his baptism but at least sometime before his death. If we understand his words correctly he no longer needs earth lives, and he "returns" as the Christ energy to those who invite him.

Practical Execution

> "What strange beings we are! Sitting in hell at the bottom of the dark, we're afraid of our own immortality. . . . You sit here for days saying, *This is strange business.* You're the strange business. You have the energy of the sun in you, but you keep knotting it up at the base of your spine." [Rumi[194]]

Armed with the Perennial Philosophy and this base of understanding about your origin, growth environment, means of growth and Natural Law, you are now ready for the more practical aspect of integrating these teachings into your daily life—not just as thoughts banging around inside your head but actually *living* them!

The principles themselves need not seem so strange. They are much like the same basis on which you (and all people) have grown into an adult human being in the past. From childhood forward you learned, step by step, to recognize, accept, identify with and submit to higher values and purposes than those to which you were previously accustomed. You did so automatically, and, we can say, largely unconsciously. The only difference now is that you will be doing it deliberately and with increased awareness of what you are doing. You will be *intentionally* taking a step toward the higher consciousness of the second realm and your truer identity.

The central principles guiding this integration were introduced above: free choice and responsibility, cause and effect (karma), love as the grand binding force, giving and receiving, forgiveness and being forgiven, continuity across levels ("as above, so below"), continuity across space and time and a few lesser ones.

The process works generally like this. As you attempt to apply each principle in your life you will come to understand how its acceptance is being retarded or blocked by attitudes or beliefs you are unintentionally holding. Thus begins the work to eradicate this block. At the same time your built-in and on-going urge toward growth and expansion keeps you motivated and helps you gradually recognize your place in the cosmic order: how you came into being, the path you are following, how you fit into the cosmic environment and how you accommodate to Natural Law, as described above. You also draw strength from the love, common sense and sense of fairness behind this grand design, which is truly an immense gift.

This recognition culminates in a greater understanding of your *life purpose*, and this frees you in turn to pursue a fresh course for your continuing growth and expansion, both day-to-day and long-term. You may already be subtly aware of this purpose in your life, even if you can't see it clearly or verbalize it well. The more it becomes conscious, however, the better you are able to trust it as personally valid, can make firm decisions based upon it and move forward in your growth without doubt or hesitation. This is the sought-for clarity that accompanies the application of the spiritual framework presented above.

If you take no more than this first intentional step you will be far ahead of the man in the street, who chooses not to think about such matters at all. He lives in ignorance of them and is unaware of how they are shaping his thoughts, decisions and therefore his entire life. His growth is reactionary and sporadic, with many needless diversions, and is typically painful.

Yearnings, Values and Ideals

On the long multi-life journey to awakening, your essence follows its own unique path. It holds to this path by *aligning* itself along one or a few particular attributes or qualities of growth at a time, which is why it undertakes successive physical incarnations. For most of its lives there are many to choose from; there is no fixed order to the learning of lessons. The qualities selected before birth normally express themselves only partially consciously, as felt *urges* or *yearnings*, a stepping down from full essence awareness. Your entire orientation toward life experiences are governed by these yearnings. They are active and conscious to a greater or lesser extent, depending upon whether and how you choose to recognize, relate to and accept them. You can probably identify right now one or more long-term yearnings that have persisted throughout your life.

Your mind translates these yearnings into a set of *higher values, ideals* or a *vision* with which you can identify and toward which you may grow. While they may be subtle and sublime they are nevertheless compelling. Once accepted from your essence you cannot easily run away from them.

You may undertake at any time a conscious formulation of your personal ideals and values—first those you are presently living by, and then those you would like to review and upgrade to a higher level, more consonant with your life's purpose and your understanding of Natural Law at this time. You do not need to create them because they already abide with your essence. Your task is only to reflect them downward into your present awareness and translate them into ongoing activities. Note that they are *guides* only; that is, they serve to set direction, stimulate motivation and help you establish priorities. They are *not* goals to be actually accomplished. Nor do they need to be understood in their entirety by your thinking mind but only acknowledged and used.

Objectives and Tasks

Once these values and ideals are consciously in place they impel almost automatically a chain reaction of specific expression, beginning with a set of *long term objectives*. They enable you to *focus consciously* your living energies, activities and decisions, without diversion or compromise. They can be looked upon as the *roles* you play with your personality and in your current life drama. Typical roles are: to be of service to others, either individuals in need or humanity at large; to be creative and expressive in communication or deed; to be involved in action as leader or follower; to be an explorer or gatherer of knowledge; and to seek devotionally a stronger connection with your Source.* These role typically endure throughout life but they may change in mid-life if you grow out of them or if your essence's intentions shift.

These long-term objectives translate in turn into specific, *short-term goals* or *tasks* that you choose to actually accomplish—not just work toward. Goals call for commitment and consciously managed effort, and imply short-term shifts in your daily interests and behavior (over months or years). They may also include regular practices for keeping an ongoing

---

* For comparison, Hindu philosophy prescribes four such patterns, called yogas: *knowledge* (or wisdom), using the mind to explore its own nature and gain true knowing of God; *devotion/divine love*, using deep meditative processes to develop your love for God and all creation; *control of body and mind* to convert mental and physical energy to spiritual energy; and *action/service*, selfless detachment from the fruits of one's actions and any thought of gain or reward. They are termed jnana yoga, bhakti yoga, raja yoga and karma yoga, respectively Other systems describe somewhat similar options.

tie with the second realm and for dealing with intellectual and emotional obstacles.

The final result of accepting these objectives and accomplishing these tasks is a grounding of your life in a purposeful, loving, joyful and fulfilling mode of living, with increased conscious awareness and control of progress toward a higher level of awareness—eventually the awakened state mentioned above.

Attitudes and Behaviors

The goals you select consist primarily of efforts to change attitudes, beliefs and behaviors you acquired or fell into when young or during the following years and decades of your life. Most of these changes will take place through interactions with other people, and the balance more or less independently. If you make no effort these changes will happen anyway, automatically and eventually, but this can be a slow and painful process for both yourself and other persons. Better to know what you are trying to do and follow accordingly.

The majority of these deliberate attempts at change are included among the specific directives Jesus gave to his apostles and followers for how to life a righteous life. A few others, appropriate in today's more complex and civilized world, derive from them.

The efforts for dealing with the attitudes and behaviors that most commonly impact *other persons* are:

- strive to love God and all your fellow men
- give of yourself in heartfelt service
- do to others what you deeply wish them to do to you
- forgive others for their errors, without condition
- practice non-violence, non-blaming, non-revenge and personal peace
- be compassionate, merciful and healing to all
- be honest, just and responsible in your relationships
- be tolerant (non-judgmental) and patient with others
- live and teach righteousness by your example
- behave harmlessly, honoring others' right of free choice

The efforts for dealing with the attitudes and behaviors that most commonly impact *yourself* are:

- seek only the kingdom of God/higher consciousness
- nurture faith, trust and alignment with God
- nurture love of yourself, God and all life
- remain open and receptive to new knowledge and experience
- seek the truth and always live in truth (Natural Law)
- focus your primary awareness on the present (not past or future)
- always be grateful, humble and patient with yourself
- remain simple, still, serene and peaceful
- practice devotion and prayer
- strive only for heavenly, not material values and "rewards"
- be self-responsible in your intentions and choices
- be self-forgiving for your errors
- accept without resistance that which you cannot change

If you are one who prefers to deliberately focus your efforts on particular traits to be developed, you may utilize these two lists as *checklists* to see where you should next place your attention. One option is to work out for yourself the reasons and lines of argument behind the tasks you commit to, so you can always be sure they are correct for you and worthy of your serious effort. Alternatively, you may commit yourself somewhat arbitrarily to achieving a chosen few of these virtues, on the assumption that you cannot make a serious mistake, for they are all worthwhile. In any case you may find help from the external resources cited in Appendix A.

For a third option you may be one who does not want to be bothered by such a fine-scale breakdown of growth possibilities as outlined here. You may prefer to live freely, fully and lovingly, and just accept your lessons, even if painful, as they arise incidentally from daily life. This approach is also valid, albeit uncontrolled and slower.

Obstacles

A fourth option is to proceed intentionally by focusing on personal *obstacles* to your growth and overcoming them one by one. This approach will appeal to those who prefer to struggle against whatever seems to oppose them instead of striving directly to acquire positive qualities.

Obstacles are revealed, usually indirectly, by their disruptive effects on daily life: conflicts in your closest relationships (spouses, parents, children, siblings, long-term friends, authority figures, etc.); activities which are not working as you expect; loneliness, depression or despondency; or more serious mental or physical conditions. Because of their separative nature obstacles *always* induce some degree of suffering, at least in yourself and often in those with whom you interact. An obstacle can be found hiding wherever you are hurting or are causing pain in others. This pain signals where you need to pay attention.

If you choose to work on your obstacles, here is another checklist which can help you identify particular ones in yourself:

selfishness	resentment	guilt/shame	anger
arrogance	specialness	grief/loss	doubt
impatience	self-punishment	judgment	hate
intolerance	jealousy/envy	vengeance	greed
hypocrisy	self-deprecation	loneliness	negativity
arrogance	deceit/dishonesty	idolatry	.. and others.

Jesus indicated that *obstacles arise from a voluntary separation of oneself from God*—that is, from the natural order of things, one's essence, the second realm or Natural Law. Each obstacle is a single facet of this chosen separation. It is typically reinforced as one accommodates to it and finds apparent justifications for it, with result that in time the separation seems natural. It is similar to becoming addicted, overweight or succumbing to bad habits; one soon adapts to his condition and forgets he has rejected other options. You are surely aware of a few of your obstacles, though the most serious ones typically reside outside of everyday awareness. To deal with them you must first find a way to identify them and accept (not deny) their presence. Then you must own them (as self-caused) and commence the effort to remove them.

Obstacles are normal and very human, of course. They are merely the most bothersome aspects of the ever-present learning process. You never need to feel guilt or judge yourself over them, and no one else has the right to judge you. Indeed, guilt and self-blame are just other obstacles.

A book could be written about the many possible human obstacles to growth and the various ways one may remove them from his life. But there is a better way . . . .

225

A Master Obstacle

> "All difficulties arise from fear, conscious or unconscious. Fear is the opposite of love, in the sense that wherever there is fear, the capacity to love is blocked. Fear is actually an illusion, but love is real. Our principal task as humans is to overcome fear. We may start with the conscious fears." [ACIM[195]]

If there is one underlying obstacle that induces all the others, it is *fear*. Every obstacle is rooted in a fear. If this fear can be confronted and dissolved then the obstacle disappears. A broader release from fear can remove several obstacles at once. *Melting out fears from your character is the most effective action you can take to eliminate your personal obstacles.*

The cloud of fear behind your obstacles may be hard to recognize at first. It usually lies just below the level of ordinary awareness which the conscious mind sees, so it is typically hidden and denied. Once fully acknowledged it is not a difficult notion to accept and deal with, for fear does not "make sense" to the conscious mind.

Fears are disruptive because they tend to crystallize themselves in the personality where they induce an over-reliance on ego (a limited notion of who you think you are), an unregulated mind (thought noise) and various attachments (unnecessary needs and desires). These traits can be taken as broad indicators of the fears you are carrying.

Specific fears can be detected in yourself because they send out signals of confusion, distress or contradiction. These signals are typically regarded as externally caused at first; you will be tempted to attribute them to other persons or your immediate environment rather than yourself, thereby denying responsibly for them. Still, the attitudes and beliefs generated by this denial are easier to detect than the fears themselves, so they are your best indicators that obstacles are asking for attention. By pursuing such warnings you may identify the underlying obstacles for yourself and see what fears lie behind them.

The consequences of melting out fears are all positive. Every fear removed from your life allows more love to manifest, in many ways, and the additional love melts out other fears more effectively than anything else. This love is not something you create directly, of course; you cannot force yourself to love anyone or anything. Love already exists inside of you and is only waiting to be awakened and released. However, you *can* choose to remove whatever obstacle is blocking this love from manifesting. This is a task you can deal with because it is under your conscious control, as just described.

Sources of Support

As you function under your chosen values and ideals, struggle to recognize your objectives, move toward your goals, achieve your tasks and continually seek to improve your attitudes and behaviors, help is near at hand at every stage. No one is ever separated from internal and external support along his personal path of growth. We have said you must "go it alone" on your long path toward awakening and ultimate perfection but this does not mean you cannot make use of guidance and other assistance along the way. You are alone only in making the choice to do so.

Modern Western society is marvelously abundant in the resources it offers for assistance to the seeker and learner. Included at this cooperative level of help are intimate and trusting human relationships, a great variety of classes, books and media programs, and various kinds of counseling and psychotherapy, to name just three. Still, all are secondary to the your personal inner reliance on prayer, intuition and mindfulness practice, provided only that these are done with the openness, surrender and trust that enables them to work effectively.

Here are some specific kinds of support you may draw upon:

Inspirational support: The strongest support comes directly from the second realm in the form of the internal presence called the *Christ*, the *Holy Spirit* or simply God. You may recognize it as a wave of pure love or light, a surge of inspiring energy, a state of being forgiven or greatly cared for. If you know how you may call upon it at any time, in any place, in any mood and at any stage of personal and essence growth. It is guaranteed to respond to your need: "Ask, and ye shall receive; knock, and the door shall be opened"[196] was Jesus' way of putting it, and his promise, "I shall be with you always."[197] This offer is found in all cultures, however, not just from Jesus. It works through the refined love presence resident within you, not from anything external. You draw upon simply by opening yourself to it.

Social and religious support: External help may be obtained in substantive ways from man's institutions. Counseling centers and similar agencies provide psychotherapy and related forms of counseling, ranging from practical techniques for coping with obstacles to deep personality change and healing for those who are receptive to this kind of assistance. Our religions, including Christianity, offer a variety of ethical and moral prescriptions and several God concepts from which to choose. They involve different belief systems, doctrines, commandments, and types of intermediaries between yourself and God—whatever might be your need and conform to your beliefs sufficiently for you to trust it. All are meaningful and useful in their own way, for different people, times and occasions.

Wisdom teachers: Should you be more mystically inclined the esoteric sides of religious and philosophic traditions offer more or less structured, more open-ended and less compromising thought systems, as well as finely tuned forms of inspirational and meditative teachings. Valuable support is available from individual counselors and wisdom teachers in the traditions of esoteric Christianity, Buddhism, Taoism, Sufism and Vedanta, for example. Many modern spiritual teachers of these traditions are available today, both in person and in their writings. (You may explore some of the latter options through the references listed in the *Recommended Reading* section in the Appendix.) The Christian or another Bible can also be a valid source, although most people find them difficult to interpret without a qualified teacher. The benefit may lie more in the teacher than the sacred book itself.

Regular practices: For accomplishing the aforementioned tasks regular personal practices such as prayer, meditation, devotion, dreamwork, mindfulness practice, certain physical disciplines and various related spiritual exercises can all be very helpful. Jesus emphasized solitary prayer and silent contemplation. All enable and strengthen one another and other growth efforts. To follow any self-improvement practice on a daily basis is certain to have positive effects since it leads to greater self-awareness.

Review

> "The only thing required on the spiritual path is your commitment
> to truth, your longing to find love of self and love of God. This one
> commitment will bring you Home, regardless of how many careless
> things you do." [Emmanuel[198]]

This broad view of human development described above is offered as a framework within which you may place yourself, and against which you may test your beliefs and your awareness about your present state of inner evolution: what you have already learned, what you are still working on and what is coming up next to take your attention. The long process of *awareness expansion* is universal, everyone's journey, and the only possibility at this earth level. We will all do well to perform it as best as we can.

This growth process may seem complex and heavy but again, it is little more than an adult version of how young children mature into adolescence and mature into old age. They learn about their world by experimenting with it, with a little guidance and protective help from parents, friends and others with whom they relate. They gradually become more conscious and self-responsible in their thoughts, choices and behavior, even though they may do it largely unconsciously.

Only rarely do we humans choose to grow ourselves into wisdom with full awareness and intention. Rather, we typically make imperfect decisions, react to pain and typically attribute our suffering to external circumstances rather than ourselves. When we take personal charge of our learning process, however, we achieve our growth more directly, consciously, responsibly and joyfully, thus with less suffering.

The principles and explanations stated above are presented factually and dogmatically as points of information, with the seeming implication that you should accept them as true and act upon them with some kind of faith. This interpretation is an unfortunate aspect of the written mode of presentation, for our intention is otherwise. The information offered here is intended mainly as ideas, possibilities and triggers to your own evolving self-awareness. We urge you strongly to reconsider it this way and assess its validity for yourself. Take it as belief if you wish, recognizing that all beliefs are just intermediate steps to knowledge. *You are never required to follow any proposed system or learning process or any particular steps.* You choose your own path.

The spiritual framework outlined here, along with its various implications, is simply a statement of how the world—your world—is working, broadly stated and according to the highest authorities available. You are invited to contemplate it, adapt it to your own inner vision and cooperate with it to whatever extent you see fit. Or you may choose to reject it all and work out your own approach.

Settling into your unique path is not so much a matter of thinking, deliberation, belief, persuasion and argument as it is a simple recognition of what is truly *real* in your world, and then choosing how you are going to relate to having recognized it. You do not doubt or deliberate whether to breathe the air around you, and it serves you not at all to resent or fight against your greater environment—physical, family, societal—in which you find yourself and attempt thereby to change it to fit yourself. A wiser option is to acknowledge it, accept it as it is and learn the many ways in which it may serve you. For guidance at this task listen carefully to your essence—a mostly intuitive act—and then move forward under its subtle guidance. After all, your essence is focused entirely on its own growth, and therefore *your* growth. It cares not at all about these various earthly conditions, which are merely temporary means and aids to this growth.

Jesus and Personal Growth

"Ye shall know the truth, and the truth shall make you free." [199]

Jesus was a very great human, and not merely because of his preaching, his confrontation with the established order, his exceptional sacrifice, his many healings and unusual deeds and the many wise sayings attributed to him. He was great because of the deep understanding he possessed and brought to humanity about what it means to be a truly human being. His words and the deeds of his life, even his death and resurrection, all testify to this central message, which may be stated like this: At the centers of our beings we are all manifestations of God, equal in our potential and our freedom to make choices about our own destiny and how we get there. Our greatest fulfillment lies in recognizing and accepting this state of being and all it implies. This is our calling, for ourselves as individuals, our societies, our species. In effect, we are being invited to recover our original divinity. In doing so we inherit all the many benefits and fulfillment that come with this recognition.

The huge religious legend which Jesus inspired emerged tangentially from this deep understanding. We still have today its residue, in various forms, and it continues to inspire those of us who choose to draw upon it. Those who do so are free to transcend the limitations of the inherited religious package and create for themselves a freshly inspired spirituality.

A NEW JESUS? Yes, certainly, but it is not Jesus who is new, for he has not changed. What may be new is your personal way of perceiving him and the lessons he taught; that is, new to you. Can you hear his central message, and allow yourself to be transformed and renewed by it?

This fundamental message comes through loud and clear to those who choose to listen to it: *your task as a human being on earth is to learn to love everyone and every experience,* with the highest priority over all possible alternatives and without conditions of any kind. It is a long road, but at the end of it you will have learned how to love not only your spouse, parents and children, your friends, associates and neighbors, God and country—including those you dislike or hate and those who cause you pain—but also your enemies (as Jesus required) and any humans, objects, places, animals, afflictions, objects, places and situations you may now detest. You will learn to love yourself, for this love is already inside of you, and needs only to be released.

If you are not clear what love is, practice its derived qualities: compassion, kindness, gratitude, forgiveness, mercy, service, harmlessness, acceptance and the other virtues discussed above. The deeper and more genuine love will make itself known to you.

What is awakening to, you see, is your *capacity to love.* This love is already inside of you, just waiting to be recognized. It has little to do what you find lovable—the things loved; they are only exemplary and temporary learning vehicles to show you how to love more and more of the total Reality in which you find yourself. This is your primary task in this life —and in all other of your earth lives, too. Everything else you might choose to do is subservient to this one transcendent objective.

Herein lies true salvation.

APPENDIX
BIOGRAPHIES OF AUTHOR AND CONSULTANT

William H. Kautz (MA, MS, ScD, M.I.T.) founded and directed the Center for Applied Intuition, a San Francisco organization which for fifteen years carried out research, training, public education and counseling/consulting on intuition and its practical application in various scientific and socially oriented problem areas. He explored especially the role of intuitive processes in science and technology, with emphasis on the enhancement of creativity through the deliberate development of intuitive skills. He conducted classes, lectures and training workshops on intuition and its applications in the U.S. and abroad for thirty years.

Before this he was Staff Scientist at SRI International (Stanford Research Institute) where he conducted and administered research in computer science, communications, geophysics and other fields for 35 years. He taught university courses at Stanford University, the Technical University of Denmark, and Tata Institute (India), and has lectured extensively throughout the world.

Kautz is the author, co-author or editor of six books and numerous journal and magazine articles. He lives in Prague, Czech Republic, and Tucson, Arizona. williamkautz@seznam.cz . . . www.appliedintuition. net. . . .

Kevin Ryerson is an acclaimed author, award winning consultant, expert intuitive, futurist and trance channel in the tradition of Edgar Cayce and Jane Roberts. He has been lecturing and teaching in the field of parapsychology and spirituality for over 30 years.

He has appeared as a guest on national and international television shows including *Oprah Winfrey* and *Good Morning America*. He is the author of the landmark book *Spirit Communication: The Soul's Path* (with Stephanie Harolde). Shirley MacLaine's best selling books *Out on a Limb, Dancing in the Light* and *It's All in The Playing* highlighted Ryerson's intuitive abilities. He was both a consultant and talent in the ABC television miniseries *Out on a Limb*. His abilities are also featured in the books *Opening the Inner Eye* by William Kautz, *Return of the Revolutionaries* by Walter Semkiw M.D., *The Tenth Insight—Holding the Vision: Experiential Guide* by James Redfield, *The Channeling Zone* by Michael Brown, *Your Sixth Sense* by Bell Ruth Naparstek and Time-Life's *Mysteries of the Unknown.*

Kevin is an eight year board member of the Intuition Network, a nonprofit organization. He is the former vice-president of the Berkeley, California, Society for Psychical Studies. He has served as faculty at the Association for Research and Enlightenment, Omega Institute, Findhorn Foundation, Interface, Lily Dale Assembly, Philosophical Research Society, Learning Annex and the Whole Life Expos.

Kevin participated actively in several research studies at the Center for Applied Intuition. He has acted as a corporate consultant for Kingston Corporation, Enchante, Whole Life Inc., Victor Grais Productions, Findhorn Foundation, Green Energy Inc., (Japan), MacLaine Enterprises, West 52nd Street, ABC Television, Newsweek and U.S. News and World Report.

Kevin is well known and respected for his balanced and integrated world view. He maintains a consulting practice in San Francisco, California.

Kevin Ryerson & Company
Office phone 415-356-9887; fax 415-267-6939
http://www.kevinryerson.com kevinryerson@mac.com

RECOMMENDED READING

Intuitive Narratives and Commentaries on Jesus: Anon 1975, Anon 1955, Bock 1980, Cummins 1937, Cummins 1949, Dowling 1972, Emmerich 1979, Furst 1970, Morgan 1989, Notovitch 1890, Cayce 2006.

Novels on Jesus: Asch 1939, Browne 2006, Caldwell 1959, Caldwell 1977, Chilton 2000, Gibran 1928, Kazantzakis 1954, Kazantzakis 1966, LeCroix 1981, Mailer, 1997.

Pre-Christian, Gnostic and Early Christian History: Armstrong 1993, Lewis 1929, Lewis 1945, Pagels 1981, Pagels 2003, Patterson 1992, Schneemelcher 1992.

Scholarly Studies of Jesus: Borg 1997, Borg 1987, Boulton 2008, Funk 1993, Funk 1998, Mitchell 1991, Thiessen 1998, Vermes 2000.

Consciousness, Parapsychology, Transpersonal Psychology: Jung 1959, Mishlove 1993, Radin 1997, Targ 1977, Vaughan 1980.

Intuition and its Development and Application: Franquemont 1999, Harman 1984, Kautz 1987, Kautz 2005, Klimo 1987, Palmer 1998, Pierce 1999, Vaughan 1979.

Living the Spiritual Life: Anon 1975, Roberts, 1970, Rodegast 1985, Ryerson 1989, Vaughan 1983, Vaughan 1993, Walsch 1996, Tolle 2005.

BIBLIOGRAPHY

The Biblical references in footnotes and endnotes employ standard abbreviations in *chapter:verse* form. They are included here only for cross-referencing, neither as Biblical support for the accuracy of channeled statements nor as channeled support for the accuracy of the Christian Bible. In-text quotes are taken from the American Standard Version.

ECW: See www.earlychristianwritings.com for texts and full citations of the four main Gospels, other portions of the Christian Bible, all known apocryphal writings such as the Gospels of Mary, Peter, Thomas, Maccabes, Egyptians and Judas, and ancient and modern commentaries.

Bibliographic support for historical and scientific statements can be found in most cases in an on-line public encyclopedia such as wikipedia (*http://en.wikipedia.org*). While not as firmly authoritative and accurate as academic sources such as the *Encyclopedia Brittanica* and the *Columbia Encyclopedia*, wikipedia is accessible, readable and well cross-referenced. Incomplete and questionable entries are usually acknowledged as such.

° Anon, *The Urantia Book* (The Urantia Foundation, 1955); Part IV; www.urantia.org/papers/index.html

° Anon., *A Course in Miracles* (Foundation for Inner Peace, 1975); http://acim.home.att.net/acim_tx-1972.html (portions only).

° Armstrong, Karen, *A History of God: The 4000-year Quest of Judaism, Christianity and Islam* (Ballantine Books, 1993).

° Asch, Sholem, *The Nazarene* (NY: Putnam, 1939).

° Barks, Coleman, Tr., & John Moyne, *The Essential Rumi* (HarperSanFrancisco, 1995).

° Barth, L.F, "Effect of constant electrical current on the regeneration of certain hydroids," *Physiol. Zool.* 7:340, 1934.

° Bock, Janet, *The Jesus Mystery* (San Ramon, CA: Aura Books, 1980); contains Notovich book.

° Borg, Marcus, Ed., *Jesus at 2000* (Boulder: Westview/HarperCollins, 1997).

° Borg, Marcus, M. Powelson & R. Riegert (Trs.), *The Lost Gospel Q: The Original Sayings of Jesus* (Berkeley: Seastone/Ulysses, 1996).

° Borg, Marcus, *Jesus, A New Vision: Spirit, Culture, and the Life of Discipleship* (HarperSanFrancisco, 1987).

° Bostock, John, Ed., *The Natural History: Pliny the Elder* (London: Taylor and Francis, 1855).

° Boulton, David, *Who on Earth Was Jesus? The Modern Quest for the Jesus of History.* (Winchester, UK: O-Books, 2008).

° Braud, William, *Distant Mental Influence* (Hampton Roads, 2003).

° Brodd, Jeffrey, *World Religions: A Voyage of Discovery* (St. Mary's Press, 2003).

° Brown, Ronald K., *The Book of Enoch* (Guadalupe Baptist Theological Seminary Press, 2000).

° Browne, Sylvia, *The Mystical Life of Jesus: An Uncommon Perspective on the Life of Christ* (Dutton, 2006).

° Caldwell, Taylor, *Dear and Glorious Physician* (Doubleday, 1959).

° Caldwell, Taylor, *I, Judas* (Atheneum, 1977).

° Cayce, Edgar, *The Complete Edgar Cayce Readings on CD-ROM, v. 2.0 for Windows* (Virginia Beach: ARE Press, 2006).

° Chilton, Bruce, *Rabbi Jesus: An Intimate Biography* (NY: Doubleday, 2000).

° Cummins, Geraldine, *The Childhood of Jesus* (London: The Psychic Book Club, 1937, 1972); www.trans4mind.com/spiritual/cummins/cummins3.html.

° Cummins, Geraldine, *The Manhood of Jesus, Parts I* & II (London: The Psychic Book Club, 1949, 1950); www.trans4mind.com/spiritual/cummins/cummins3.html.

° Dowling, Levi H., *The Aquarian Gospel of Jesus the Christ* (DeVorss & Co., 1972); www.sacred-texts.com/chr/agjc/index.htm.

° Duquesne, Jacques, *Jesus: An Unconventional Biography* (Liguori Publications, 1997).

° Emmerich, Anne Catherine, Klemens Brentano (Rec.) & Carl. E. Schmöger (Ed.), *The Life of Jesus Christ and Biblical Revelations* (Rockford, IL: Tan Books and Publishers, 1979, 1986; original: Lille & Paris: Desclée, de Brouwer & Co., Paris, and New York: Sentinel Press, 1914); four volumes.

○ Franquemont, Sharon, *You Already Know What To Do* (Tarcher, 1999).

○ Fuller, John Grant, *Arigo: Surgeon of the Rusty Knife* (Crowell Co. Books, 1974).

○ Funk, R.W. & the Jesus Seminar, *The Acts of Jesus: The Search for the Authentic Deeds of Jesus* (HarperSanFrancisco, 1998).

○ Funk, R.W., R.W. Hoover & the Jesus Seminar, *The Five Gospels: The Search for the Authentic Words of Jesus* (Macmilllan, 1993).

○ Furst, Jeffrey, *Edgar Cayce's Story of Jesus* (Edgar Cayce Foundation, 1968; Coward-McCann, 1970).

○ Gauquelin, Michael, *Neo-Astrology: A Copernican Revolution* (Arkana/ Penguin Books, 1991).

○ George, Margaret, *Mary, Called Magdalene* (Viking, 2002).

○ Gibran, Kahlil, *Jesus, the Son of Man: His Words and His Deeds as Told and Recorded by Those who Knew Him* (Alfred A. Knopf, 1928).

○ Gibson, Mel, Dir., *The Passion of the Christ*, film (Newmarket Films, 2004)

○ Harman, W.W., & H. Rheingold, *Higher Creativity: Liberating the Unconscious for Breakthrough Insights* (Putnam, 1984).

○ Helminsky, Kabir, Ed., *The Pocket Rumi* (Shambala, 2008).

○ Hock, Ronald F., *The Infancy Gospels of James and Thomas: with Introduction, Notes, and Original Text Featuring the New Scholars Version Translation* (Polebridge Press, 1996).

○ Huxley, Aldous, *The Perennial Philosophy* (Harper & Bros., 1945)

○ Jansen, Katherine Ludwig. *The Making of the Magdalen: Preaching and Popular Devotion in the Later Middle Ages* (Princeton University Press, 2000).

○ Jefferson,, Thomas, *The Life and Morals of Jesus of Nazareth* (Dover, 2006; orig. 1895); commonly known as the Jefferson Bible.

○ Josephus, Flavius, *Antiquities of the Jews* and *War of the Jews*, in *The Works of Josephus, Complete and Unabridged*, William Whiston (Tr.) (Peabody, MA: Hendrickson Publishers, Inc., 1987).

○ Jung, C. G., *The Archetypes and the Collective Unconscious*, Collected Works, Vol. 9.1, Bollingen Series XX (Princeton Univ. Press, 1959).

○ Kautz, William H., and Melanie Branon, *Channeling: The Intuitive Connection* (Harper and Row, 1987).

○ Kautz, William H. *Opening the Inner Eye: Experiments on the Practical Application of Intuition in Daily Life and Work* (New York: iUniverse, 2005).

○ Kautz, William H., *The Life of Jesus: An Intuitive Anthology (tent.) (2011).*

° Kazantzakis, Nicolas, *The Greek* Passion (Simon & Schuster, 1954; Ballentine, 1965); republished in UK as *Christ Recrucified* (Oxford: Bruno Cassirer, 1954; London: Faber & Faber, 1962).

° Kazantzakis, Nicolas, *The Last Temptation of Christ* (Simon & Schuster, 1960).

° King, Karen L., *The Gospel of Mary of Magdala: Jesus and the First Woman Apostle* (Santa Rosa: Polebridge Press, 2003).

° King, Karen L., *What is Gnosticism?* (Harvard University Press. (2003).

° Klimo, Jon, *Channeling: Investigations on Receiving Information from Paranormal Sources* (Tarcher, 1987).

° LaCroix, Mary, *The Remnant* (Virginia Beach, VA: ARE Press,1981).

° Lehner, Mark, *The Complete Pyramids: Solving the Ancient Mysteries* (Thames & Hudson, 1997).

° Lewis, H. Spencer, *The Mystical Life of Jesus* (San Jose: Rosicrucian Press, 1929).

° Lewis, H. Spencer, *The Secret Doctrines of Jesus* (San Jose: Rosicrucian Press, 1945).

° Lund, E.J., *Bioelectric Fields and Growth.* (Austin: Univ. of Texas Press, 1947).

° Mailer, Norman, *The Gospel According to the Son* (Random House, 1997).

° Martin, Harvey H. III, "Unraveling the Enigma of Psychic Surgery" (and other books); see http://www.metamind.net/enigmaipsysur.html

° Meyer, Marvin, & James M. Robinson, *The Nag Hammadi Scriptures: The International Edition* (HarperSanFrancisco, 2007).

° Meyer, Marvin, *The Secret Teachings of Jesus: Four Gnostic Gospels* (Vintage/ Random House, 1984).

° Miller, David Ian, "Finding My Religion: Religious scholar Elaine Pagels on how the newly discovered Gospel of Judas sheds new light on the dawn of Christianity," San Francisco Chronicle website, April 2, 2007; http://www.sfgate.com/cgibin/article.cgi?f=/g/a/2007/04/02/findrelig.DTL

° Mishlove, Jeffrey, *The Roots of Consciousness: Psychic Exploration Through History, Science and Experience* (New York: Marlowe & Co., 1975, 1993); revised edition online at: http://www.williamjames.com/Intro/CONTENTS.htm.

° Mitchell, Stephen, *The Gospel According to Jesus: A New Translation and Guide to His Essential Teachings for Believers and Unbelievers* (Harper-Collins, 1991).

○ Morgan, James Coyle, *Jesus and Mastership: The Gospel According to Jesus of Nazareth* (Tacoma, WA: Oakbridge Univ. Press, 1989).

○ Murakami, Kazuo, et al., "Fukutin gene mutations cause dilated cardiomyopathy with minimal muscle weakness," *Ann. Neurol.* Vol. 60(5), pp. 597-602 (Nov 2006).

○ Murakami, Kazuo, *The Divine Code of Life: Awaken Your Genes and Discover Hidden Talents* (Beyond Words/Atria, 2006a).

○ Notovitch, Nicolas, J. H. Connelly & L. Landsberg (trs.), *The Unknown Life of Jesus Christ* (Quill Driver Books, 2004; orig. 1890); www. reluctant-messenger. com/issa.htm

○ Ormond, Ron, & Ormond McGill, *Into the Strange Unknown* (Hollywood: Esoteric Foundation, 1959).

○ Pagels, Elaine and Karen L. King, *Reading Judas: The Gospel of Judas and the Shaping of Christianity* (Viking Penguin, 2007).

○ Pagels, Elaine, *Beyond Belief: The Secret Gospel of Thomas* (Random House, 2003).

○ Pagels, Elaine, *The Gnostic Gospels* (Random House 1979).

○ Palmer, Helen, Ed., *Inner Knowing: Consciousness Creativity, Insight and Intuition* (Tarcher/Putnam, 1998).

○ Parikh, Jagdish, *Intuition: The New Frontier of Management* (Oxford: Blackwell's, 1994).

○ Patterson, Stephen & Marvin Meyer, "The Gospel of Thomas," from *The Complete Gospels: Annotated Scholars' Version* (Polebridge Press, 1992, 1994).

○ Peirce, *The Intuitive Way* (Hillsboro OR: Beyond Words, 1997).

○ Radin, Dean, *The Conscious Universe: The Scientific Truth of Psychic Phenomena* (HarperSanFrancisco, 1997).

○ Reimarus, H.S., & C.H. Talbert, Ed., *Fragments, No. 64* (Philadelphia: Fortress Press 1971).

○ Roberts, Jane, *ESP Class Sessions,* 1969.

○ Roberts, Jane and Robert F. Butts, *Seth Speaks: The Eternal Validity of the Soul* (San Rafael, CA: Amber-Allen Publishing, 1972).

○ Roberts, Jane, *The Early Sessions, Volume 2* (Manhasset NJ: New Awareness Network, 1997).

○ Roberts, Jane, *The Seth Material* (Prentice Hall, 1970).

○ Robinson, James M., *The Secrets of Judas: The Story of the Misunderstood Disciple and his Lost Gospel* (HarperSanFrancisco, 1989).

◦ Robinson, James M., Ed., *The Nag Hammadi Library in English* (San Francisco: Harper & Row, 1988).

◦ Robinson, James M., & Helmut Koester, *Trajectories Through Early Christianity* (Philadelphia: Fortress Press, 1971).

◦ Rodegast, Pat & Judith Stanton, *Emmanuel's Book: A Manual for Living Comfortably in the Cosmos* (Bantam Books, 1985) ; see also Book II (1989) and Book III (1994).

◦ Ryerson, Kevin & Stephanie Harolde, *Spirit Communication: The Soul's Path* (Bantam Books, 1989).

◦ Sanders, E. P., *Judaism: Practice and Belief, 63 BCE–66 CE* (London: SCM Press, 1992).

◦ Sanders, E.P., *The Historical Figure of Jesus* (Penguin, 1993).

◦ Schneemelcher, Wilhelm, Ed., R.McL. Wilson (Tr.), *New Testament Apocrypha: Gospels and Related Writings* (Louisville: John Knox Press, 1992); pp. 391-395.

◦ Schweitzer, Albert, *The Quest of the Historical Jesus: A Critical Study of the Progress from Reimarus to Wrede* (Macmillan, 1968; orig. 1906 with various later additions).

◦ Scorcese, M., Dir., *The Last Temptation of Christ*, film (Universal Pictures, 1988).

◦ Smith, Huston, *The World's Religions: The Great Wisdom Traditions* (HarperSanFrancisco, 1991).

◦ Smith, S.D. 1967, "Induction of partial limb regeneration by galvanic stimulation," *Anat. Rec.* 158:89, 1967.

◦ Smoley, Richard, *Inner Christianity; A Guide to the Esoteric Tradition* (Boston: Shambala, 2002).

◦ Strauss, D.F., P.C. Hodgson, Ed. & Marian Evans (Tr.), *The Life of Jesus Critically Examined* (London 1973; orig. 1860).

◦ Targ, R., & H. E. Puthoff, *Mind Reach: Scientists Look at Psychic Ability* (Delacorte Press, 1977).

◦ Thiessen, Gerd & Annette Merz, *The Historical Jesus: A Comprehensive Guide* (Minneapolis: Fortress Press, 1998).

◦ Tolle, Eckhart, *A New Earth: Awakening to Your Life's Purpose* (Penguin, 2005).

◦ Vaughan, Frances and Roger Walsh, *Gifts from a Course in Miracles* (Tarcher, 1983,1995)' consists of selections from Anon, *A Course in Miracles*.

◦ Vaughan, Frances, *Awakening Intuition* (Anchor/Doubleday, 1979).

◦ Vaughan, Frances, *The Inward Arc* (Shambala, 1986).

○ Vermes, Geza, *The Complete Dead Sea Scrolls in English* (Pelican, 1962; Penguin 1965, 1987)

○ Vermes, Giza, *Jesus and the World of Judaism* (Penguin, 1983).

○ Vermes, Giza, *The Changing Faces of Jesus* (Penguin, 2000).

○ Walsch, Neale Donald, *Conversations with God: An Uncommon Dialogue* (Hampton Roads, 1995); see also Books II and III.

○ Walsh, Roger, *Essential Spirituality: The Seven Central Practices to Awaken Heart and Mind* (Wiley, 1999); pp. 6-9.

○ Webber, Andrew Lloyd, *Jesus Christ Superstar*, rock opera and film (1970).

○ Wilber, Ken, The Marriage of Sense and Soul: Integrating Science and Religion (Random House, 1998).

○ Williamson, G.A. (Tr.), *The Jewish War*, and *Jewish Antiquities* (Penguin, 1981).

○ Wise, Michael, Martin Abegg, Jr., & Edward Cook, *The Dead Sea Scrolls: A New Translation* (HarperSanFrancisco, 1996).

○ Wrede, William, *The Messianic Secret* (Cambridge, 1971; orig. 1901).

○ Yarbro, Chelsea Quinn, *Messages from Michael* (Berkeley Publishing, 1985).

○ Yogananda, Paramahansa, *Autobiography of a Yogi* (Los Angeles: Self-Realization Fellowship, 1985).

○ Yonge, Charles Duke, Tr., *The Works of Philo* (Hedrickson Publishers, 1995)

ENDNOTES

For full citations and explanation of abbreviations see the Bibliography.

1. Ryerson 1989.
2   Kautz 2011.
3   Ryerson 1989.
4   Funk 1993, p. 2.
5   Reimarus 1971, Strauss 1972, Wrede 1971.
6   Jefferson 2006.
7   Scheitzer 1968.
8   Josephus 1987, Vermes 1983; Sanders 1933, pp. 15-48; Williamson 1981, Bostock 1855; for a non-academic perspective see: http://www.jesuscentral.com/ji/historical-jesus/jesus-firstcenturycontext.php.
9   See ECW.
10 Robinson 1988.
11 Robinson 1989, Pagels 2007.
12 Vermes 1987, Meyer 2007, Pagels 1981, Meyer 1984.
13 Funk 1993, 1998.
14 Walsch 1996.
15 Helminski 2008, p. xiii.
16 Huxley 1945, Smith 1991, Walsh 1999.
17 Huxley 1945, Walsh 1999. This restatement follows Walsh with a few changes.
18 Matt 6:33; Mark 12:30, also Luke 10:27, 22:37.
19 Borg 1996 and ECW: Gospel Q.
20 Matt 5:1-6:34, Luke 6: 20-45.
21 Borg 1996, p. 28.
22 Smith 1991.
23 Luke 6:20-26, 29-35, 37-38; Matt 5:3-12, 39-42, 6:14-15, 7:1-2, 12, ; Thom 6:3, 54, 68, 69, 95; Mark 4:24, 11:25.

24 Pagels 2003, Paterson 1992.

25 E.g., Thom 4, 18, 30, 105.

26 Matt 12:31, Mark 3:28-9, Luke 12:10.

27 Luke 6:37, Acts 10:43; Matt 12:31, Mark 3:28-9, Luke 12:10.

28 Matt 3:7, 12:34, 23:33, Luke 3:7, John 8:43.

29 Matt 16:11-12, 23:13-29, Mark 7:6-15, Luke 11:42-52, 12:1.

30 Luke 4:1-13, Matt 4:1-11, Mark 1:12.

31 Luke 2:19, 2:51.

32 Smith 1991, Armstrong 1993, Brodd 2003.

33 Palmer 1998, Peirce 1997, Franquemont 1999.

34 Klimo 1987, Mishlove 1993, Parikh 1994, Kautz 2005, see www.appliedintuition. net.

35 Ryerson 1989, p. 10.

36 Kautz 2011 (book in progress).

37 Roberts 1964, Session 81, p.3.

38 Ryerson 1989, p. ix.

39 Apparently refers to Mark 13:11, Matt 10:19, Luke 12:11.

40 Acts 12:12, 25; 15:37,39.

41 Patterson 1992, Pagels 2003.

42 Pagels 2005, p. 114.

43 Patterson 1992, 22, 106.

44 Borg 1996 and ECW: Gospel Q.

45 Isaiah 7:14.

46 Luke 1:27.

47 Matt 1:18, Luke 1:31-35.

48 Matt 1:23.

49 Matt 2:2-10.

50 Matt 2:8.

51 See wikipedia: astrology for a basic description.

52 Cayce 2006, rdgs. #5749, 1541, 1151.

53 Matt 2:2-10.

54 See wikipedia: astrocartography for a fuller description.

55 Targ 1977.

56 Luke 2:39.

57 Matt 2:13-15.

58 Matt 2:16.

59 Dowling 1972, 5:20, & 7:6 to 12:22.

60 Matt 1:1,17, Luke 20:41, John 7:42.

61   Matt 1:1-16, Luke 3:23-37.

62   Perhaps Jude 1:14.

63   Matt 13:44.

64   Mark 6:3.

65   Philo 1995, Williamson 1981.

66   Vermes 1965, 2000.

67   Furst 1970.

68   Pagels 1981

69   Matt 5:3.

70   John 19:26.

71   Hock 1996.

72   Luke 2:46-47

73   Luke 2:41-50

74   ECW: Gospels of the Infancy.

75   ECW: Gospels of the Infancy, IV, IX.

76   ECW: Gospels of the Infancy, II-III.

77   Matt 15:26-27, Mark 7:27-28.

78   John 8:3-11.

79   Anon 1955, Chs. 130, 132.

80   Dowling 1972, 47:11-16.

81   Furst 1970.

82   Furst 1970, Dowling 1972, Ch. 21-43; Cayce 2006; Wheeler 1994; Notovitch 2004, Chs. 5-8; Lewis 1929, Ch. 10.

83   Notovitch 2004.

84   Furst 1970.

85   Ryerson 1989, pp. 91, 126-30, 144, 169-72.

86   Ryerson 1989, p. 127.

87   Matt 4:1-11, Mark 1:12, Luke 4:1-13.

88   Matt 17:1-8, Mark 9:1-8, Luke 9:28-36.

89   Matt 3: 13-17, Mark 1: 1-11, Luke 3:21-22, John 1: 28-34.

90   Isai 40:3-5..

91   Matt 11:5, Luke 7:22

92   ECW: Gospel of Mary.

93   Isai 9:6, 53:4-5; Dan 7:9-14, Mica 5:2.

94   Matt 26;39, Mark 14:33-36, Luke 22:41.

95   John 15:13.

96   Matt 22:37, Mark 12;30, Luke 10:29

97   Matt 10:34.

98   Matt 10:21, 35, Mark 13:8, 12, 24:7, Luke 12:52-53, 21:10.

99   Matt 21:42, Mark 12:10, Luke 20:17, Acts 4:11.

100   Jer 31:15, cited in Matt 2:17.

101   Hos 11:1, cited in Matt 2:15.

102   Luke 4:16-30.

103   Luke 4:24.

104   John 2:1-11.

105   Luke 8:27-39, Mark 5:1-20, Matt 8:28-34.

106   Mark 9:14-29, Luke 9:37-43, Matt 17:14-20.

107   Mark 7, Matt 15.

108   Mark 1:23-26.

109   Matt 17, Mark 9.

110   Matt 8, Matt 12.

111   Matt 8: 28-33, Mark 5: 11-13, Luke 8:32-33.

112   Matt 3:17.

113   Luke 4:40.

114   Matt 12, 15, 21, Mark 10, John 5, 9.

115   Matt 9, 15, Mark 2, Luke 5, John 5.

116   Matt 15, 21, John 5.

117   Mark 1, Matt 8, Luke 5, 17.

118   Mark 1, 3, 8, Luke 4, John 4.

119   Mark 5, Luke 8.

120   Matt 15, Mark 3, Luke 6.

121   Luke 7, 8, John 11.

122   Ryerson 1989, p. 134.

123   John 11:39.

124   John 11:43.

125   Matt 9:22, Mark 5:34 and many others.

126   Matt 19:9.

127   Luke 8:2.

128   Matt 27:55, 28:5, Mark 15:41, Luke 23:55.

129   Janssen 2000; ECW: Gospel of Mary.

130   Kazantzakis 1960, Webber 1970, George 2002, Scorcese 1988, Gibson 2001 & others.

131   Matt 5:27.

132   John 8:7.

133   John 8:3-11.

134   Matt 21:21.

135 Matt 9:22.

136 Matt 21:22

137 Heb 11:1.

138 Ryerson 1989, p. 156.

139 Matt 11:29-30.

140 John 1:1-3.

141 Mark 9:24.

142 Matt 17:21.

143 See www.st-francis.org/prayer.htm and www. holywellsanctuary.co.uk/ Serenity%20Prayer.htm

144 Matt 9:37, Luke 10:2.

145 Matt 25:1-15.

146 Matt 15:25-28.

147 Mark 6:4, Matt 13:57.

148 John 9:1-3.

149 Matt 12:31-32; also Luke 12:10, Mark 3:28-29, Thom 44.

150 For this well known saying in Tendai Buddhism see: www.stumbleupon.com/url/ www.101zenstories.com/index.php%3Fstory=46.

151 Mark 3:29, Luke 12:12.

152 John 8:58; Matt 11:14, 16: 12, Mark 9:13.

153 Jer 1:5.

154 John 16:25.

155 Patterson 1992, #22, #144.

156 Patterson 1992, #18, #19, #50.

157 John 3:6.

158 John 9:1-2.

159 John 8:58.

160 See www.near-death.com/experiences/origen049.html.

161 John 1:1.

162 Gen 5:22-29, Gen 4:17.

163 Jud 1:14-15, Heb 11:5.

164 Job 1-42.

165 John 14:12.

166 Gen. 14:18-20.

167 Heb 7:3.

168 See, e.g., http://en.wikipedia.org/wiki/String_theory for an usually clear description.

169 Caldwell 1977.

170 Pagels 2007, Robertson 1989.
171 John 13:27.
172 ECW: Macc I and II.
173 Matt 16:15, Mark 8:27-29, Luke 9:18-20.
174 Matt 26:39, 42, Mark 14:36, Luke 22:42, John 18:11.
175 John 10:10.
176 Matt 27:46, Mark 15:34;.
177 Matt 12:40, 26:60, 27:40, 63, Mark 8:30, 9:31, 10:34, 14:58, 15:30, John 2:19-21.
178 For an example see Yogananda 1985.
179 Perhaps Matt 27:33-34, Mark 15:23.
180 John 19:34, Luke 8:25.
181 See, for example: www.uoguelph.ca/zoology/devobio/210labs/regen1.html.
182 Lund 1947, Barth 1934, Smith 1967.
183 Matt 28: 9-10, Mark 16:9-19, John 20:26-31, John 21:1-23, Luke 24:15-31, 36-51.
184 Matt 6:5-6.
185 Probably Matt 10:29-31.
186 Exod 19:6.
187 Roberts 1969.
188 Anon 1975, Anon 1955, Dowling 1972, Rodegast 1985, Yarbro 1985, Roberts 1970, Walsch 1996, Tolle 2005.
189 Walsh 1999.
190 Matt 6:33.
191 Barks 1995, p. 2
192 Gal 6:7.
193 Matt 6:6.
194 Barks 1995.
195 Vaughan 1995.
196 Matt 7:7-8, Luke 11:9-10.
197 Matt 28:20.
198 Rodegast 1985.
199 John 8:32.

OPENING THE INNER EYE
EXPLORATIONS ON THE PRACTICAL
APPLICATION OF INTUITION IN DAILY
LIFE AND WORK

William H. Kautz, Sc.D.

Opening the Inner Eye presents the latest discoveries in the workings of intuition and its applications to individual daily life and in all professional areas that depend upon information and knowledge for their advances. Most of these new findings were obtained from a team of "expert intuitives," individuals who developed their natural intuitive ability into a refined skill. This book describes the broad conditions under which intuition can be used to access almost unlimited information, and the results of applicational experiments in counseling, business consulting, science, medicine and other fields.

> "I believe this is the best single book available on intuition and its applications. While there are many books out on the subject, no one book other than William Kautz's provides as knowledgeable and comprehensive a balance between a solid examination of the nature of the subject and a rich description of how it can be used. . . . Kautz has had more experience than anyone I know in using expert intuitives to successfully bring their unusual information accessing abilities to problem solving tasks in the real world." [Prof.

William H. Kautz, Sc.D.

Jon Klimo, Ph.D., author of *Channeling: Investigations on Receiving Information from Paranormal Sources*]

OPENING THE INNER EYE may be ordered from the publisher, iUniverse, 1663 Liberty Drive, Bloomington, IN 47403, or through www. iuniverse.com, www.amazon.com or www.bn.com

THE STORY OF JESUS
AN INTUITIVE ANTHOLOGY

William H. Kautz, Sc.D.

The Story of Jesus offers a narrative account of Jesus' life from the perspective of twelve contemporary individuals who have developed their natural intuitive skills to a high level and are able to bring forth detailed information not accessible by ordinary means. In prior work in history, literature and poetry these *expert intuitives* and a few similar contributors have demonstrated an unusual skill to probe deeply into the personal lives of historical individuals. They apply their abilities here to discover information about Jesus and his contemporaries that did not find its way into the New Testament Gospels and other historical accounts. They present illuminating new insights, a more spiritual understanding of Jesus' deeper teachings and a much richer view of the man Jesus than that available from conventional Christian sources.

THE STORY OF JESUS: AN INTUITIVE ANTHOLOGY will be available in fall 2011 from Trafford Publishing, 1663 Liberty Drive, Bloomington, IN 47403, or through www.trafford.com, www.amazon. com or www.bn.com.